No Longer
Disabled

NO LONGER DISABLED

The Federal Courts
and the
Politics of
Social Security
Disability

SUSAN GLUCK MEZEY

STUDIES IN SOCIAL WELFARE POLICIES AND
PROGRAMS, NUMBER 7

GREENWOOD PRESS
NEW YORK • WESTPORT, CONNECTICUT • LONDON

Library of Congress Cataloging-in-Publication Data

Mezey, Susan Gluck, 1944–
    No longer disabled : the federal courts and the politics of social
security disability / Susan Gluck Mezey.
        p.   cm. — (Studies in social welfare policies and programs,
ISSN 8755–5360 ; no. 7)
    Bibliography: p.
    Includes index.
    ISBN 0–313–25424–9 (lib. bdg. : alk. paper)
    1. Disability evaluation—Law and legislation—United States.
2. Insurance, Disability—Law and legislation—United States.
3. Judicial review of administrative acts—United States.   4. United
States. Social Security Administration.   I. Title.   II. Series.
KF3649.M49   1988
344.73'021—dc19
[347.30421]   87–31783

British Library Cataloguing in Publication Data is available.

Library of Congress Catalog Card Number: 87–31783
ISBN: 0–313–25424–9
ISSN: 8755–5360

First published in 1988

Greenwood Press, Inc.
88 Post Road West, Westport, Connecticut 06881

Printed in the United States of America

The paper used in this book complies with the
Permanent Paper Standard issued by the National
Information Standards Organization (Z39.48–1984).

10 9 8 7 6 5 4 3 2 1

To Paula Gluck
Whose strength has always inspired me

In Memory of Felix Gluck
and
Lilli and Charles Rand

Contents

Tables

Preface

In 1980, tired of a career of part-time teaching, interspersed with inter-
mittent postdoctoral fellowships, I entered law school. Graduating in 1983,
I discovered that law firms were not lining up to offer jobs to women lawyers
with Ph.D.s in political science, even those who graduated at the top of
their law school class.

Although the financial rewards of private law practice were enticing, because of my background in political science and my interest in public policymaking, I was primarily interested in working on the legal staff of a federal
agency. This feeling was reinforced by the fact that federal government
interviewers were the least sexist and most professional of all those I en-
countered. I would have liked to work for an agency whose politics were
compatible with mine—such as the Equal Employment Opportunity Commission or the Environmental Protection Agency—but with continual hiring
freezes all federal jobs were scarce and I did not have the luxury of satisfying
my ideological "druthers." I eventually secured a position with the Department of Health and Human Services—in the Social Security Litigation Unit.
The job involved writing legal briefs to persuade federal magistrates and
judges to affirm the Social Security Administration's decisions to terminate
disability benefits.

I must confess that when I accepted the job, I was unaware of the enormity
of the disability termination enterprise and, as I became aware, I became
acutely uncomfortable with the Department's litigation posture and my role
in it. I believe I would be accurate in reporting that many, if not most, of
my colleagues felt a good deal of discomfort as well about their roles in the
benefits termination process. Fortunately, within a few months, the Social
Security Administration called a halt to the terminations and I no longer
had to write briefs in defense of an essentially indefensible position.

Even more fortunately, within another few months, I was offered, and
accepted, a teaching position in the political science department at Loyola
University of Chicago. In September 1984 I began teaching undergraduates

about courts and the law and began as well to consider a number of different research projects that would allow me to combine my legal training with my interest in judicial policymaking. It soon occurred to me that the recent struggles between the courts and the Social Security Administration over the disability benefits termination policy would serve my purposes admirably. Throughout my work on the book, my interest in the topic remained high and my admiration for the federal courts continued to grow as I learned more about their role in the disability policymaking process.

The topic was first introduced in a paper presented at the American Political Science Association meeting in New Orleans in September 1985. The paper was next transformed into an article in the March 1986 issue of the *Policy Studies Journal* and now, much expanded, has become this book. Although the process of writing a book is often lonely, tedious, and anxiety-producing, these feelings are ameliorated by the help and encouragement one receives during the ordeal. I would like to take this opportunity to publicly thank those who provided these relief-giving measures.

Let me begin by expressing my gratitude to Loyola University for giving me a leave of absence for a semester that relieved me of teaching responsibilities and allowed me to work on the book full time. I'd also like to thank Roy Fry of Loyola's Cudahy Library who assisted me in securing the government documents that I needed. Thanks also to Bill Stant, my graduate research assistant, for his diligence in checking citations, finding cases, and reading the government documents, as well as his editing suggestions. Bill spent a year engaged in the process of working on this book and performed the invaluable service of listening to me talk about disability terminations and presenting me with his views on the subject.

I received encouragement from a number of people and let me now add my thanks in print to the verbal thanks they have already received: to Robert Katzman, who commented on my APSA paper and whose book on transportation disability policy provided a model for my book; to Lowell Arye, on the staff of the House Aging Committee, who expressed great enthusiasm for the idea of writing a book on this subject; to Angus MacIntyre, whom I never met but who wrote to me from Australia after reading my piece in *Policy Studies Journal* and sent me his work on judicial statutory policymaking; to David Rosenbloom, who also proclaimed interest in the topic and read an early draft of the manuscript; to Beverly Cook, who read and commented extensively on a later draft of the manuscript. Much appreciation also goes to the federal court judges, especially Judge James Moran, the attorneys, and congressional staffers who patiently answered questions about the parts they played in the disability termination drama. Needless to say, any errors of omission or commission contained in the book are mine and mine alone.

Finally, the family that I am extremely fortunate to have deserves more thanks than I can adequately express on these pages. My children, Jennifer and Jason, two terrific teenagers, always encouraged me and, even more important, were always proud of me. And they were usually understanding when I put my work ahead of them temporarily. They knew that what I most needed from them was the opportunity to work without feeling guilty and their numerous successes in their own lives allowed this to happen. And last, my husband, Michael, who has always been my professional mentor, for reading and commenting on all the drafts I thrust at him. Much more significantly, he deserves my gratitude for, uncomplainingly, often taking on an unequal share of responsibilities for our children and our home so that I could work on whatever needed to get done at the time: whether it was law school, teaching, or the research and writing of this book. In fact, what I owe him for his dedication and devotion to our family above all, I can never repay.

No Longer Disabled

1

Prologue

The social security disability insurance program was created in the mid–1950s to provide financial support for members of the labor force who were totally incapacitated for work. After a stormy beginning, the disability program became a relatively noncontroversial benefits program that enjoyed steady growth and received bipartisan approval for about twenty years. However, as more beneficiaries were incorporated into the program and monetary awards were increased, concern for costs and increasing worker dependency arose and the support for the steadily expanding disability program began to erode. Responding to reports that large numbers of disability recipients were improperly receiving benefits, in 1980 Congress authorized a stepped-up periodic review of current social security disability beneficiaries to determine continued eligibility for benefits. It was not made clear whether, in such cases, the Social Security Administration (SSA or Agency) had to demonstrate that the disabled individuals had improved from the condition which initially rendered them disabled.

The Social Security Administration interpreted the 1980 legislation as a directive to reduce the number of disability recipients and proceeded to terminate benefits in such great numbers that the process soon took on the proportions of a national crisis. Terminated recipients attempted to combat the mass cessation of disability funds by seeking judicial review of SSA termination decisions as permitted under the Social Security Act. Because of the generally favorable treatment accorded to disability claimants in federal court, the judiciary became a preferred forum for resolution of these issues.

Beginning in the Ninth Circuit in 1982 and ultimately expanding into all circuits by the end of 1984, federal courts of appeal ruled that the Social Security Administration used improper standards to determine that current beneficiaries were no longer disabled. The courts decreed that SSA restore benefits to thousands and thousands of plaintiffs. Although required by statute to defer to administrative agency findings of fact if supported by substantial evidence, the courts also ordered the Social Security Administration to apply a medical improvement standard in reviewing the eligibility of current recipients.

The Social Security Administration disputed the appellate courts' authority to mandate standards for a national insurance program and refused to adopt the judicial interpretation of eligibility for continuing disability. Because the legislature had not specified the standard of eligibility for the periodic review process, a struggle for interpretation of legislative intent between the courts and the social security bureaucracy ensued. Tension mounted as accusations of judicial interference in social security policy were leveled at the courts by Agency officials and by high-ranking members of the executive branch.

NONACQUIESCENCE

The conflict over the correct adjudicative standard in the continuing disability review procedure was exacerbated by SSA's policy of nonacquiescence which was used to circumscribe judicial authority over the Agency's adjudication process. Nonacquiescence is legal terminology that describes a standoff between an administrative agency and a court in which the agency refuses to incorporate the judicial interpretation of the enabling legislation and regulations in its administrative procedures.

The Social Security Administration's nonacquiescence policy forced each terminated beneficiary to seek judicial review of SSA findings of nondisability; although the Agency followed the appellate court's ruling in the litigated case and awarded benefits to the plaintiff, it did not acknowledge the legitimacy of the court's order to apply the medical improvement standard in its administrative reviews of other beneficiaries in the same judicial circuit. Nonacquiescence thus created two standards of adjudication in continuing eligibility cases: beneficiaries who appealed their terminations to the federal courts were judged on a medical improvement standard while those who failed to appeal were judged by the Agency's standard in which medical improvement was irrelevant.

Because of nonacquiescence, litigants' courtroom victories were not immediately translated into disability policy reform. Eventually litigants were able to circumvent SSA's nonacquiescence policy by following a strategy that combined litigation with extrajudicial activity and included arousing public sympathy through media exposure, lobbying in state and national policymaking arenas, and filing tens of thousands of individual (and class action) lawsuits.

The increasing number of hostile interactions between the federal courts and the bureaucracy, primarily over nonacquiescence, accompanied by mounting constituent pressure, eventually persuaded Congress to step in to mediate the conflict between the courts and the Agency and explicate the proper standards for the disability review process. By the end of 1984 Congress had reexamined the termination issue and enacted legislation supporting the appellate courts' interpretation of the medical improvement standard for the disability review process.

THE COURTS AS CATALYST

The social security disability beneficiaries used their judicial victories as part of their arsenal against the Social Security Administration. Although they were not able to rely solely on courtroom victories, the litigation played a crucial role in their struggle against the bureaucracy; it allowed them to capitalize on the litigation activity to generate publicity and bring the plight of the disability beneficiaries to public awareness. In so doing, they succeeded in eventually persuading elected governmental officials to support their policy goals.

While litigation may not immediately accomplish the policy changes that litigants seek, it often sets in motion a chain of events that prompts the legislature or other government agencies into action. The litigation triggered by the Social Security Administration's termination policy offers an opportunity to explore the "catalytic" effects of federal court decisions on administrative and legislative policymaking. This study examines the interactions among actors in the disability policymaking process and highlights the role of the judiciary in formulating social security disability policy.

Although the court's position was ultimately vindicated, the social security disability litigation also demonstrated the limitations on the court's ability to secure compliance with its orders. Because litigation is not always successful in accomplishing social reform, the impact of litigation activity must be assessed by examining indirect or cumulative results of the litigation.

The litigation activity that arose in response to SSA's benefits cessation policy abruptly began and ended within a few years, was highly visible, and concluded with a dramatic shift in the disability review process. The limited duration and high visibility of the litigation provides an opportunity to examine a case study of judicial policymaking in a relatively controlled environment.

Although the results of a single case study must be viewed with caution, it is hoped that providing empirical data on the judicial-administrative-legislative relationship will allow future scholars to engage in more systematic assessments of judicial policymaking.

THE DEBATE OVER JUDICIAL POLICYMAKING

The social security litigation raises questions about the appropriate role of the judiciary in overseeing administrative decisionmaking through interpretation of the enabling legislation. Charges that the courts are using their power of judicial review to invade the prerogatives of other institutions of government are not novel and the problem of finding agreement on the proper role of the courts in exercising judicial oversight of administrative agencies is certainly not unique to the Social Security Administration. The controversy generated by the battle over the medical improvement standard in the periodic review process stems from a sharply divided view over the position and authority of the federal courts in the American political system.

Judicial review has been a source of dispute in the United States since

1803 when Chief Justice Marshall declared in *Marbury v. Madison*[1] that "it is emphatically the province and duty of the judicial department to say what the law is." Justice Marshall's proclamation of judicial supremacy has since served as authority for judicial declarations of unconstitutionality when, in the court's view, the acts of other governmental officials are inconsistent with the Constitution.

Judicial Activism and Restraint

Most studies of, and debates over, judicial review have centered on the role of the courts in assessing the constitutionality of the actions of state and federal governments. The controversy over judicial review centers on the proper role of an appointed judiciary in a democratic society. The term "judicial activist" is usually applied to one who applauds searching judicial scrutiny over the acts of other governmental officials; "judicial restraint" is the position that urges a more subdued role for the courts in overseeing other governmental decisionmakers.

Controversy over judicial review is primarily touched off by judicial nullification of legislative and executive actions through constitutional adjudication. It typically revolves around the *degree* to which the judiciary should substitute its views for the views of other government officials and the *extent* to which the Court should limit itself to textual analysis of the Constitution and hold itself within the strict confines of the framers' intentions.

The ongoing debate over judicial constitutional review has generated much heat but comparatively little light and judicial activism and restraint remain terms that reflect a state of mind rather than empirical referents.[2] Nevertheless, at least two distinct, yet related, measures of activism and restraint can be identified. One measure involves the court's adherence to the textual parameters of the Constitution, that is, the degree to which constitutional provisions are interpreted according to the language of the document and the intent of the framers. Another measure concerns the degree to which an appointed judiciary defers to politically accountable branches of government and refrains from judicial negation of democratically adopted policies.[3]

Adherents of judicial restraint describe the present judicial role as one in which judges allow themselves "carte blanche to govern on whatever matters they [see] fit, permitting the policy choices made through the political process to prevail only so long as the judges, like the military in some other countries, find those choices agreeable."[4] These critics of judicial policymaking portray judicial review as an infringement upon the democratic principle of majority rule but grudgingly assent to it when courts restrict themselves to overturning legislative enactments "in accordance with an inference whose underlying premise is fairly discoverable in the Constitution itself."[5] Absent constitutional commands, they argue, courts indulge themselves in policymaking when they impose values that negate popular choices.[6]

Proponents of an activist court have argued that the judiciary is in the best position to address the problems that legislatures have neglected or refused to solve. They stress that the framers intended democracy to coexist with a restriction on the legislative or popular will implemented by the courts through judicial review. Judicial activists urge the courts to act "as the expounder of basic national ideas of individual liberty and fair treatment, even when the content of these ideals is not expressed as a matter of positive law in the written Constitution."[7]

Judicial activists charge that advocates of restraint elevate form over substance and ignore the reality that the federal courts can provide an antidote for the political system's inability or unwillingness to respond to certain groups. While judicial review may be incompatible with majoritarianism, a principle at the heart of a democratic system, proponents assert that federal courts provide a forum for the demands of minorities to be heard. They insist that the judiciary is "the most effective guarantor of the interests of the unpopular and unrepresented precisely because it is the most politically isolated judicial body."[8] And they argue that binding courts to constricted views of deference to representative institutions and rigid parameters of framers' or legislative intent forgoes an opportunity to redress individual grievances and satisfy demands of groups unable to achieve their goals in the politically accountable majoritarian institutions.[9]

An ardent exponent and practitioner of judicial activism, Appellate Court Judge Frank Johnson of the Eleventh Circuit, maintains that federal courts have always been "activist." He argues that judicial discretion is a necessary concomitant of constitutional interpretation unless judges are to be limited to voicing the expressed intent of the framers, a restriction he considers totally inappropriate for interpreting "an enduring charter of government."[10]

The controversy over the federal court's role in the disability litigation echoed, in many ways, the familiar debate over the role of the judiciary in making public policy through constitutional adjudication. For while the social security disability litigation did not revolve around issues of constitutional doctrine, it raised related questions about separation of powers and judicial deference.

STATUTORY INTERPRETATION AS JUDICIAL ACTIVISM

Despite the attention to constitutional adjudication, the reality is that the major role courts play in overseeing the actions of other governmental institutions lies in fixing the meaning of words in statutes and regulations and deciding which party's interpretation is the "better" one. "In this sense judicial review is the power to declare an act or decision of a government official not unconstitutional but simply illegal—not beyond the totality of powers that government may legitimately exercise, but simply beyond the authorization of the statute or other legal rule by which he is supposed to conduct himself."[11] An assessment of the federal courts' role in public policymaking is not complete without an examination of the relatively neglected area of the federal court's role in statutory interpretation because it "no less than constitutional adjudication, is the exercise of power to 'say what the law is.' "[12]

Judicial interpretation of legislative enactments often involves interpolation from the statutory language and requires courts to discern legislative intent from the words of the statute and legislative history. By interpreting legislative acts, therefore, as well as by interpreting constitutional provisions, courts frequently function as coordinate policymakers, especially when the question presented to them arises from circumstances that have changed since enactment or were unanticipated by the legislature.[13]

Statutory Limits on Administrative Procedure

The court's function of statutory interpretation frequently encompasses the oversight of administrative decisionmaking when judges are called upon to fix the limits of administrative power within the confines of the enabling legislation. Administrative agencies are legislative creations with powers delegated to them by the enabling statute and agencies may only exercise power consistent with the statute. The problem of reconciling bureaucratic power with the legislative framework is confounded because administrative agencies, like courts, are responsible for interpreting the legislative design and are statutorily entrusted with a great deal of discretion in implementing the legislation.

Both courts and bureaucracy legitimately claim the right to interpret the legislature's intention and conflict is generated when interpretations of congressional intent clash.[14] In such cases bureaucrats often assert moral superiority over the courts because, they argue, their accountability to the president makes them more democratic than the appointed-for-life judiciary. Because neither courts nor agencies are democratically elected or constituted, it is not readily apparent which of these two nonelected institutions has the better claim to legitimacy under principles of democratic governance.

Judicial Activism in Administrative Review

Although reports of conflict between judges and bureaucrats, arising over the exercise of judicial oversight of bureaucratic decisionmaking, are highly visible in the literature, Martin Shapiro's study of courts and administrative agencies provided a somewhat different picture of the relationship between the two institutions. Shapiro described both courts and agencies as "supplementary lawmakers" that "ought to be considered as two alternative and parallel structures for the administration of government programs."[15] Although Shapiro envisioned modern (post–New Deal) courts and agencies as roughly two sides of the statutory interpretation coin and sought to accentuate their similarities, it cannot be denied that the exercise of judicial review diminishes administrative autonomy.[16]

Borrowing from Shapiro's work on courts and administrative policymaking, Angus MacIntyre enumerated five conditions in which judges are "most tempted to intervene and substitute their own judgment for that of an administrative agency. . . . "[17] According to MacIntyre, judicial policymaking through statutory interpretation thrives in the following environment: a vaguely worded statute; self-serving policy interpretations by the bureaucracy; an unwillingness by Congress to step in to correct administrative implementation of the statute; sufficient resources to mount a judicial challenge; and, lastly, a sympathetic judiciary armed with appropriate remedial tools.[18]

The circumstances of the disability litigation show that an active judicial role in disability policymaking was precipitated by virtually identical factors: an ambiguity of legislative intent in the 1980 Amendments mandating the periodic review of current beneficiaries to determine continued eligibility; an expansive and somewhat questionable interpretation of the statute by the bureaucracy that served other interests beyond ensuring current eligibility of disability recipients; an initial unwillingness by Congress to intercede in bureaucratic implementation of the statute despite the bureaucracy's overzealousness in purging the disability rolls; the ability of beneficiaries, greatly enhanced by automatic fee-withholding provisions in the statute, to seek judicial review of the deprivation of their benefits; and, finally, statutory entitlement to judicial review accompanied by an abundance of sympathetic judges who were able to reverse the termination of benefits.

MacIntyre also noted that, to deflect criticism of judicial interference in agency decisionmaking, the courts frequently disguised their policymaking by grounding their decisions in agency procedural errors or deficiencies. In reversing the Social Security Administration's determination that beneficiaries were no longer disabled, the courts typically relied upon SSA's failure to support its findings with substantial evidence, thus obscuring the fact that it was imposing a new standard of adjudication upon the Agency.

The debate over judicial oversight of administrative actions has shifted attention from the Supreme Court to the lower federal courts, particularly the trial courts, because while these courts were formerly more deferential to legislators and administrators, they are now less hesitant about imposing a "new administrative law [that] is based on the premise that administrators cannot be trusted to carry out the mission assigned to them by law."[19]

Notwithstanding the prevalence and importance of statutory interpretation as an opportunity for judicial policymaking, empirical evidence on judicial "statutory" activism remains scarce.[20] Given the significance of the lower courts in statutory interpretation, especially as it is applied to administrative decisionmaking, it is important to repair this omission with data on how the lower federal courts exercise authority over administrative agencies through their power of statutory interpretation.

OUTLINE OF THE STUDY

This study is devoted to two themes: it provides an opportunity for empirical analysis of the lower federal court's role in the political system by looking at the circumstances associated with active judicial involvement in a policymaking area; it also examines litigation as a form of political activity to illustrate the means by which litigants make demands on the political system through filing lawsuits as well as through pursuit of traditional political lobbying. Because litigation activity and judicial decisionmaking have formed a symbiotic relationship in public policymaking, these two themes will be interwoven throughout the study.

The analysis is divided into three parts. The first part presents a brief picture of the debate over judicial review and focuses on the role of the courts in judicial oversight of administrative agencies. In discussing litigation activity, it notes that even successful litigants may not achieve policy reform immediately and are required to exert pressure on several fronts to influence public policy. Because of the limits on the judiciary's ability to secure bureaucratic compliance, litigation virtually requires accompanying political activity. The section concludes by examining new patterns of litigation activity and assessing their effect upon policy changes.

The second section begins with a history of the disability program and an analysis of the administrative process, including the role that the federal courts play in judicial review of disability claims. Because congressional intent plays a vital role in an assessment of judicial policymaking, an examination of the passage of the 1980 Social Security Amendment concludes this section.

The final section details the judicial decisionmaking that led to the conflict between the courts and SSA over the medical improvement standard. In discussing nonacquiescence, this section illustrates the problems that arise when the courts and an agency clash over the parameters of the judicial role. The book ends by examining the extrajudicial litigation activity in which terminated disability beneficiaries applied pressure in a number of policymaking arenas to create the environment that led to enactment of the 1984 Social Security Disability Benefits Reform Act.

NOTES

1. 5 U.S. (1 Cranch) 137, 177 (1803).

2. See Bradley Canon, "A Framework for the Analysis of Judicial Activism," in Stephen Halpern and Charles Lamb, eds., *Supreme Court Activism and Restraint* (Lexington, Mass.: Lexington Books, 1982), pp. 385–419, and Charles Lamb, "Judicial Restraint on the Supreme Court," in Halpern and Lamb, eds., *Supreme Court Activism and Restraint*, pp. 7–36; but see Gregory Caldeira and Donald McCrone, "Of Time and Judicial Activism: A Study of the U.S. Supreme Court, 1800–1973," in Halpern and Lamb, eds., *Supreme Court Activism and Restraint*, pp. 103–32 for an empirical analysis of activism and restraint.

3. Interpretivism (applying a literal or near literal interpretation of the words of the Constitution) and deference (subordinating judicial value judgments to the judgments of elected government officials) are often used interchangeably and "their indiscriminate coupling is a fertile source of confusion in debates on judicial restraint." Stanley Brubaker, "Reconsidering Dworkin's Case for Judicial Activism," *Journal of Politics* 46(1984):505. Brubaker, acknowledging that the two concepts are not "un-

related," suggests a sliding scale relationship between the two by stating that "the very question of activism and restraint would seem resolvable only through an interpretation of the Constitution's meaning. And the latitude of permissible judgment must vary with the meaning that can be given to a particular constitutional provision." Ibid. For a discussion of the problems of intertwining these two dimensions, see Ronald Cass, "The Meaning of Liberty: Notes on Problems within the Fraternity," *Journal of Law, Ethics & Public Policy* 1(Summer 1985):777–812; see also Ronald Dworkin, *Taking Rights Seriously* (Cambridge: Harvard University Press, 1977). For a discussion of how judicial restraint is associated with noninterpretivism and deference to legislative institutions, see John Hart Ely, *Democracy and Distrust* (Cambridge: Harvard University Press, 1980).

A third popular definition of activism is divergence from precedent, that is, failure to conform to stare decisis. Other criteria have been suggested in the literature but these two dimensions seem to occupy a central role in almost all analyses. See also Richard Posner, *The Federal Courts* (Cambridge: Harvard University Press, 1985), and Vincent Blasi, "The Rootless Activism of the Burger Court," in Vincent Blasi, ed., *The Burger Court* (New Haven: Yale University Press, 1983), pp. 198–217.

4. Lino Graglia, "In Defense of Judicial Restraint," in Halpern and Lamb, eds., *Supreme Court Activism and Restraint*, p. 141.

5. Robert Bork, "The Impossibility of Finding Welfare Rights in the Constitution," *Washington University Law Quarterly* (1979):695.

6. For other advocates of judicial restraint, see William Rehnquist, "The Notion of a Living Constitution," *Texas Law Review* 54(May 1976):693–706; Nathan Glazer, "Towards an Imperial Judiciary," *The Public Interest* 41(Fall 1975):104–23; John Agresto, *The Supreme Court and Constitutional Democracy* (Ithaca, N.Y.: Cornell University Press, 1984); Raoul Berger, *Government by Judiciary* (Cambridge: Harvard University Press, 1977); Lino Graglia, *Disaster By Decree: The Supreme Court's Decisions on Race and Schools* (Ithaca, N.Y.: Cornell University Press, 1976); Alexander Bickel, *The Supreme Court and the Idea of Progress* (New Haven: Yale University Press, 1978).

7. Thomas Grey, "Do We Have an Unwritten Constitution?" *Stanford Law Review* 27(February 1975):706. Arthur Miller, *Toward Increased Judicial Activism* (Westport, Conn.: Greenwood Press, 1982), is one of the strongest proponents of an active judiciary. He argues that an activist court must not be encumbered by problems of divining the framers' intentions or concerned about the courts treading on the institutional toes of the other branches of government. Miller is openly result-oriented and urges the courts to assume policymaking roles because the political process does not satisfy policy demands sufficiently. He believes that a nonelected court is "democratic" as long as "its decisions further the concept of human dignity that is the essence of democratic theory." Ibid., p. 101.

For the views of another advocate of judicial activism, see Michael Perry, *The Constitution, the Courts, and Human Rights* (New Haven: Yale University Press, 1982). Perry is more concerned than Miller about the nondemocratic features of judicial activism but is also willing to allow federal courts to follow their own values in human rights cases rather than merely searching for values constitutionalized by the framers. He justifies an active judiciary because it "serves a crucial governmental function, perhaps even an indispensable one, that no other practice can realistically be expected to serve—and serves it in a manner that accommodates the principle of electorally accountable policymaking—that function constitutes the justification for this practice." Ibid., pp. 92–93.

According to Perry, the federal courts are best suited to perform the task of protecting human rights from governmental encroachment because elected members of democratic institutions, concerned about their political futures, are less able and less willing to confront the moral dilemmas plaguing society. Because the federal courts are not accountable to the electorate, they can best articulate the "right" answers for society's problems. See also Richard Neely, *How Courts Govern America* (New Haven: Yale University Press, 1981); Jesse Choper, *Judicial Review and the National Political Process* (Chicago: University of Chicago Press, 1980) for additional arguments in favor of judicial activism.

8. Choper, *Judicial Review and the National Political Process*, p. 69.

9. See Ely, *Democracy and Distrust*, for discussion of a judicial role in which the courts explicitly act as a counterweight on behalf of groups inadequately represented in the political process. A less committed activist than either Miller or Perry, Ely urges a more restricted role for federal courts. He would allow courts to stray beyond the text of the document only to redress the deficiencies of the pluralist system to ensure that the political process is open to all participants.

Relying heavily upon Justice Stone's famous footnote four in *U.S. v. Carolene Products*, 304 U.S. 144 (1938), Ely notes that the political system, based upon the principle of majority rule, does not always effectively protect minorities. Because a minority group requires assistance in preserving effective representation in a democratic system, a court can engage in activism to protect minority rights of expression and enfranchisement and to overturn legislative and administrative acts that are motivated by hostility to minority groups.

District of Columbia Circuit Judge Robert Bork and Seventh Circuit Judge Richard Posner question the existence of a class of unrepresented people in the American political system that have to rely on the federal courts for representation. Posner argues that because all groups are represented in, and have benefited from, the political process, the search for the appropriate balance between equality and other competing values belongs in the representative institutions and not in the courts; see Posner, *The Federal Courts*. Similarly, according to Bork, "the poor and the minorities have had access to the political process and have done very well through it." Bork, "The Impossibility of Welfare Rights in the Constitution," p. 701.

10. Frank Johnson, "In Defense of Judicial Activism," *Emory Law Journal* 28(1979):910.

11. Martin Shapiro, *The Supreme Court and Administrative Agencies* (New York: Free Press, 1968), p. 3.

12. Note, "Intent, Clear Statements, and the Common Law: Statutory

Interpretation in the Supreme Court," *Harvard Law Review* 95(1982):892. For a classic work on statutory interpretation, see Reed Dickerson, *The Interpretation and Application of Statutes* (Boston: Little, Brown, 1975).

13. Judge Posner has a less restrictive view of statutory interpretation. See Posner, *The Federal Courts*. Posner has suggested an approach to statutory interpretation called "imaginative reconstruction." He urges judges to begin with a routine analysis of statutory language, legislative intent, and purpose as gleaned through legislative history but to consider also the values of the period in which the legislation was enacted to attempt to discern how the authors of the bill would have wanted the law to be applied in later unforeseen circumstances. If such information is unavailable or discord among the framers of the legislation makes this process unyielding, the judge must determine which interpretation of the statute "will yield the most reasonable result in the case at hand." Ibid., p. 287.

Another approach to statutory interpretation argues that courts should "view statutes as statements of consensually agreed-upon principles... [and] explicitly reason from and develop statutory principles in the tentative, incremental fashion of the common law." Note, "Intent and the Common Law," p. 913. See also Guido Calabresi, *A Common Law for the Age of Statutes* (Cambridge: Harvard University Press, 1982). Calabresi argues that the courts should simply consider statutes as common law precedent, and either update or revise them, or urge the legislature to do so. He is not troubled that this method places courts on a more equal footing with policymakers because the legislature still retains the ability to overrule the judicial decision.

14. See Jonathan Casper, *Lawyers before the Warren Court* (Urbana, Ill.: University of Illinois Press, 1972) and Canon, "A Framework for the Analysis of Judicial Activism."

15. Shapiro, *The Supreme Court and Agencies*, p. 44. Shapiro draws a distinction between these two creatures of Congress primarily to the extent that courts are policy generalists and agencies are policy specialists.

16. Shapiro views the conflicts between courts and agencies arising not from their functions but from "the essentially conflicting ideologies of their personnel." Ibid., p. 93.

17. Angus MacIntyre, "A Court Quietly Rewrote the Federal Pesticide Statute: How Prevalent is Judicial Statutory Revision?" *Law and Policy* 7(April 1985):251.

18. Ibid. MacIntyre's analysis of statutory interpretation of federal pesticide statutes supported his hypothesis that these five factors were present and contributed to judicial policymaking in this area of environmental policy.

19. R. Shep Melnick, *Regulation and the Courts: The Case of the Clean Air Act* (Washington, D.C.: Brookings, 1983), p. 393.

20. MacIntyre, "A Court Quietly Rewrote the Federal Pesticide Statute," p. 250.

2

The Politics of Litigation Activity

Judicial review of administrative agencies was initially viewed with suspicion by liberal interests in society who welcomed the creation of the New Deal executive agencies and were appalled at the restrictions inherent in the process of judicial oversight. Proponents who saw administrative agencies as agents of change were opposed to provisions for judicial review because they believed that courts would block executive branch public welfare policy innovations. The debate over judicial oversight of agency decision-making has continued but positions have been reversed and the courts are now viewed as supportive of public rather than special interests. Ironically, "liberal reformers now attack the federal agencies their predecessors proudly created [and] they invoke the aid of the courts against the same interests that earlier fought for access to the courts."[1]

In the 1935 case of *Schechter Poultry Corporation v. United States*,[2] the Supreme Court struck down the National Industrial Recovery Act of 1933 by holding that Congress had unconstitutionally delegated power to an administrative agency. This case, now seen as the epitome of judicial overreaching, has never been reversed but has clearly been eclipsed by the passing years and remains an anachronism in administrative law. The expansion of post–New Deal administrative power would have been impossible without the demise of the *Schechter* rule of law, and, by ignoring its precepts, the courts eventually allowed the expansion of bureaucratic power within the American system of government.[3]

The judiciary's concern for separation of powers peaked during the New Deal *Schechter* days. As agencies became more entrenched, the court's diminishing concern with the delegation doctrine led to an expansion of agency power; had the courts continued to wink at administrative policymaking, judicial influence might have declined until the courts were reduced to merely rubberstamping agency actions. Gradually, as the dominating influence of the executive branch in public policymaking created apprehensions about excessive bureaucratic power, the courts began to exert more authority over administrative decisionmaking and judicial review became instrumental in restricting the hegemony of administrative agencies.

JUDICIAL REVIEW OVER ADMINISTRATIVE AGENCIES

While the lion's share of cases seeking judicial review of agency action has traditionally involved regulatory programs, an increasing source of litigation has revolved around adjudication of individual claims for entitlement to government spending programs.[4] Through judicial review, the courts have helped foster the growth of individual rights by articulating the principle that, as clients of the administrative state, persons have cognizable interests in government benefits and that these benefits may not be withdrawn without proper procedure.[5]

The reliance on judicial scrutiny of agency action to protect individual rights has evolved with the rise of the modern administrative state. Judicial review of administrative procedure frequently involves balancing the enhanced protection of individual rights against the possible loss of bureaucratic efficiency and expertise resulting from judicial oversight. Despite its potential interference with bureaucratic autonomy, judicial review has become more prevalent as "courts are increasingly asked to review administration action that touches on fundamental personal interests in life, health, and liberty. . . . "[6] Endorsing the growth of judicial power to protect individual rights, Chief Judge David Bazelon of the Court of Appeals of the District of Columbia criticized courts for showing too much deference to administrative decisions. In a 1971 case brought by the Environmental Defense Fund under the Federal Insecticide, Fungicide, and Rodenticide Act asking for agency action to ban the use of pesticide DDT, Judge Bazelon urged an expanded role for the courts in oversight of bureaucratic policy by endorsing a broader interpretation of judicial authority in the review process.[7]

Legal challenges to agency actions have been facilitated by federal statutes specifying judicial review as a remedial mechanism to aid administrative enforcement. Aside from creating statutory rights of action, federal legislation has also encouraged litigation by easing restrictions on standing (particularly for private attorneys general), allowing successful plaintiffs to collect attorney's fees from defendants, permitting plaintiffs to combine resources in class action suits, and perhaps most importantly, making available government-funded legal services for low income people.[8]

THE DEBATE OVER JUDICIAL CAPACITY

"Americans have always resorted to the courts to challenge the action of government, but only from the late 1950s on has the use of litigation as an instrument of social reform become so widespread that it can be called a movement."[9] The bulk of the recent litigation activity aimed at social policy reforms has been directed against the federal bureaucracy to challenge administrative implementation of the statutory design.[10]

Judicial review of administrative policy often stems from litigation involving a class action suit, or at least large numbers of litigants, and assumes a posture of adjudicating or legislating for the society as a whole. The expansion of litigation as a source of social policymaking has led to a more influential role for the courts in determining public policy outcomes because litigation has become a forum for determining "whether or how a government policy or program shall be carried out."[11]

Increased reliance on litigation to achieve social policy goals has in turn generated charges that courts lack the capacity to play a major role in formulating and implementing public policy and that their assumption of this role comes at the expense of institutions more suited to these tasks.[12]

Opponents of judicial involvement in social policymaking claim that courts are not equipped to perform the functions they have undertaken because they cannot effectively select among competing public policy options. Lawsuits, they say, are inappropriate vehicles for formulating social policy because judges are trained to focus on narrow questions of rights and duties and are not encouraged to consider alternatives and weigh costs and benefits as other policymakers are forced to do. They argue that litigation does not allow for the introduction of information outlining likely problems of implementation and therefore courts often make decisions that translate into public policy without awareness of practical constraints. Consequently, courts ignore practical funding problems and impose unrealistic and unattainable goals upon government agencies. Critics point out that the judicial implementation order has negative consequences for bureaucratic efficiency because it upsets the chain of command in the agency by allowing courts to assume final authority over the decisions of agency officials.

In sum, the criticism of the court's ability to create social policy centers around two major themes: first, the adjudicatory model does not lend itself to effective social policy formulation, especially regarding the allocation of public resources; second, courts issue unwise and impractical implementation orders because the judiciary's expertise and ability to assimilate technical data is inferior to the bureaucracy's.

Defenders of judicial capacity claim that the critics' allegations of incapacity appear to be motivated at least as much by ideological disagreement with the output of recent judicial decisionmaking as by concern over the court's deficiencies in creating social policy.[13] They contend that the court's detractors are not persuasive because they assume rather than prove lack of capacity and do not actually demonstrate that courts are *less* capable of dealing with social policy issues than other institutions.[14]

The portrayal of the court's incapacity is further distorted, they insist, because the court's detractors "compare real courts, warts and all, with an ideal vision of other government institutions."[15] Moreover, they assert, the criticism misses the mark because the court's actual performance does not square with the model of adjudication depicted by the critics. Judges devote a great deal of time and energy to fostering settlement agreements and the judicial decrees in social reform litigation are much more conciliatory than the critics indicate.[16]

Additionally, courts' supporters stress that claims of judicial incapacity do not recognize that the judiciary possesses skills for making social policy decisions that other decisionmakers lack.[17] They maintain that judges are better able to assess fairness in administrative procedures because they can be more objective than administrators involved in the daily activity of the agency who are pressured to achieve greater efficiency at lesser costs. Furthermore, judges can be more dispassionate about bureaucratic policy because they are not "subject to the political pressures from a 'clientele.' "[18]

These charges and countercharges about judicial capacity, focusing on the court's capability for formulating sound social policy decisions, are somewhat academic. Despite their real or imagined limitations, courts are unlikely to markedly reduce their influence on social policymaking in the foreseeable future. A more realistic concern about the judiciary's role in the public policymaking arena lies in the court's limited ability to obtain bureaucratic compliance with its decisions.

LIMITATIONS ON JUDICIAL REMEDIES

Judicial decisions are not self-enforcing. A judicial remedy will often fail to produce the desired results because courts frequently confront problems in securing bureaucratic compliance with their decrees. A major obstacle to the implementation of a judicial ruling can be traced to the court's difficulty in countering bureaucratic discretion in carrying out the judicial order. The bureaucracy's ability to thwart the envisioned relief typically arises from vague statutory language and administrative regulations, as well as from the complexity of bureaucratic structures—especially those, like the Social Security Administration, in which power is divided between state and federal agencies.[19] The uneasy relationships between the courts and administrative agencies are often compounded by the bureaucracy's refusal to obey changes mandated by judicial decree; indeed, "experienced administrative lawyers report that administrative agencies are notorious for ignoring court rules."[20]

Because of the difficulty of transforming a judicial decree into a policy output, a victory in the courtroom can be ephemeral. But while litigation by itself may not be sufficient to achieve bureaucratic compliance, a broadly-defined litigation strategy improves a group's ability to bargain more effectively in a pluralist society. A strategy directed toward creating changes in public policy often succeeds by initiating public debate and arousing public interest, creating group solidarity, placing the administrative policy under public scrutiny, and ultimately prompting legislative action to solidify the results of the judicial order.

A realistic picture of litigation therefore requires a broad perspective in which it is viewed as a catalyst for political activity that ultimately leads to social reform.[21] The catalytic, often remote effect of litigation on public policy, makes it difficult, if not impossible, to prove that it "caused" the policy change. It can be shown, however, that the litigation "influenced" the change in public policy without attributing causation solely to it. Exploring the interactions among the social security disability policymakers will help determine whether "it is reasonable to believe that litigation 'made a difference.' " Without claiming that the lawsuits against the Social Security Administration were solely responsible for the adoption of the medical improvement standard, it can be plausibly argued that the social security litigation was "a substantial contributor" to the change in Agency policy.[22]

LITIGATION STRATEGY AS POLITICAL ACTIVITY

Even successful lawsuits do not easily achieve the intended social reform goals. Experienced litigators recognize that litigation must be supplemented by political activity aimed at the executive and legislative branches. They advocate the adoption of a multitargeted approach to litigation strategy that includes lobbying and political bargaining. Viewed in this perspective, a victory in the courtroom is not the sole measure of accomplishment because litigation is only one tactic in a broad-based strategy used by social reform groups.[23]

The ultimate aim of a lawsuit directed against a government agency is a change in the behavior of government officials. While a winning suit is more likely to achieve this goal, it is not critically important if the lawsuit is won or lost because benefits may be derived merely by bringing an action within the court's purview.[24] A losing suit can be instrumental in achieving social reform because judicial involvement provides a countervailing force to bureaucratic power by bolstering adherents inside the bureaucracy and fortifying litigants for the next legal confrontation.[25]

A strategy centered around litigation activity is advantageous because of the benefits that flow from presenting a legal claim regardless of the outcome in the courtroom; attracting public sympathy and raising the consciousness of administrators and legislators are positive results that are derived from litigation—whether the lawsuit ends in victory or defeat. Unsuccessful lawsuits, far from consigning plaintiffs to legal oblivion, produce unforeseen benefits, the greatest of which is increased societal attention to a problem.

Publicity is one of the most important by-products of a lawsuit and plays a key role in the litigants' arsenal of weapons against an administrative agency. The "publicity generated by public interest law intervention can have a strong influence on public opinion and on the behavior of legislatures, [and] government administrative agencies. . . . "[26] Public attention is a natural consequence of litigation because each stage in a lawsuit—from the initial filing of the complaint to the final stage of the judicial decree—becomes part of a public record. "By serving as a window on an agency whose operations would otherwise be largely invisible," litigation obliges government agencies to defend the wisdom of their policies.[27]

A number of strategies are available for arousing public interest and generating support for a legal issue; the litigants' relationship with the media is an important component of a successful litigation strategy. When litigants are portrayed as legally and morally deserving, as the social security disability litigants were, their task in achieving their ultimate goal of policy reform is greatly facilitated. Filing a class action suit also serves as a highly visible way of applying pressure on bureaucratic decisionmakers and is especially significant in lending credibility to the legal complaint.[28]

MODELS OF LITIGATION ACTIVITY

With the Supreme Court's commitment to individual rights, beginning in the late 1930s and continuing through the Warren Court era, the courts were seen as a forum for demands by individuals who lacked the resources to pursue their goals in representative institutions. Most studies of litigation activity have looked at the strategy pursued by such "disadvantaged" individuals forced to rely upon judicial intervention in the policymaking process. The major focus of these studies has been directed at advocates of "liberal" policy changes, such as the Legal Defense Fund (formerly the National Association for the Advancement of Colored People Legal Defense Fund), the American Civil Liberties Union Women's Rights Project and Reproductive Freedom Project, primarily working to expand rights of women and racial minorities through declarations of constitutional rights.[29]

More recently, attention has also been paid to "conservative" social and economic interest groups whose positions have typically been well represented in the state legislatures and Congress and who are now turning to the courts to solidify their legislative gains.[30] Litigants such as the National Association of Manufacturers, Citizens for Decency through Law, and Americans United for Life Legal Defense Fund have joined their liberal adversaries in seeking judicial support for their policy goals. They acknowledge their political influence and seek to enhance their power in the judicial arena because they perceive themselves as disadvantaged *there*.

These two models tend to view litigation as a discrete activity with the courts essentially separate from the political environment. A more accurate model of litigation is one in which litigation is seen as a political activity, and part of a more or less simultaneous multistrategy effort, to exert pressure on the bureaucracy and legislature for policy changes. The social security disability litigation more closely resembles the latter model with litigants using the legal arena as a springboard for accomplishing their policy goals in the political arena. The disability litigants' strategy recognized a need for integrating litigation with other political activity and reflected an accurate sense of judicial capability in implementing the judicial decree.

The Disability Litigation

In 1978, Jerry Mashaw noted that disability beneficiaries were "not, by and large, an organized group capable of identifying, much less bringing to public or congressional attention, aspects of the administrative process that may be in need of reform."[31] While the disability litigants may have initially lacked political clout, this picture changed as thousands of disability claimants assaulted the public consciousness and presented their demands for disability reform in the congressional arena as well as in the courtroom. What was striking about the social security litigation was the immediacy of the legislative response to the litigation activity and the congressional acknowledgement of the litigation as an impetus to the legislation.

Unlike the coordinated litigation activity typified by the civil rights litigation, the social security disability litigation was characterized by a multitude of decentralized lawsuits. Each suit asked the courts to order a specific remedy—the reversal of a disability termination—rather than a broad constitutional remedy. It included a strategy whereby the lawsuits were accompanied by political activity and arousal of public opinion to exert pressure on the government agency.[32]

The social security litigation was complicated by SSA's nonacquiescence policy which created added pressure to supplement the courtroom activity. Litigants were spurred to greater efforts to initiate interest group activity and multiple-plaintiff lawsuits. Although public interest litigation has traditionally involved class action suits, the legal ramifications of nonacquiescence engendered a greater need for this type of litigation. The social security disability litigants relied on class action suits to increase the effectiveness of their demands on the bureaucracy; the number of litigants involved in the statewide and circuitwide class suits became a powerful argument in favor of imposing legislative policy changes upon SSA procedure.

Litigation strategists realize that the impact of litigation is not always immediately felt; the Social Security Administration's policy of nonacquiescence created a situation in which it was especially difficult to determine whether the litigation was effective or not. The outcome of the social security litigation could reasonably be described as both victory and defeat: victory for the individual litigant and defeat for the ultimate goal of changing the administrative policy. Eventually, litigants were forced to transcend the narrow principle of reversal of the termination decision and make demands upon disability policymakers to initiate changes in SSA's administrative procedure.

NOTES

1. Donald Horowitz, "The Courts As Guardians of the Public Interest," *Public Administration Review* 37(March-April 1977):149.

2. 295 U.S. 495 (1935). See Theodore Lowi, *The End of Liberalism* (New York: W. W. Norton, 1969), chapter 5 for a discussion of the implications of the demise of the *Schechter* doctrine in the American political scheme.

3. See David Rosenbloom, "The Judicial Response to the Rise of the American Administrative State," *American Review of Public Administration* 15(Spring 1981):29–51.

4. An explosion of litigation against government agencies followed in the wake of the 1970 *Goldberg v. Kelly*, 397 U.S. 254 (1970), decision and the clamor for an expansive interpretation of the due process clause of the Fourteenth Amendment. The due process clause became the basis for a myriad of suits filed against the government when litigants demanded formal hearings prior to deprivation of "rights" such as jobs, licenses, or public assistance benefits. For further discussion on the expansion of procedural

due process in entitlement programs, see Charles Reich, "The New Property," *Yale Law Journal* 73(1964):734–87; William Van Alstyne, "The Demise of the Right-Privilege Distinction," *Harvard Law Review* 81(1968):1439–64.

5. Rosenbloom, "The Judicial Response to the Administrative State."

6. *Environmental Defense Fund v. Ruckelshaus*, 439 F.2d 584, 598 (D.C. Cir. 1971).

7. *Environmental Defense Fund*, 439 F.2d at 584.

8. See Abram Chayes, "Public Law Litigation and the Burger Court," *Harvard Law Review* 96(November 1982):4–311. See also J. Craig Youngblood and Parker Folse III, "Can Courts Govern? An Inquiry into Capacity and Purpose," in Richard Gambitta, Marlynn May, and James Foster, eds., *Governing through Courts* (Beverly Hills: Sage, 1981), pp. 23–65. They defend judicial activism by pointing to laws such as the Education of All Handicapped Children Act, 20 U.S.C. §§1411–20 (1984), and the Rehabilitation Act of 1973, 29 U.S.C. §§790–95 (1984), in which Congress included a role for the federal courts in enforcing provisions of the Act. More broadly, the Equal Access to Justice Act, 28 U.S.C. §2412 (1984), which allows payment of attorneys fees to prevailing parties in suits against the government when its position was not "substantially justified," provides further evidence of congressional approval of litigation to redress grievances.

9. Joel Handler, *Social Movements and the Legal System* (New York: Academic Press, 1978), p. 1.

10. Ibid. According to Handler, litigation activity is used for demanding policy changes or protesting the implementation of policy by street-level bureaucrats. See also John Denvir, "Toward a Political Theory of Public Interest Litigation," *North Carolina Law Review* 54(1976):1133–60.

11. Abram Chayes, "The Role of the Judge in Public Law Litigation," *Harvard Law Review* 89(May 1976):1295.

12. For arguments that courts lack capacity for social policy decision-making, see Donald Horowitz, *The Courts and Social Policy* (Washington, D.C.: Brookings, 1977); Nathan Glazer, "Should Judges Administer Social Services?" *Public Interest* 50(Winter 1978):64–80. Horowitz's attack focuses on the difficulty of introducing "social facts," that is, historical perspectives, and "consequential facts," that is, implementation constraints, into the litigation. Because litigants influence the introduction of relevant facts into the case, courts often make decisions that translate into public policy without awareness of realistic constraints. Moreover, because courts must passively await litigants and adjudicate only on the facts presented to them, they cannot ascertain if they have all the available information and if the litigant's injuries are representative of others similarly situated.

Glazer also believes that judicial policymaking strains the limits of judicial capacity. Like Horowitz, he criticizes the courts because judges are removed from practical knowledge of problems faced by social welfare or administrative agencies, that is, they are permitted to "ignore the impact of [their] decisions and intervene upon the structure of policy." Glazer, "Should Judges Administer Social Services?" p. 67. The dilemma is sharply illustrated when courts attempt to reorganize governmental services by intruding into the allocation of societal resources and requiring budgetary realignment in the agency. Glazer contends that judicial activism has added to the difficulties of creating effective social policy by reducing the authority and discretion of experienced administrators and substituting for it the theoretical knowledge, speculation, and laboratory research of distant professionals.

In his study of the role of the federal courts in environmental litigation, R. Shep Melnick summed up the problem by noting that "the debate over judicial activism has [largely] focused on the ability of the adjudicatory process to supply generalist judges with information sufficient for solving complex social problems." R. Shep Melnick, *Regulation and the Courts: The Case of the Clean Air Act* (Washington, D.C.: Brookings, 1983), p. 367. Burton Weisbrod's study of public interest law, however, suggests that judges are aware of their limitations and often have been "reluctant to override the judgments of administrative agencies because of the complexity of technical issues involved." Burton Weisbrod, Joel Handler, and Neil Komesar, *Public Interest Law* (Berkeley: University of California Press, 1978), p. 557.

13. See Youngblood and Folse, "Can Courts Govern?" in Gambitta, May, and Foster, eds., *Governing through Courts*. Horowitz has been criticized for not providing empirical evidence of incapacity and instead presenting a normative argument against judicial activism. See Charles Lamb, "Book Review: The Courts and Social Policy," *University of California at Los Angeles Law Review* 26(1978):234–52; Stephen Wasby, "Book Review: The Courts and Social Policy," *Vanderbilt Law Review* 31(1978):727–61; J. Woodford Howard, "Book Review: The Courts and Social Policy," *Washington University Law Quarterly* 4(1978):833–39.

14. Lief Carter is one of the few scholars who attempts to compare relative institutional capacity and in doing so offers a more dispassionate view of the relative capabilities of courts compared to other institutions. His criteria are related to technical competence (policies that express themselves in legal language), ability to assimilate information relative to the problem and to reformulate policy in light of new information (impact and implementation problems), and the last, a legitimacy criterion, that is, whether the policy will be acceptable to the receiving public. Underlying these criteria is the broader question of whether any other policymaking institution has undertaken to deal with the problem. He concludes that courts are well equipped to provide a solution for certain kinds of issues such as legislative malapportionment and criminal procedure but are not the best policymaking institution to deal with such issues as substantive due process, national security, and abortion. See Lief Carter, "When Courts Should Make Policy: An Institutional Approach," in John Gardiner, ed., *Public Law and Public Policy* (New York: Praeger, 1977), pp. 141–57. See also J. Woodford Howard, "Adjudication Reconsidered As a Process of Conflict Resolution: A Variation on Separation Of Powers," *Journal of Public Law* 18(1969):339–70; Timothy O'Neill, "The Imperial Judiciary Meets the Impotent Congress," *Law and Policy* 9(1987):97–117.

15. Richard Posner, *The Federal Courts* (Cambridge: Harvard University

Press, 1985), p. 213. Horowitz admits that he does not compare relative institutional capacity and acknowledges that "parallel research along some of the same dimensions of decision that we have explored would seem very much in order." Horowitz, *Courts and Social Policy*, p. 297.

16. Despite "the rhetoric of their opinions, courts have not relied on coercion, almost never invoking serious sanctions even in the face of persistent recalcitrance." Colin Diver, "The Judge As Political Powerbroker: Superintending Structural Changes in Public Institutions," *Virginia Law Review* 65(1979):45. In their discussion of institutional litigation, Theodore Eisenberg and Stephen Yeazell, "The Ordinary and the Extraordinary in Institutional Litigation," *Harvard Law Review* 93(January 1980):493, point out that often "cases considered to be part of the new litigation are little more than judicial opinions blessing settlements requested by the parties." Concerns about judicial expertise are also somewhat misleading because judges are not solely preoccupied with adjudication within the courtroom. They are perpetually engaged in the process of settling cases outside the adjudicatory framework and remedies that appear to be imposed by judicial fiat are often merely the conferral of judicial approval upon the parties' own resolution of their dispute. Austin Sarat suggests that evaluations of judicial capacity be based upon the judiciary's ability to promote settlements and persuade the parties to enter into consent decrees, that, but for the judicial intervention, would not have come about. Austin Sarat, "Judicial Capacity," in Richard Dubois, ed., *The Analysis of Judicial Reform* (Lexington, Mass.: Lexington Books, 1982), p. 35. See also Michael Churgin, "Mandated Change in Texas: The Federal District Court and the Legislature," in Joel Handler and Julie Zatz, eds., *Neither Angels Nor Thieves: Studies in Deinstitutionalization of Status Offenders* (Washington, D.C.: National Academy Press, 1982), pp. 872–98. In the complex and seemingly interminable litigation over the Texas juvenile justice system, District Court Judge William Justice refrained from issuing injunctive relief and asked the parties to submit implementation plans and engage in settlement negotiations before a final decree was issued. Ibid. Others point out that, questions of capability aside, concern about capacity misses the point because courts have been forced to involve themselves in social policymaking and only began to specify details of institutional reform when it was apparent that state and local governments were not prepared to obey vaguer and more gentle directives. See Eisenberg and Yeazell, "The Ordinary and Extraordinary," p. 493.

17. See Chayes, "The Judge in Public Law Litigation," who points out that legislatures are not well suited for decisionmaking that deals with specific situations, while bureaucracies, often committed to a particular policy, are not able to balance conflicting policy agendas. Unlike both legislatures and bureaucracies, the judiciary has experience with "the task of balancing the importance of competing policy interests in a specific situation." Ibid., p. 1308.

18. Denvir, "Toward a Political Theory," p. 1158. Judges are also not locked into traditional bureaucratic models of decisionmaking with "a rigid,

multilayered hierarchy of numerous officials. . . . " Chayes, "The Judge in Public Law Litigation," p. 1309.

19. See Handler, *Social Movements and the Legal System*; Joel Handler, *Protecting the Social Service Client* (New York: Academic Press, 1979).

20. Handler, *Protecting the Social Service Client*, p. 53.

21. Few impact studies have examined the role that litigation can play as a catalyst for public policy change. The typical targets of judicial impact studies are local school boards (in their compliance with school prayer or integration decisions) and police departments (in their compliance with criminal procedure decisions). Such studies report varying degrees of non-compliant behavior such as avoidance, evasion, and delay.

Classic studies of judicial impact include Kenneth Dolbeare and Phillip Hammond, *The School Prayer Decisions: From Court Policy to Local Practice* (Chicago: University of Chicago Press, 1971); Richard Johnson, *The Dynamics of Compliance: Supreme Court Decision-Making from a New Perspective* (Evanston, Ill.: Northwestern University Press, 1967); David Everson, ed., *The Supreme Court as Policy-Maker: Three Studies on the Impact of Judicial Decisions* (Carbondale, Ill.: Southern Illinois University Public Affairs Research Bureau, 1968); Neal Milner, *The Court and Local Law Enforcement: The Impact of Miranda* (Beverly Hills: Sage, 1971); Harrell Rodgers and Charles Bullock, III, *Coercion to Compliance* (Lexington, Mass.: Lexington Books, 1976); Michael Wald, et al., "Interrogations in New Haven: The Impact of Miranda," *Yale Law Journal* 76(July 1967):1519–1648. See Kathryn Moss, "The Catalytic Effect of a Federal Court Decision on a State Legislature," *Law and Society Review* 19(1985):147–57 for an example of a study that looked at the way in which judicial policy "catalyzed" the Texas State Legislature into making changes in mental health policy. See also Michael Churgin, "Mandated Change in Texas," in Handler and Katz, eds., *Neither Angels Nor Thieves*.

Without offering specific evidence, Michael Perry also noted that judicial activism "in institutional reform cases has served as an important catalyst to legislative and other actions." Michael Perry, *The Constitution, the Courts, and Human Rights* (New Haven: Yale University Press, 1982), p. 155.

22. Denvir, "Toward a Political Theory," p. 1135, n. 5.

23. Handler urges a broader view of the attainments of social reform groups and recommends judgment based upon three perspectives: the first, and perhaps easiest to measure, is the tangible benefit—the won and lost column; the second, the realization of indirect results that are not immediately apparent, including increased publicity and consciousness raising; and the third, the most remote and difficult to measure, greater access to the decisionmaking process by traditionally unrepresented groups. See Handler, *Social Movements and the Legal System*.

24. "A judicial victory does not guarantee a policy change because it is "neither necessary nor sufficient for bringing about the change in behavior toward which the public interest law effort is directed." Wesibrod, Handler, and Komesar, *Public Interest Law*, p. 554. See also Richard Gambitta, "Lit-

igation, Judicial Deference, and Policy Change," in Gambitta, May, and Foster, eds., *Governing through Courts*, pp. 259–82.

25. See Susan Olson, *Clients and Lawyers* (Westport, Conn.: Greenwood Press, 1984). Jeffrey Berry, *The Interest Group Society* (Boston: Little, Brown, 1984), p. 199, cites the effectiveness of lawsuits filed by the transportation-disabled in encouraging the government to settle because it "preferred direct negotiation to the uncertainty of a court decision. Stuart Scheingold was especially enthusiastic about using litigation as leverage against executive agencies as well as creating publicity through litigation as a policial weapon. Stuart Scheingold, "The Politics of Rights Revisited," in Gambitta, May, and Foster, eds., *Governing through Courts*, pp. 193–224.

26. Weisbrod, Handler, and Komesar, *Public Interest Law*, p. 555; see also Robert Mnookin, "Final Observations," in Robert Mnookin, ed., *The Interest of Children* (New York: W. H. Freeman, 1985), pp. 510–27.

27. Jerry Mashaw, et al., *Social Security Hearings and Appeals* (Lexington, Mass.: Lexington Books, 1978), p. 137.

28. See Marie Failinger and Larry May, "Litigating against Poverty," *Ohio State Law Journal* 45(1984):2–56.

29. The seminal work in this area is Clement Vose, *Caucasians Only* (Berkeley: University of California Press, 1959); other studies include Karen O'Connor, *Women's Organizations' Use of the Courts* (Lexington, Mass.: Lexington Books, 1980); Ruth Cowan, "Women's Rights through Litigation: An Examination of the American Civil Liberties Union Women's Rights Project, 1971–1976," *Columbia Human Rights Law Review* 8(1976):373–412; Richard Kluger, *Simple Justice* (New York: Alfred A. Knopf, 1976); Jonathan Casper, *Lawyers before the Warren Court* (Urbana, Ill.: University of Illinois Press, 1972); Richard Cortner, "Strategies and Tactics of Litigants in Constitutional Cases," *Journal of Public Law* 17(1968):287–307. Most of these appraisals of litigation activity are based upon models of constitutional litigation in which organizations attempt to achieve their goals by urging courts to adopt a free-wheeling interpretation of a constitutional principle.

30. For a recent study of conservative interest groups, see Lee Epstein, *Conservatives in Court* (Knoxville, Tenn.: University of Tennessee Press, 1985). See also Karen O'Connor and Lee Epstein, "The Rise of Conservative Interest Group Litigation, *Journal of Politics* 45(1983):479–89.

31. Mashaw, et al., *Social Security Hearings and Appeals*, p. 137.

32. The social security disability litigation was similar to the pattern of litigation established in the suits brought by the disabled during the 1970s seeking statutory entitlement to accessible public transportation. The transportation lawsuits sought judicial enforcement of plaintiffs' rights rather than a declaration of constitutional rights. The litigation was characterized by numerous uncoordinated suits seeking specific remedies such as specially designed accessible buses and trains, elevators in subway systems, or an alternative public transportation system for the disabled. Recognizing that the judicial outcome was not sufficient to produce the desired policy changes, litigants combined lawsuits with extrajudicial political activity to increase leverage on the bureaucracy. See Susan Olson, "The Political Ev-

olution of Interest Group Litigation," in Gambitta, May, and Foster, eds., *Governing through Courts*, pp. 225–58. See also Olson, *Clients and Lawyers*; Robert Katzman, *Institutional Disability* (Washington, D.C.: Brookings, 1986). Olson and Katzman provide analyses of public policymaking for the transportation disabled; their approach looks at the litigation as part of the effort to enforce the legislation guaranteeing rights to public transportation and prohibiting discrimination against the handicapped. See also Neal Milner, "The Right to Refuse Treatment: Four Case Studies of Legal Mobilization," *Law and Society Review* 21(1987):447–85, for a discussion of the process of legal and political mobilization on the issue of the rights of mental patients to refuse treatment.

3

The Shaping of Social Security Disability Policy

The social security disability program arose out of the Social Security Act of 1935,[1] an Act that "constituted an unprecedented expansion in the role of the federal government in only twenty-nine pages. . . . "[2] The linchpin of the Social Security Act was the old age insurance program which, as the Supreme Court noted in 1937, was intended "to save men and women from the rigors of the poor house as well as from the haunting fear that such a lot awaits them when the journey's end is near."[3]

Franklin Roosevelt, consumate politician that he was, realized that affixing the notion of insurance to his social security program would generate current support and help insulate it from attack in the future.[4] His instincts proved sound and wage earners have continued to regard the social security program as "a solemn government contract—not welfare, but an earned right."[5]

In any social insurance program, the American experience no exception, policymakers must initially resolve the problem of allocating benefits "according to need" (the "adequacy" principle) or "giving them in proportion to individual tax payments" (the "equity" principle).[6] In the early years of the social security program, inconsistency ruled and neither choice was clearly preferred nor implemented by policymakers. American social security benefits never rose to the level of support in the European concept of social insurance. But, as the program developed, the adequacy principle generally prevailed as the private insurance concept became more attenuated and the social insurance notion expanded. "Once the concept of individual equity was dismissed as the guiding principle for the program, almost any future change, whether demanded by special interest groups or recommended by public suppliers, could be rationalized on the grounds of social justice or welfare arguments."[7]

Distinguishable from welfare or public assistance, social insurance programs are also distinct from private insurance plans because they are not governed by a rigid formula of return on premiums nor by other strict

revenue considerations.[8] Martha Derthick attributed the shift away from
equity principles in the social security program to the bureaucracy's desire
to attain "welfare objectives" and the congressional desire to provide benefits
to as many people as possible to keep social security payroll taxes as low as
possible.[9] These two goals converged and succeeded in creating a clientele
for the social security program that not unexpectedly viewed any attempts
at fiscal restraint with disfavor.

DISABILITY INSURANCE

The social insurance concept was expanded when disability protection
was grafted onto the original social security program in 1954. While the
rhetoric of the disability program emphasized its strict criteria for entitlement, there was, for about twenty years, a gradual expansionist movement
as benefits were increased and additional beneficiaries were added; here
too, as in the social security program, adequacy (albeit, somewhat limited)
triumphed over strict equity.

The Social Security Act authorizes the payment of benefits to individuals
able to prove their disability to the satisfaction of the Social Security Administration—first, to officials within the state agencies and ultimately to administrators within the federal social security bureaucracy. Unlike the
veterans' disability program in which disability is measured in percentages
and benefits are awarded according to the degree of disability, a social security disability beneficiary must be totally disabled. Total disability precludes a capacity to work at *any* meaningful job in the national economy.[10]

The concept of disability coverage was not unique in the United States
when disability insurance became part of the social security umbrella of
protection. Various disability programs, such as veterans, railroad worker's,
worker's compensation, and civil service, as well as private insurance plans,
already existed to provide models for the social security disability program.[11]

The social security disability insurance (SSDI or DI) program functions
as an income maintenance scheme that attempts to replace all or part of
income lost due to disability; benefits are related to predisability income.
By way of contrast, an income support, or welfare, program is designed to
maintain individuals at a predetermined income level—regardless of income
prior to disability.[12] The DI program differs from a public welfare program
because benefits are larger; they are awarded without consideration of other
income in the family; and unlike benefits in welfare assistance programs,
disability insurance benefits are contingent upon an employment history.[13]

The distinction between the DI program and public welfare is not as
obvious for some. For while the disability program is titled an insurance
plan, it is tenuously connected to market insurance concepts. Indeed, Robert Dixon has argued that, "despite their semicontributory nature," it is a
"misnomer" to apply the term insurance to the social security retirement
and disability programs.[14] It is especially "misleading," he insists, to talk
about an insurance concept in the disability program because while disability benefits are financed through payroll deductions, they are primarily
awarded to the older, the poor, and the unskilled worker. In his view, the

disability insurance plan qualifies more as a welfare program than an insurance program.[15]

Disabled persons may also receive benefits from the federal government under the Supplemental Security Income (SSI) Program. SSI benefits became available to former recipients of state public assistance when a number of disparate state welfare programs were "federalized," that is, brought under the auspices of the Social Security Administration, in 1972.[16] With federal payments beginning in 1974, SSI now provides benefits for persons unable to meet the work history requirements of social security; eligibility requires classification as aged, blind, or disabled and is need-based.

Disabled persons receiving benefits under state welfare programs before July 1973 were automatically covered or "grandfathered in" by SSI when payments began in January 1974; applicants after July 1973 were required to meet the federal disability standards. Today, disabled persons may receive benefits concurrently from the supplemental income program as well as the disability insured program if they meet disability and need standards.

The creation of the SSI program has helped blur the conceptual distinction between disability insurance and public welfare.[17] Moreover, since July 1973, the legal standard for adult disability has been identical under both programs. Nevertheless, differences between SSDI and SSI still exist for purposes of distribution of benefits. SSI benefits are only paid to the disabled individual, not to dependents or family survivors. In contrast, in keeping with the insurance scheme, the DI program provides benefits to nondisabled family members; spouses of disabled insured workers are eligible for dependents' benefits if they are either sixty-two years old or are caring for a minor or disabled child. Minor children of insured workers also receive dependents' benefits. Additionally, disabled surviving spouses of deceased insured workers are eligible for benefits.[18]

DISABILITY PROGRAM BENEFICIARIES

The distribution of disability insurance beneficiaries by sex and age, shown in Table 3.1, indicates that the average age of recipients has declined since the inception of the program, in part because of eased restrictions on age requirements.

The table shows that workers between the ages of fifty-five and fifty-nine were most frequently awarded benefits, and about half the beneficiaries were fifty-five or older when *first* awarded benefits. Because entitlement to disability benefits ends when the disability ends, at death, or at age sixty-five,[19] most beneficiaries receive disability benefits for a maximum of ten years.

Benefit Awards

Disability insurance benefits represent a fraction of the total sums expended under the social security program. At the end of January 1985, the combined old age, survivors, and disability insurance program (OASDI) was paying over $15 (15.1) billion in monthly cash benefits to over 36 million

Table 3.1
Characteristics of Disability Recipients (1960–1982)

Year	Total #	Average Age	Total %	Percent of Disabled Workers By Age*								
				Under 30	30–39	40–44	45–49	50–54	55–59	60–61	62–64	65**
				MEN								
1960	168,466	54.5	100	0.8	7.0	6.5	10.5	16.7	20.0	11.8	21.3	4.1
1965	186,808	53.0	100	1.8	8.2	7.9	11.1	17.1	25.7	14.0	13.0	1.0
1970	258,072	52.1	100	6.7	7.6	6.5	10.1	14.7	23.5	12.3	16.1	2.6
1975	408,531	51.5	100	7.7	8.6	6.2	9.5	15.7	23.1	12.1	14.6	2.5
1980	275,185	51.2	100	8.3	9.7	6.0	8.4	14.7	24.6	12.3	14.2	1.8
1981	244,984	50.8	100	8.6	10.2	6.2	8.4	14.5	24.3	13.0	13.1	1.7
1982	207,453	50.9	100	8.4	10.4	6.3	8.4	14.1	24.6	12.9	13.6	1.2

WOMEN

Year	Number											
1960	39,339	52.5	100	0.7	8.1	8.0	13.3	21.9	24.6	12.4	10.1	0.8
1965	66,691	53.2	100	1.1	6.5	7.4	11.7	19.3	28.3	14.1	10.9	0.6
1970	92,312	52.8	100	4.2	6.3	6.1	11.0	17.5	27.2	13.0	12.9	1.7
1975	183,518	52.1	100	6.1	7.3	6.1	10.1	17.7	25.5	12.2	12.9	2.1
1980	121,374	51.1	100	7.4	9.7	6.4	9.3	16.3	25.5	11.7	12.2	1.5
1981	106,863	50.8	100	7.8	10.2	6.5	9.5	16.4	25.1	12.0	11.1	1.4
1982	89,678	50.5	100	8.0	10.9	6.8	9.5	15.6	24.9	11.7	11.4	1.1

* Age in year of award.

** Awards to workers 65 or older with entitlement preceding 65.

SOURCE: 1984-1985 Annual Statistical Supplement, Social Security Bulletin.

31

(36,598,394) beneficiaries. Of these, retired workers numbered a little over 22 million (22,001,641) or 60 percent. Disabled workers constituted 7 percent of the total, or about two and one-half million (2,603,382) persons. The average monthly benefits paid in January 1985 were similar, with $461.10 going to retired workers and $470.44 paid to disabled workers.[20]

A comparison of benefits arising out of each program, illustrated in Table 3.2, shows that the number of monthly benefits awarded out of the DI trust fund constituted only about 4 percent of the OASDI program in 1960. Although the proportion of DI monthly awards would grow to 13 percent of OASDI, after 1980 the percentage began declining about 1 percent a year. By the end of 1985 the number of monthly benefits paid out of the disability trust fund comprised about 10 percent of the total number of OASDI monthly benefit awards. Similarly, the amount of monthly benefits paid to DI beneficiaries as a percentage of benefits paid to all OASDI beneficiaries decreased from 1980 to 1981 after a steady rise after 1960.

Average Monthly Benefits

SSA statistics, seen in Table 3.3, reveal a steady increase in the amount of the average monthly disability benefit. By the end of 1985, the average monthly award to a disabled wage earner was $483.86. Monthly payments rose in part because the earnings base of workers' contributions were raised and because benefits were indexed to the Consumer Price Index.[21] The precise amount of a disability award is calculated on the basis of additional factors such as number of dependents, the duration of the disability, and the age of the worker at the onset of disability. It was estimated in 1979 that the average value of a successful disability application was about $30,000.[22]

THE POLITICS OF EXPANSION

The disability program is today an integral part of the American social insurance scheme. Spawned amid great controversy, disability insurance was initially under attack in Congress from medical and business groups fearing an expansion of social insurance benefits. Within a relatively short time, Congress was subjected to pressure from the opposite direction and acceded to constituents' demands to increase the number of beneficiaries and ease restrictions on eligibility.

The Disability Freeze

Although disability insurance had been under discussion at the top levels of the Social Security Board and Advisory Councils as early as 1938, the concept of national disability insurance was not accepted until almost twenty years after passage of the Social Security Act.[23]

In 1954 Congress enacted a program allowing a freeze on the social security retirement contributions of disabled workers.[24] Under this "disabil-

Table 3.2
Comparison of Monthly Benefits of Programs within SSA (1960–1985)

End Of Year	Number			Amount (In Thousands)		
	Total	OASI*	DI**	Total	OASI*	DI**
1960	14,844,589	14,157,138	687,451	936,321	888,320	48,000
1965	20,866,767	19,127,716	1,739,051	1,516,802	1,395,817	120,986
1970	26,228,629	23,563,634	2,664,995	2,628,326	2,385,926	242,400
1975	32,084,511	27,732,311	4,352,200	5,727,758	5,047,656	680,102
1980	35,618,840	30,936,668	4,682,172	10,694,022	9,432,299	1,261,723
1981	36,006,371	31,550,097	4,456,274	12,255,310	10,901,677	1,353,632
1982	35,840,411	31,866,946	3,973,465	13,320,815	11,997,917	1,322,899
1983	36,084,823	32,271,893	3,812,930	14,173,441	12,834,854	1,338,587
1984	36,478,971	32,657,167	3,821,804	15,025,756	13,636,246	1,389,510
1985	37,058,353	33,151,184	3,907,169	15,901,643	14,441,737	1,459,906

* Benefits paid from the Old-Age and Survivors Insurance Trust Fund to retired workers and their spouses and children and to all survivors.

** Benefits paid from the Disability Insurance Trust Fund to disabled workers and their spouses and children.

SOURCE: Table M-8, Social Security Bulletin 49(April 1986):35.

Table 3.3
Average Amount of Monthly Benefits (1960–1985)

End of Year	Disabled Workers	Spouses	Children
1960	$ 89.31	$ 34.41	$ 30.21
1965	97.76	34.96	31.61
1970	131.29	42.55	38.63
1975	225.89	67.42	61.95
1980	370.74	110.48	104.41
1981	413.15	121.62	123.40
1982	440.60	129.24	127.93
1983	456.20	129.17	135.53
1984	470.67	130.92	138.51
1985	483.86	132.58	141.79

SOURCE: Table M-12, Social Security Bulletin 49(April 1986):39.

ity" plan, disabled workers could collect benefits at retirement as if they had continued working until then. The program, an indirect approach to the ultimate goal of providing cash benefits for disabled workers, was "the first step down a slippery slope" and part of the gradual insertion of disability insurance into the American social security program.[25] And "for the Social Security Administration, the freeze represented a step along the incremental path to disability insurance."[26]

Cash Benefits

With the enactment of the freeze, disability advocates continued their efforts to achieve their long-term goal of cash benefits. The House of Representatives had passed a disability insurance measure approving cash benefits in 1955; the bill authorized the distribution of cash benefits to all eligible disabled insured wage earners. Funds were to be generated from a slight increase in payroll taxes committed to a separate disability trust fund.

The disability proposal soon became enmeshed in political battle as congressional Democrats, especially in the Senate, saw an opportunity to create a campaign issue in the November 1956 election and embarrass the Republican presidential candidate. The cash awards program became an issue upon which Senate Democrats were able to capitalize on their 1954 congressional successes and form a coalition under the leadership of Senate Majority Leader Lyndon Johnson. After achieving a narrow (47–45) victory in the Senate in July 1956, the Democrats now had a campaign weapon against the Republican Party. Their "party platform boasted of having improved social insurance over the Republicans' opposition."[27]

Supported by organized labor, the Democrats were able to shepherd the legislation through Congress despite the opposition of the National Association of Manufacturers, the American Medical Association, the Chamber of Commerce, and large segments of the insurance industry who lobbied against the cash benefits program. Advocates of the cash benefits program relied heavily on the concept of incrementalism and argued that the benefits, initially available only to those between fifty and sixty years old, should merely be thought of as early retirement benefits to individuals who could no longer work because of disability. Opponents warned of the undeterminable costs of the program and the problems of fostering dependency upon government largesse.[28]

Although successfully emerging from the congressional battleground, the legislation that was enacted in 1956 had been compromised to "accommodate conservative opposition."[29] Because they were wary of the discretionary authority invested in federal program executives, conservatives had initially, when agreeing to the 1954 freeze, insisted on a major role for the states in eligibility determinations; this scheme remained in place when cash benefits were introduced. Compromise was eventually reached with the decision that eligibility would be determined by state agencies and kept under federal supervision to maintain uniformity of standards.

Conservatives were also successful in establishing a six-month waiting period and an eligibility threshold age of fifty years.[30] Moreover, benefits were restricted to disabled insured workers with no compensation for dependents. Despite their initial victory in setting limits on benefits and terms, the conservatives were eventually defeated by the program expansionists.

Program Executives

It was not surprising that the program executives of the social security bureaucracy played an inordinately powerful role in setting the social security policy agenda and determining its outcome. Their dominance in the policymaking process stemmed from their virtually unchallenged control over the instruments of analysis including "the timely identification of social needs, the invention of policy responses, and the projection of costs."[31]

As part of their efforts to constrain the social security bureaucracy, congressional conservatives had demanded the creation of Social Security Advisory Councils. The first council met in 1938 with future councils serving at sporadic intervals until 1956 when they became statutorily mandated. The councils had been intended to restrain the power of the social security bureaucrats. But as events later proved, the supposedly detached Advisory Councils, meeting periodically with representatives from various interested groups—business, labor, the insurance industry, and the public—actually "functioned so as to foster program-serving attitudes and choices."[32]

Conservatives were correct in fearing program aggrandisement by the SSA bureaucracy; the continuous expansion of the disability program was accelerated by the efforts of the social security program executives. Enjoining his staff not to be overly influenced by a conservative philosophy, in 1960, the head of Disability Operations indicated that his primary fear was the disallowance of proper claims. He instructed his employees to give claimants "the benefit of the doubt" in situations "where there is a reasonable doubt in a close case."[33] Similarly, testifying before the Ways and Means Subcommittee on Social Security in 1960, Robert Ball, Social Security commissioner, stated: "I can assure you the general attitude of people in the district office is wanting to pay claims."[34]

Opposition Subsides

Guided by these principles, the disability program assumed increasing importance to the American labor force. In contrast to the hard-fought battle over its initial creation, the "post–1956 liberalization of the law . . . suddenly seemed to lose its political salience."[35] The controversy dissipated in large part because the policy changes and the program's growth were incremental. The disability plan had been attacked by the American Medical Association as a first step toward socialized medicine because physicians were to make eligibility determinations under the supervision of the federal government.[36] Opposition from physicians' groups diminished as members became aware that their fears about socialized medicine were unfounded. Additionally, the medical profession began to focus its attention on the next perceived threat: health insurance for the aged or the Medicare program.

New Beneficiaries

By extending the payment of monthly cash benefits to dependents of disabled workers, the 1958 Amendments created a new class of beneficiaries.[37] Eligible dependents now included spouses who reached retirement age or were caring for minor or disabled children as well as unmarried dependent children, including older children who became disabled before age twenty-two. Divorced spouses who had been married to an insured worker for at least ten years were also now eligible for benefits.[38]

Table 3.4 shows the number of monthly benefits awarded each year to disabled workers and their dependents from 1960 to 1985.

Number of Monthly Benefit Awards

Table 3.5 illustrates the number and amount of monthly benefits in current payment status for disabled workers and eligible family members from 1960 to 1985.

Eligibility Is Eased

The fifty-year-old threshold was repealed in 1960 to allow workers under fifty to become eligible for benefits.[39] Congress again eased eligibility in 1965 by imposing a twelve-month duration requirement to replace the more re-

Table 3.4
Number of Monthly Benefits Awarded to Disabled Workers and Dependents per Year (1960–1985)

Year	Total	Disabled Workers	Spouses	Children
1960	366,302	207,805	54,187	104,310
1965	520,298	253,499	69,183	197,616
1970	763,234	350,384	96,304	316,546
1975	1,256,606	592,049	148,741	515,216
1980	883,984	389,152	108,502	386,330
1981	787,321	345,254	96,207	345,867
1982	641,397	298,531	78,246	264,620
1983	620,688	311,491	80,085	229,112
1984	679,461	357,141	81,834	240,486
1985	713,907	377,371	83,511	253,025

SOURCE: Table M-16, Social Security Bulletin 49(April 1986):42.

Table 3.5
Monthly Benefits in Current Payment Status for Disabled Workers and Dependents

End Of Year	Total Number*	Disabled Workers	Total Amount* (In Thousands)	Disabled Workers (In Thousands)
1960	687,451	455,371	$ 48,000	$ 40,668
1965	1,739,051	988,074	120,986	96,599
1970	2,664,995	1,492,948	242,400	196,010
1975	4,352,200	2,488,774	680,102	562,180
1980	4,682,172	2,861,253	1,261,723	1,060,792
1981	4,456,274	2,776,519	1,353,632	1,147,113
1982	3,973,465	2,603,713	1,322,899	1,147,186
1983	3,812,930	2,568,966	1,338,587	1,171,950
1984	3,821,804	2,596,535	1,389,510	1,222,110
1985	3,907,169	2,656,500	1,459,906	1,285.386

*Includes disabled workers, spouses, and children.

SOURCE: Table M-11, Social Security Bulletin 49(April 1986):38.

strictive "long-continued and indefinite duration" language of the 1956 Amendments.[40] The change meant that entitlement no longer required a finding of "permanent" disability. Finally, in 1967, another group of beneficiaries was added to the program when disabled surviving spouses of insured workers became entitled to benefits; they were required to meet a stricter standard of disability by demonstrating that they could not engage in *any* gainful employment activity.[41]

THE POLITICS OF RETRENCHMENT

Congressional statements during debate over the disability program show that Congress had intended a restrictive interpretation of disability entitlement.[42] When originally enacted, eligibility was limited to the totally and permanently disabled and benefits were paid only to persons unable "to engage in any substantial gainful activity by reason of any medically determinable physical or mental impairment which can be expected to result in death or to be of long-continued and indefinite duration."[43]

Although content for the most part to go along with the expansionist philosophy, as costs continued to increase, there were some stirrings of congressional unrest over the size and expense of the disability program in the latter part of the 1960s. And around this time, Congress saw the need to reiterate its original position that disability insurance should not be viewed as a substitute for unemployment insurance.

Kerner v. Flemming

When the disability insurance program had originated, it was accompanied by a House Ways and Means report that stressed the need for "a clear distinction between this program [disability insurance] and one concerned with unemployment...."[44] As the program matured, however, would-be beneficiaries began challenging the concept of social security as an insurance program only for the totally disabled.

Supported by the Second Circuit's opinion in *Kerner v. Flemming*[45] as well as other appellate court cases, claimants advocated that the strict medical definition of disability be expanded to allow consideration of employability.

In *Kerner*, the Second Circuit had essentially taken the position that disability benefits might substitute as unemployment compensation for disabled persons who are *unable to find work*. The case revolved around a sixty-year-old furniture repairman with diabetes and a severe heart condition who could not return to his old job but was willing to seek other employment. As most employers were reluctant to hire individuals with his impairments, he was not able to find another job. The Secretary denied disability benefits and Kerner sought judicial review. The court held that the Secretary had not shown that Mr. Kerner would be able to *find* an available job and remanded the case for the taking of additional evidence on this issue.

The 1967 Amendments

Rejecting the *Kerner* approach by enacting the 1967 Amendments, Congress reiterated its position that disability benefits were intended only for those totally incapable of working. The Amendments made it clear that job availability was not part of the definition of disability. Disability meant that there was *no* job in the national economy that the claimant could perform; local employment opportunities were irrelevant as was the likelihood that the disabled person might actually secure work.

The 1967 Amendments constituted the first legislative restriction on eligibility. Reflecting congressional concern with the expansion of the disability insurance program, the more restrictive eligibility requirements were intended to reinforce the original legislative intent and separate the concept of disability from the practical consideration of job availability.

The difficulty of establishing an unambiguous definition of disability proved to be a constant source of concern to members of Congress. The 1967 Amendments required consideration of vocational evidence in the disability determination process and, following passage of this legislation, the Secretary developed administrative guidelines for the state agencies. However, because these guidelines were not uniformly applied by the agencies, eligibility determinations remained inconsistent.

ADMINISTRATIVE RESTRICTIONS

The 1967 Amendments represented the last statutory alteration in the definition of disability. In the following years, social security disability policymaking was primarily in the hands of Agency officials who no longer looked for ways to expand the disability program but instead moved to slow down its growth.

The "Grid"

Reflecting congressional unrest over lack of uniform standards, Congress ordered SSA to promulgate regulations establishing uniform guidelines of eligibility. In 1979 the Social Security Administration proposed a formula for determining eligibility for benefits based upon a combination of medical and vocational factors. Known in social security parlance as the "Grid," the medical-vocational guidelines became effective as final regulations on February 26, 1979.[46]

The "Grid" became the final determination in a new administrative procedure specified in a sequential five-step evaluation.[47] It was designed to ensure uniformity, fairness, and predictability in decisionmaking by setting forth criteria to determine if claimants met eligibility requirements. By creating a matrix of vocational factors—age, education, and prior work experience—in combination with medical determinations of a claimant's residual functional capacity (RFC) for work, the regulations were designed to allow adjudicators to consult a table to determine eligibility.[48]

Individuals could challenge one of the categories in which they were placed but once the categories were fixed, the final decision on eligibility was prescribed by the "Grid." The regulations explaining the "Grid" stipulated that all criteria of a classification must be satisfied before it could be used; where any of the findings of fact did not conform to the requirements of the classification, the "Grid" could not be applied and could only serve as a guide in the disability determination.[49]

The "Grid" was attacked for eliminating individual consideration from the disability review process but most courts upheld it as a valid exercise of the Secretary's rule-making authority.[50] In 1983 the Supreme Court placed its stamp of approval on the "Grid" by holding that the Secretary's reliance on rule-making to resolve issues in the individual's disability determination did not conflict with the Social Security Act's requirement of individual consideration of eligibility.[51]

The Agency's stricter approach to disability entitlement was also evidenced in increased denials on the basis of the no severe impairment stage of the sequential evaluation and, with a further revision of the regulations in 1980, a new formulation of the standard used to evaluate pain.[52] The criteria for assessing pain as well as the interpretation of the severity step have provided the impetus for major confrontations between the Social Security Administration and disability program beneficiaries; these two issues have also been a source of controversy between SSA and the federal courts.

Thus, about twenty years after the disability insurance program was begun, it appeared that the Social Security Administration's enthusiasm for growth faded and was replaced by an increasingly restrictive attitude toward disability entitlement. And by the middle of the 1970s, a new disability era had begun.

NOTES

1. Social Security Act of 14 Aug. 1935, ch. 531, Pub. L. No. 74–271, 49 Stat. 620 (1935). The Act consisted of three parts: a welfare program, an old age retirement program, and an unemployment compensation program. Each involved different degrees of federal/state involvement. See Carolyn Weaver, *The Crisis in Social Security* (Durham, N.C.: Duke University Press, 1982), chapter 5; and Edward Berkowitz, *Disabled Policy* (Cambridge: Cambridge University Press, 1987), chapter 2, for a discussion of the original provisions of the Social Security Act.

2. Weaver, *The Crisis in Social Security*, p. 92.

3. *Helvering v. Davis*, 301 U.S. 619, 641 (1937).

4. Robert Dixon, *Social Security Disability and Mass Justice* (New York: Praeger, 1973), p. 21.

5. Paul Light, *Artful Work: The Politics of Social Security Reform* (New York: Random House, 1984), p. 34.

6. Martha Derthick, *Policymaking for Social Security* (Washington, D.C.: Brookings, 1979), p. 213.

7. Weaver, *The Crisis in Social Security*, p. 124.

8. Dixon, *Mass Justice*, p. 21; Edward Berkowitz and Kim McQuaid,

Creating the Welfare State (New York: Praeger, 1980), pp. 106–10; see also Weaver, *The Crisis in Social Security*, chapters 6 and 7.

9. Derthick, *Policymaking for Social Security*, p. 215.

10. Under current law, an individual is entitled to benefits upon presenting proof of an inability "to engage in any substantial gainful activity by reason of any medically determinable physical or mental impairment which can be expected to result in death or which has lasted or can be expected to last for a continuous period of not less than 12 months." 42 U.S.C. §423(d)(1)(A) (1984). To satisfy this test, the impairment must be of such severity that it prevents the individual from returning to prior work and also, considering his or her age, education, and prior work experience, precludes a person from "engag[ing] in any other kind of substantial gainful activity which exists in the national economy. . . . " 42 U.S.C. §423(d)(2)(A) (1984).

11. Deborah Stone, *The Disabled State* (Philadelphia: Temple University Press, 1984), p. 69.

12. William Johnson, "Disability, Income Support, and Social Insurance," in Edward Berkowitz, ed., *Disability Policies and Government Programs* (New York: Praeger, 1979), p. 80.

13. Ibid., p. 120; see Edward Berkowitz, "The American Disability System in Historical Perspective," in Berkowitz, ed., *Disability Policies*, pp. 16–74.

14. Dixon, *Mass Justice*, p. 4.

15. Ibid., pp. 21–23.

16. Social Security Amendments of 1972, Pub. L. No. 92–603, 86 Stat. 1329 (1972) (taking effect on January 1, 1974).

17. Berkowitz, *Disabled Policy*, chapter 2.

18. The disability insurance program is contained in Title II of the Social Security Act (42 U.S.C. §§401–33 (1984)); the supplemental security income program is contained in Title XVI of the Act (42 U.S.C. §§1381–83 (1984)). Benefits under the SSDI and SSI programs are paid to five categories of disabled individuals with standards of eligibility cutting across type of program and type of beneficiary. The SSDI programs includes insured disabled wage earners, disabled surviving spouses of insured wage earners, and disabled children of insured wage earners. The SSI program includes disabled needy adults and disabled needy children. The legal standard of disability is the same for the insured wage earner, the disabled child of an insured wage earner, and the adult SSI beneficiary. The disabled surviving spouse and the disabled SSI child must meet a stricter test of eligibility to receive benefits.

19. 20 C.F.R. §404.316 (1986).

20. "Program Operations," *Social Security Bulletin* 48(April 1985):2.

21. Mordechai Lando, Alice Farley, and Mary Brown, "Recent Trends in the Social Security Disability Insurance Program," *Social Security Bulletin* 45(August 1982):3–4. The maximum taxable earnings rose from $14,100 in 1975 to $25,900 in 1980. Cost of living increases were instituted in 1972 and have been factored into the benefit awards each June since 1975. Ibid., p. 4.

22. General Accounting Office, *Report on Controls over Medical Examinations Necessary for Better Determinations of Disability by the Social Security Administration*, HRD–79–119 (October 9, 1979).

23. In 1950 Congress had enacted welfare legislation that made money available to the states for distribution to claimants who were classified as totally and permanently disabled as well as poor. Berkowitz, *Disabled Policy*, p. 70.

24. Social Security Amendments of 1954, Pub. L. No. 83–761, 68 Stat. 1052 (1954).

25. Stone, *The Disabled State*, p. 77.

26. Berkowitz, *Disabled Policy*, p. 73.

27. Derthick, *Policymaking for Social Security*, p. 306.

28. Weaver, *The Crisis in Social Security*, p. 138.

29. Derthick, *Policymaking for Social Security*, p. 308.

30. As a result of a legislative change in 1972, the current waiting period is five months; see 20 C.F.R. §404.315 (1986). The fifty-year-old minimum age requirement was dropped in 1960.

31. Gary Freeman and Paul Adams, "Ideology and Analysis in American Social Security Policymaking," *Journal of Social Policy* 12(January 1983):80–81.

32. Derthick, *Policymaking for Social Security*, p. 101. There were six Councils between 1938 and 1971; see chapter 4 for a discussion of the Social Security Advisory Councils.

33. Ibid., p. 310.

34. Ibid.

35. Ibid., p. 311.

36. In a 1949 proposal, federal administrators had been given the responsibility of making the eligibility determinations. Because of concern about federal control over the medical profession, Congress had also side-stepped this contentious political issue at that time.

37. Social Security Amendments of 1958, Pub. L. No. 85–840 §§301–304, 72 Stat. 1013, 1026–29 (1958). The number of monthly benefits awarded to the wage earner constituted about two-thirds of the total number of monthly disability benefits awarded. The actual amount of money distributed to wage earners compared to dependents was a great deal more than two-thirds; insured workers received as much as 85 percent of the dollar amount awarded as benefits in 1985. See Table M–11, *Social Security Bulletin* 49(April 1986):38.

38. According to current regulations, the wife's or husband's monthly benefit is half of the insured person's primary insurance amount. Widows' and widowers' benefits, however, are equal to the entire primary insurance amount of the insured person while a child's disability benefits are based upon one-half the primary insurance amount if the insured worker is alive and three-fourths of the primary insurance amount if the worker has died. See 20 C.F.R. §§404.330 to 404.355 (1986).

39. Social Security Amendments of 1960, Pub. L. No. 86–778, §401, 74 Stat. 924, 967 (1960).

40. Social Security Amendments of 1965, Pub. L. No. 89–97, §303(a)(2), 79 Stat. 286, 367 (1965).

41. Social Security Amendments of 1967, Pub. L. No. 90–248, §104, 81 Stat. 821, 828–33 (1967).

42. Landon Rowland, "Judicial Review of Disability Determinations," *Georgetown Law Journal* 52(1963):51–52.

43. Social Security Amendments of 1956, Pub. L. No. 84–880, §103(c)(2), 70 Stat. 807, 815 (1956).

44. Subcommittee on the Administration of Social Security Laws, House Committee on Ways and Means, 86th Congress, 2d Sess. (1960); cited in Stone, *The Disabled State*, p. 84.

45. 283 F.2d 916 (2d Cir. 1960). The dispute over the *Kerner* doctrine represented a battle over domination of the social security policymaking process as SSA was forced to accept the court's interpretation until Congress intervened with the 1967 Amendments. For a discussion of the relations between the courts and SSA during this period, see Dixon, *Mass Justice*, pp. 95–99; and Stone, *The Disabled State*, chapter 5.

46. 43 Fed. Reg. 55,349 (1979); 20 C.F.R. §404.1520 (1986).

47. If a finding of nondisability is made at any step of the determination, the evaluation ceases and the claim is denied. The process requires that an initial decision must be made to determine whether the claimant is currently engaged in substantial gainful activity; if so, a finding of nondisability is proper. Second, it must be determined whether the claimant has a severe impairment—one that significantly limits his or her ability to perform work-related functions; if the impairment is not severe, the claimant is deemed not disabled on the basis of the medical evidence alone. If a severe impairment is found, it is compared to those listed in the regulations (the Listings) to see if the claimant can be considered disabled solely on the basis of the medical evidence. If the impairment is not severe enough to meet (or equal) the Listings, an inquiry is made about whether the claimant can perform past relevant work. If so, the claimant is considered not disabled. If the claimant cannot perform past relevant work, the last step of the process requires the adjudication to consider whether the claimant can perform other work in economy. This determination is made by assessing the claimant's residual functional capacity (RFC), that is, the maximum work capability or level of exertion. The last step of the sequential evaluation utilizes the RFC to find the appropriate "Grid" matrix to determine whether the individual is disabled or not. See Jerry Mashaw, "The Definition of Disability from the Perspective of Administration," in Berkowitz, ed., *Disability Policies*, pp. 160–67.

48. The "Grid" consists of four tables, each based on work capability ranging from sedentary to heavy work. The tables are composed of matrices of age, education, and occupational skills.

49. Before the "Grid" was instituted, the Secretary was required to present a vocational expert to identify the type of jobs the claimant could perform. In determining the availability of jobs for use in the "Grid," the Secretary has taken administrative notice of the number of jobs that exist throughout the national economy at the various functional levels by referring to the

same sources as vocational experts; this has eliminated the need for vocational experts to testify to the existence of work in the national economy that the individual could perform. The Sixth Circuit ruled in *Kirk v. Secretary of Health and Human Services*, 667 F.2d 524 (6th Cir. 1981) that use of the "Grid" did not impermissibly shift the burden of proof away from the Secretary. Moreover, courts have held that the "Grid" produces more uniform decisionmaking because it eliminates the need for subjective judgments by vocational experts and administrative law judges about the claimant's abilities. The Secretary's burden of proof is met by supporting with substantial evidence the finding that the claimant meets each category within the "Grid"; the "Grid" then serves to direct a conclusion that the individual is or is not disabled within the meaning of the statute.

50. See, for example, *McCoy v. Schweiker*, 683 F.2d 1183 (8th Cir. 1982); *Cummins v. Schweiker*, 670 F.2d 81 (7th Cir. 1982); *Kirk*, 667 F.2d at 524.

51. *Heckler v. Campbell*, 461 U.S. 458 (1983). In an earlier case dealing with the medicare provisions of the Social Security Act, the Supreme Court held that Congress has "conferred on the Secretary exceptionally broad authority to prescribe standards for applying certain sections of the Act." *Schweiker v. Gray Panthers*, 453 U.S. 34, 43 (1981). Because the statute explicitly entrusted the Secretary with the task of implementing a statutory definition of disability by regulation, the Court ruled in *Gray Panthers* that its review was limited merely to determining whether the regulations exceeded the statutory grant of authority and to finding whether they were capricious and arbitrary. In *Campbell*, the Court ruled that the "Grid" met this standard. The Court's recent decision in *Bowen v. Yuckert*, 107 S.Ct. 2287 (1987) held that stage two of the sequential evaluation, the severity step, was consistent with the language and legislative history of the Act and was not capricious or arbitrary.

52. See Alan Goldhammer and Susan Bloom, "Recent Changes in the Assessment of Pain," *Administrative Law Review* 35(Fall 1983):454–56.

4

The Adjudication of Disability Claims

The social security disability program encompasses a majority of the working population in the United States and the number of potential and actual claimants is immense. While the volume of claims alone presents enormous obstacles to program administrators, the difficulties of rational administration are enhanced by the necessity of making individual judgments of claimant eligibility. Despite the requirement of programmatic consistency, the demand for individualized determinations of eligibility means that "subjectivity is an essential characteristic of disability [a fact which]...has caused substantial problems, pressures, and public misunderstanding with the disability program in recent years."[1]

Since the early planning stages of the disability program, determinations of eligibility have been enveloped in a political debate that reflects the inherent tension within the social security program and uneasiness about the extent of the social insurance concept. This tension has been characterized by "a constant struggle of the boundaries which manifests itself in shifting pressure for expansion and contraction of the disability category."[2] When supporters of the program urged its adoption, they promised that abuse and fraud would be contained by allowing benefits only in cases that successfully passed strict medical criteria. Despite their assurances of keeping the program in check, and using its resources only to compensate those with clinically proven impairments, there has been a steady increase in benefits and beneficiaries.

Pressure for expansion arose from disability claimants; at times, although not recently, from disability bureaucrats; as well as from the courts that were called in to mediate disputes over the boundaries of eligibility. The disabled have fared better than beneficiaries of other government programs because they are generally perceived as more deserving (they are, by definition, willing to work) and less culpable (they are prevented from working by medical circumstances beyond their control) than public welfare recipients.[3] Despite this image of worthiness, disability beneficiaries are nevertheless still subject to periods in which contraction of the program is the desired political goal. The policymaking see-saw is accompanied by alternating rhetoric about society's obligation to the disabled or the necessity of maintaining the fiscal integrity of the program.

With the magnitude of government spending for social programs, concern over the allocation of societal resources has enormously expanded. The conflict over the Social Security Administration's disability review policy that triggered the litigation activity can be traced to differing perceptions of the program's goals and unresolved differences over the question of how widely to cast the definitional net over physical and mental disability.

The disagreement over distribution of disability resources is reflected in the anxiety over the bureaucracy's role in administering the program consistently and efficiently and in generating confidence that it will give individual consideration and impartiality to all claimants. Concern about administrators making numerous judgments about eligibility, often subjective, has led to procedural safeguards that added to the complexity of the program.

Disability adjudication consists of several levels of administrative review within the Agency and a final appeal of the bureaucracy's decision to the courts of the United States. Although the Social Security Act provided for judicial oversight of Agency procedure to ensure that it conformed with constitutional requirements of due process and was consistent with the statutory language, it did not authorize a judicial role in SSA policymaking. As the events of the early 1980s demonstrated, when dissatisfaction with the Agency's performance in the achievement of the twin goals of efficiency and consistency steadily increased, an enormous number of disability beneficiaries took advantage of the provision in the Act authorizing final appeal of the administrative process to the courts and turned to the federal courts for relief. These factors created the conditions that ultimately drew the judiciary into active participation in social security policymaking.

ADJUDICATION OF CLAIMS

The Social Security Administration's major task is to adjudicate individual claims for disability benefits.[4] Adjudication of a disability claim involves four administrative steps or levels; the procedure is identical for individuals claiming initial entitlement to benefits and for current beneficiaries contesting the Agency decision to terminate benefits.

State Officials

The first judgment about the individual's entitlement to disability is made by the Disability Determination Service (DDS), a state agency under contract to SSA. The decision about eligibility for benefits is made by a DDS physician and a lay disability examiner and issued in the name of the Social Security Administration. Concerned about disparate standards among state agencies, in 1980, Congress attempted to increase federal control over DDS determinations by providing for a federal preeffectuation review (prior to notification of the claimant or payment of benefits) of a specified sample of DDS allowance decisions.[5]

After denial or termination at the state level, an individual may apply for reconsideration of the DDS decision. Before 1984 all state decisions were based on paper reviews only, that is, claimants were unable to appear in person to present their case. In January of that year, legislation went into effect that allowed claimants a face-to-face evidentiary hearing at the reconsideration stage.[6] The 1983 Act also provided for payment to beneficiaries through the administrative hearing stage and now allows a claimant to appear at the reconsideration stage with a representative.[7]

Federal Officials

Claimants denied at reconsideration (and most are, following an initial denial) then encounter the federal bureaucracy by appearing before an administrative law judge (ALJ) for a de novo hearing in which the claimant may present new evidence, call witnesses, and be represented by counsel. During the administrative hearing, the ALJ performs many of the functions of a trial judge, including fact finding, assessing witness credibility, and reaching legal conclusions. Disability hearings before an administrative law judge are intended to be nonadversarial and while the claimant may be represented by counsel, SSA is not. The ALJ is charged with the obligation of developing the record and acting as an impartial arbiter, rather than as a representative of SSA. When dissatisfied claimants pursue their claim in federal court, the process becomes adversarial with representation on both sides—the United States, that is, SSA, is represented by the local U.S. Attorney.

The last administrative stage consists of a final review of the files (a paper review) by SSA's Appeals Council (AC). The Appeals Council's judgment (even if it denies the request for review) is the final decision of the Secretary for purposes of establishing the required exhaustion of administrative remedies. The Appeals Council, a fifteen-member body, and the administrative law judges together form SSA's Office of Hearings and Appeals (OHA). The AC exists as the final overseer of Agency action and is authorized to conduct an own-motion review of the ALJ's decision to ensure consistency of Agency policy.

The final step in asserting a disability claim is the appeal for judicial review of the Secretary's decision to a United States District Court followed by appeal to a Circuit Court of Appeals. Appeal of an Agency denial of benefits to the United States Supreme Court is theoretically possible but is very unlikely because the vast majority of cases appealed contest the factual conclusions of Agency decisionmakers rather than challenge a Constitutional or statutory interpretation of the Act.

ADMINISTRATIVE LAW JUDGES

The Social Security Administration employs the largest single contingent of administrative law judges. In 1981, a total of 29 agencies used the services of 1,119 administrative law judges, and, of these, SSA employed 61 percent, or 695.[8] One year later, 810 of 1,156, or 70 percent of the corps of administrative law judges were assigned to the Social Security Administration.[9] Much of the controversy over the continuing disability review process revolved around the role of administrative law judges within the Social Security Administration: their accountability, their decisional independence, and their professional status.

Conflict over these areas was a key element in the mounting turmoil within SSA during the early 1980s. By the time the termination crisis was resolved in 1984, SSA's relationship with its ALJs had deteriorated into virtual open warfare and the Agency's policy toward the ALJs was threatening to destroy the autonomy of the administrative law judges assigned to the Social Security Administration.

Authority over ALJs

Historically—before the enactment of the Administrative Procedure Act (APA)[10] in 1946—ALJs were subject to control by the Agency that employed them as hearing judges. The APA was enacted in part to create a corps of adjudicators beyond the reach of agency influence and, since 1946, ALJs have become quasi-independent; they are "employed" by the agency and charged with enforcing its policies, but are not within its control.[11] ALJs may only be removed from office for "good cause" as defined and judged by the Merit Systems Protection Board (MSPB) and have a right to a hearing before removal. Although attached to individual agencies, administrative law judges are under the jurisdiction of the Office of Personnel Management (OPM) for salary, tenure, and promotion decisions. Their independence, however, is not absolute as the agency is entitled to exert control over a number of "perquisites of the job (for example, office space, parking privileges, and travel to seminars)."[12]

Around 1975 when SSA was faced with an expanding caseload, burgeoning costs, and lengthy processing time, demands for higher productivity as well as greater decisional consistency between federal and state agencies (often a euphemism for a reduction in ALJ reversals of initial denials by the state agencies) resulted in the creation of a Quality Assurance Program under the leadership of director Robert Trachtenberg.[13] The program was based upon own-motion reviews by the Appeals Council to appraise "erroneous" ALJ decisions. These decisions were defined then, as now, as decisions that granted (or restored in the case of termination) benefits. ALJs perceived these measures as attempts to subvert the decisional independence they were guaranteed under the APA.

Bellmon Review

The adjudication of disability terminations emphasized the fragility of the ALJ's independence within the Social Security Administration. The Agency view was that ALJs "attached" to SSA were accountable to the Agency for

their hearing decisions and production quotas and that they could be sanc-
tioned for failure to meet quality and quantity goals. The Bellmon Amendment to the Social Security Amendments of 1980[14] brought matters to a
head by requiring the Secretary of Health and Human Services to "implement a program of reviewing, on his own motion, decisions rendered by
administrative law judges as a result of hearings under . . . the Act, and . . .
[to] report to the Congress . . . on his progress." Passage of the Bellmon
Amendment reflected congressional concern with a growing ALJ allowance
rate as well as the disparity in decisionmaking standards among ALJs.
Pursuant to the congressional mandate, SSA began a review of ALJ reversals
of state denials in preparation for its report to Congress.[15]

The conflict over ALJ allowance decisions was, in essence, a conflict for
control of Agency policy. While SSA exerted ultimate authority over the state
agencies, it could not firmly control its federal "employees" for two reasons:
first, ALJs were protected by their independent status under the APA, and
second, as lawyers and officers of the court, they often felt bound, to a greater
extent than SSA thought necessary or desirable, to the rulings of the federal
courts. When the termination review process began to generate more heat
after 1980 and SSA tried to exert more authority over the ALJs, the relationship became even more strained.

The Social Security Administration's review in accordance with the Bellmon Amendment consisted of two parts: initial review and ongoing review.
The former looked at ALJ allowance and denial decisions and found that
"the decisions rendered by the ALJs were not wrong, but just different,
based on different criteria, and evaluated with different procedures."[16] The
ongoing review, begun in October 1981, targeted high allowance judges and
put them under "Bellmon Review." SSA justified this focus on ALJs with
higher awards records in two ways. First, the Agency contended that it was
instructed to do so by the Bellmon Amendment and second, the Agency
maintained that the allowance decisions of high allowance judges were more
likely to be erroneous. By April 1982, the survey population was expanded
to include other ALJs in addition to the high allowance judges; the original
ALJs remained under scrutiny however, and the inquiry was still focused
on allowance decisions.

The Bellmon Report

The Social Security Administration's attention was focused entirely on
allowance decisions because it claimed that allowances were more likely to
be erroneous. The Bellmon Report submitted to Congress in 1982 attempted
to justify the Agency's concentration on ALJ allowance. Based on an analysis
of allowance rates, the sample of ALJs was divided into high, medium, and
low allowance judges. Comparing the ALJ allowance rates with the Appeals
Council allowance rates, the study found that the AC allowance rates were
relatively consistent and that they diverged most from the high allowance
ALJs. Using the AC decisions as the "criterion," the analysts found that the
most incorrect decisions were allowance decisions by high allowance ALJs.

The Report concluded by reminding Congress that these data justified SSA's focus on the awards made by high allowance ALJs during Bellmon Review.[17]

Despite SSA's insistence that many ALJs erroneously granted disability benefits, factors other than ALJ error contributed to the mounting number of state agency reversals by administrative law judges. A high ALJ allowance rate could be traced to, among other things, a "lack of state [DDS] record development; the introduction of new evidence into the record after state determination; differences between the state guidelines and the SSA statute and regulations used by ALJs; the use of vocational rules by ALJs; or the increase in ALJ caseloads."[18] As the caseload reached massive proportions, especially after 1980 with the onset of the cessation review process, state agency decisions became more error-prone and ALJs were increasingly forced to reverse state denials. These events coincided with SSA's preoccupation with high allowance judges under Bellmon Review.[19]

The Social Security Administration's claim that it was following the intent of Congress in limiting its scrutiny to the decisions of high allowance ALJs was not entirely warranted. Although the introduction of the Bellmon Amendment in Congress had been accompanied by a written statement from Senator Bellmon indicating his intention that SSA review allowance decisions of high allowance ALJs, the statement was deleted by the Conference Committee. Because the language of the amendment did not specify which type of decisions should be targeted, and because there was no floor debate on the amendment, there was little support for the Agency's insistence that Congress intended to place only high allowance ALJs under Bellmon Review.[20]

ALJ Productivity

Another source of friction between SSA and its administrative law judges revolved around the latters' productivity. The Agency's policy toward ALJ productivity raised questions about whether SSA was in fact conducting a performance rating of ALJs—a violation of the APA. The tension between the ALJs and the Agency manifested itself in at least two major lawsuits brought against SSA by the Association of Administrative Law Judges.[21] The complaints in these suits alleged interference with the judges' guaranteed right to independence.

Allegations in the first suit accused SSA of improperly pressuring administrative law judges to increase their productivity and decrease their allowance rates. The case was settled before trial with an order prohibiting SSA from publicizing ALJ case dispositions or setting production goals and quotas.

This negotiated settlement did not remove the problem of conflict between the Agency and the administrative law judges. Processing the tremendous number of cases initiated by the continuing eligibility policies caused a backlog that led to increasing pressure on ALJs to produce decisions. Arguing that it was necessary to bring greater efficiency and accuracy to the review process, the Agency brought a number of ALJs before the MSPB on charges of low productivity. Although low productivity had not been previously considered "good cause" for removal of an ALJ, SSA argued that it constituted "good cause" because it served as evidence of incompetence. The Merit Systems Protection Board dismissed the charges against the ALJs under review, but ruled that twenty cases a month was an acceptable minimum standard. At the time, however, SSA was setting goals of sixty cases a month.

Although these ALJs were cleared by the MSPB because the evidence against them was insufficient, the Association of Administrative Law Judges filed a second suit against SSA and the MSPB alleging violations of the APA and Social Security Act. The ALJs claimed that the Agency was illegally monitoring their performance ratings and violating their right to be removed only for "good cause." The Agency raised as its defense its obligation to process claims quickly and argued that its concern with productivity was instrumental in achieving that goal. Moreover, the SSA claimed that it had been mandated to review high allowance ALJs by the terms of the Bellmon Amendment.[22] The district court judge held in favor of the Agency in part because, by the time the case was heard, SSA had ceased to focus entirely on high allowance judges and was reviewing a broader sample of ALJs.

In June 1983, the Subcommittee on Oversight of Government Management of the Senate Committee on Governmental Affairs held hearings on the role of the administrative law judge in the disability insurance program. The Subcommittee found that the Agency had succeeded in reducing the allowance rate of the administrative law judges from 67.2 percent in mid-1982 to 51.9 percent by June 1983.[23] It concluded that SSA had jeopardized their decisional independence and recommended repeal of the Bellmon Amendment.

JUDICIAL REVIEW OF DISABILITY CLAIMS

During the planning stages of the disability program, policymakers were presented with evidence of the judiciary's role in the expansion of the disability concept in private insurance plans. The courts played a similar role in the social security disability program, sometimes, as in the *Kerner* case, in the face of contrary legislative intent.

According to Deborah Stone, there are three explanations for the courts' behavior: first, legal reasoning and standards of proof allow them to apply a looser chain of causality between the medical condition and the inability to work. Second, the court's consideration of subjective experiences permits individuals to prove a variation from an average person standard; this allows claimants to show that they are less able to deal with their symptoms than others might be. And lastly, the courts adopt a due process notion that interprets the disability program as a contract between individuals and their government. The latter focuses on the reasonable expectations of citizens who pay taxes and expect the government to honor their "contract" by providing income support when they are no longer able to work.[24]

The judiciary's record in disability adjudication prompted legislative reservations about judicial participation in disability entitlement; yet, despite these, judicial review was incorporated in the Social Security Act as part of the appeals process. Implementation of the continuing disability review process by the Social Security Administration in 1981 brought an onslaught of disability appeals to the federal courts and tested the limits of judicial oversight over Agency decisionmaking in a way that few other administrative procedures had.

Opponents of judicial review of social security disability adjudications often point to the veteran's disability program because adjudicative hearings on entitlement to veteran's benefits are not subject to judicial review. Judge Jack Weinstein, a federal district court judge who strongly favors judicial oversight of the Social Security Administration's disability program, argues that the two programs cannot be compared because veterans have electoral clout that acts as a check on bureaucratic power and helps to compensate for the lack of judicial oversight.[25]

Recognizing that judicial review may detract from effective administration of the adjudication process, some nevertheless consider it necessary to ensure that "the massive systems below work properly."[26] Illinois District Court Judge Prentice Marshall believed it essential to have "review mechanisms for adjudication of individual claims for fairness and accuracy." He added that while he approved of judicial review for all agencies, an even "stronger case can be made" for judicial review of the Social Security Administration's decisions.[27]

Deference to Administrative Action

The judiciary's efforts on behalf of individuals' rights are balanced, to a large extent, by statutory requirements of judicial deference to administrative agencies. The protectionist role of the federal courts is therefore offset by this countervailing force that limits the effectiveness of judicial oversight. The standard of review for judicial oversight is determined either by the enabling legislation or, more generally, in the absence of specific statutory directions, by the Administrative Procedure Act. Under the terms of the Administrative Procedure Act, the court's posture in judicial review of agency rule-making or adjudication must be a respectful one that acknowledges the primacy of administrative decisionmaking and accords a great deal of deference to agency expertise by using a lenient standard of review.

The APA specifies that rules or regulations promulgated by an administrative agency in its rule-making function may be set aside when the rules exceed statutory authority, are unconstitutional, constitute an abuse of discretion, or are arbitrary or capricious.[28] Courts must sustain the validity of regulations issued by an agency invested by Congress with authority to implement a statute, if among other things, the regulations are reasonably related to the purpose of the enabling legislation.[29]

According to the provisions of the Administrative Procedure Act, judicial review of agency action simply permits a court to determine if the agency's findings of fact on the evidence presented are reasonable. In *E.I. duPont de Nemours v. Train*, the Fourth Circuit stated that a "court may not substitute its judgment for that of any agency . . . [and that] if the agency's construction of the controlling statute is 'sufficiently reasonable,' it should be accepted by the reviewing court."[30] Specifically, the APA states that factual determinations reached by an agency in the rule adjudication process after an evidentiary hearing shall be set aside only if "unsupported by substantial evidence."[31] "Substantial evidence," according to the Supreme Court, is "such evidence as a reasonable mind might accept as adequate to support a conclusion."[32] Even more strongly the Court stated in *Consolo v. Federal Maritime Commission*, that "the possibility of drawing two inconsistent conclusions from the evidence does not prevent an administrative agency's findings from being supported by substantial evidence."[33]

Like other administrative agencies, the Social Security Administration promulgates rules and regulations but its major effort is devoted to individual determinations of eligibility for benefits. Under the substantial evidence rule, courts are precluded from making their own (de novo) factual determinations of the evidence and substituting their judgment for the Secretary's. Translated into social security disability terms, this means that the Secretary's findings should be reversed only when a reviewing court determines that the evidence does not reasonably support a conclusion that the claimant is not disabled.

Despite the deference courts owe to SSA findings of fact, judges are often at odds with SSA adjudicators over determinations of disability because agencies and courts have different perspectives on eligibility and are not subject to the same constraints:

Judges . . . need not consider the program as a whole or its annual budget. Their inquiry is normally focused on an individual claimant, whose story is often sympathetic, whose perseverence in carrying the case so far is evidence of a sincere claim, and who will not be on Easy Street even if he wins the appeal.[34]

Given the idiosyncratic nature of an individual's ability to deal with sickness and pain, decisions about entitlement to disability benefits are often subject to dispute. The problem is compounded because determinations of eligibility are not simply based upon the state of the individual's medical condition but also include consideration of such factors as age, employment experiences, and education.

The variability of these individual factors means that eligibility determinations often become subjective because adjudicators can have honest differences of opinion about entitlement—even when they use the same criteria to judge all applicants. This is especially true for the borderline claims that are more likely to be denied at the lower levels and appealed to administrative law judges and the courts.[35]

The substantial evidence rule requires courts to defer to the Agency's findings of nondisability; failure to do so gives rise to charges of judicial interference in administrative decisionmaking. Given the nature of the adjudicatory process, it is not remarkable that assessment of medical and vocational data by the courts and by the Agency may well result in disparate conclusions. It is also not surprising that these differences have led to contention between the courts and SSA over the proper role of the judiciary in bureaucratic decisionmaking.

The Effectiveness of Judicial Review

Opponents of a far-reaching judicial review, such as Jerry Mashaw, argue that judicial oversight of administrative adjudication undermines the effectiveness of bureaucratic decisionmaking.[36] In their 1978 book on adjudication within the Social Security Administration, Mashaw and his collaborators recognized that judicial review promotes accuracy in administrative decisionmaking by correcting erroneous decisions and providing guidance for lower levels of adjudicators.[37] They also acknowledged that judicial review serves to legitimize administrative decisions by providing a conduit between the bureaucracy and its clientele. Despite these positive features, because of the relatively few cases seeking judicial review *at the time*, they questioned its effectiveness in correcting and regulating future errors in administrative decisions. On balance they concluded that "judicial review as currently practiced in disability claims does not paint a very cheerful picture."[38]

In Mashaw's *Bureaucratic Justice*, a 1983 book that focuses on administrative decisionmaking in the social security disability program, he took a firmer stance against judicial review. He contended that "the judiciary, assisted by congressional conferrals of broader and broader jurisdiction, became a hospitable forum for reform-minded bureaucracy fighters of every persuasion."[39]

Mashaw would prefer a system of "bureaucratic rationality" that relied on internal agency controls to lend fairness and accuracy to the program— thereby obviating the need for judicial review. He proclaimed satisfaction with SSA's administration of the disability program, a system encompassing bits and pieces of the three models of bureaucratic justice: the professional treatment model (judgment largely in the hands of service-oriented professionals); the moral judgment model (resolution of conflict by adversarial judicial procedures); and the bureaucratic rationality model (implementation of the legislative will through accurate and efficient decisionmaking). Mashaw concluded that "bureaucratic rationality—at least as practiced by SSA in the disability program—is a promising form of administrative justice." In his view, due process hearings before administrative law judges and appeal to the courts through judicial review as "external modes of reform are wrongheaded."[40]

While Mashaw would prefer to see internal reform of the disability adjudication system, rather than relying on ALJ hearings or judicial review to promote better decisionmaking, it is unlikely that sufficient pressure for reform can be generated within the bureaucracy. Moreover, his study of SSA was published before the onslaught of termination cases created a national uproar and cast doubt upon the fairness and accuracy of Agency decisionmaking.

Mashaw's views prompted reaction from scholars who expressed skepticism about the fate of bureaucratic policymaking if the external check provided by judicial review were removed. They rejected his conclusions because, in their view, judicial oversight lends legitimacy to social security disability policymaking. They also warned against leaving eligibility decisions entirely to members of the social security bureaucracy "whose main claim to this power is that they passed a civil service test?"[41]

Others argued that the ability to litigate against the bureaucracy, absent congressional intervention, is one of the most effective ways of applying pressure to higher level bureaucratic policymakers.[42] Discussing the role of the courts in exercising judicial review, Judge Richard Posner pointed out that the judiciary can more easily resist pressure from the political branches to conform to the current desires of the legislature and bureaucracy and is less likely to identify with the goals of the government policy.[43] Writing specifically of social security adjudication, Judge Posner expressed a preference for strengthening the Appeals Council of SSA's administrative process as a way of lessening the need for judicial review. He conceded, however, that, because the Appeals Council did not provide the same quality of review as the judiciary, it would not do as a substitute for the courts.[44]

Legislation to Limit Judicial Review

Arguments against judicial review also arose from governmental circles. In 1979 the Carter administration proposed legislation to limit judicial review to questions of constitutional or statutory interpretation and leave factual determinations to the administrative agency. Under this plan, the claimant was considered sufficiently protected by the final appeal to the Appeals Council. The administration bill also proposed to replace the Social Security Act's substantial evidence standard of review with an arbitrariness standard; that is, the Secretary's findings of fact would be conclusive for the reviewing court unless they were found to be capricious or arbitrary.

Defending this proposal, Commissioner Stanford Ross of the Social Security Administration indicated that few social security cases involved questions of law. He charged that courts take advantage of judicial review to engage in their own factfinding despite the strictures of the substantial evidence rule. In his view, this kind of judicial intrusion led to court congestion and a situation of "haphazard intervention by Federal district judges for the benefit of a small minority of claimants."[45]

Persuaded of the wisdom of abandoning the substantial evidence standard, the Senate voted to adopt the arbitrary or capricious standard in the Senate version of the administration-proposed bill.[46] When the bill went to Conference Committee, the Senate proposal to limit the scope of judicial review was rejected "because of the uncertainty as to the ramifications of the rule proposed and the concern that the administrative process is not operating with the degree of credibility which would justify elimination of the 'substantial evidence rule.' "[47]

The debate over judicial review and the proper standards of judicial deference to agency decisionmaking became especially relevant to SSA's conflict with the federal courts as problems within the Agency surfaced during the decade from 1975 to 1985. Because the Agency was legally required to submit its final decisions to them, the federal courts were caught in the upheaval caused by the Agency's changing standards for judging disability entitlement. The process of judicial review of SSA adjudications became more conflictual during the latter part of the 1970s and, when the termination reviews began in earnest in 1981, the relationship between these two branches of government had sharply deteriorated.

DISPARITIES IN ADJUDICATIVE STANDARDS

The controversy over the court's review of the Agency's adjudicative process can be traced in part to the mounting state of disarray within SSA over the conflicting standards used by the various levels of administrative decisionmaking. Determining eligibility for disability benefits has always been a problem of "flexibility, uncertainty, and opportunity for inconsistency."[48] The complexity inherent in the multiple stages of review was compounded by the fact that the standards for determining eligibility differed for the ALJs and the state agencies. Some of the problems were also attributable to a variance of Agency standards from state to state and from state to federal jurisdictions within SSA. SSA acknowledged the difference in standards between state and federal levels of adjudication and admitted to an inconsistency in eligibility determinations even with all adjudicators applying the same standards.

The POMS

State agencies are governed by statute and court opinions, regulations, and Social Security Rulings (SSRs).[49] To interpret these various sources of law, SSA issues a set of administrative instructions—the Program Operating Manual System (POMS)—to state agencies. "The POMS is theoretically written to implement the statutes and regulations, but there are glaring examples of POMS provisions which are in direct conflict with the statutes or regulations and with Federal court decisions interpreting the Social Security Act. Yet the states follow this manual whose provisions are neither published nor subject to rulemaking under the APA."[50]

Unlike regulations and rulings, the POMS is an internal Agency document; it is not published in the Federal Register and does not have the force of law. Moreover, administrative law judges are not bound by the provisions in the POMS. This peculiar arrangement not surprisingly has created tension between the state and federal levels of adjudication.

Social Security Rulings

The Social Security Administration attempted to reconcile the inconsistency in state and federal standards by incorporating the POMS into Agency rulings that are binding on ALJs. Consequently, since 1981, when this process was begun, Social Security Rulings began to differ from the regulations published in the Federal Register. The disparity forced ALJs to deal with conflicting instructions in determining eligibility for disability. The difference in standards was accentuated by the fact that state DDS examiners were not made aware of case law resulting from judicial review.[51]

The Social Security Administration acknowledged this problem in its report to Congress pursuant to the Bellmon Amendment (the Bellmon Report):

SSA has long recognized that the standards and procedures governing decisions by DDSs and ALJs are not entirely consistent. Where inconsistencies exist, they are, at least in part, an outgrowth of two somewhat different systems of adjudications. The rule governing DDSs, on the one hand, have developed over time as detailed instructions governing an administrative system. This system is not an independent adjudicative body, and the decisionmaker has no direct face-to-face contact with the claimant. The standards and procedures followed by ALJs, on the other hand, to some degree reflect the status of the ALJ as an adjudicator having decisional independence, conducting hearings in a quasi-judicial setting involving face-to-face contact with claimants, their representatives, and expert witnesses, *and takes cognizance of rulings of the U.S. District and Circuit Courts on individual disability claims* (emphasis added).[52]

These divergent paths in a program that prides itself on uniform decisionmaking have obviously exacerbated tensions between the state and federal bureaucracies as well as between the Agency and the federal courts.

A DECREASE IN AWARDS

An examination of disability program indicators shows that it had grown rapidly from 1966 to 1975 with disabled worker awards peaking in 1975. The year 1975 marked the end of an era of relative generosity and the beginning of a period of relative austerity. During the decade from 1965 to 1975, the number of program beneficiaries increased by more than 230 percent with costs rising more than four and a half times by 1975.[53] The number of initial determinations, initial allowances, and total awards all fell between 1975 and 1980 even though the insured population grew between 1975 and 1980 and applications remained relatively constant.[54] The average annual percent change in these two five-year periods is illustrated in Table 4.1 which shows the relative decrease in several program indicators in the second half of the decade compared to the first half.

Because the statutory definition of disability had not changed from 1975 to 1980, other explanations have been sought for the decline in program beneficiaries after 1975. A 1982 study of recent trends in the SSDI program offered three possible explanations for the decline in disability awards after 1975: first, an improvement in the population's health; second, an increase in nonmedical denials; and third, tighter standards established by SSA for state agencies. The study concluded that "it is quite possible that state agencies and disability examiners have become more conservative in the way in which they interpret and apply the standards."[55]

Table 4.1
Average Annual Percent Change for Program Indicators

INDICATOR	1970–1975	1975–1980
Insured Workers	2.9	2.8
Applications	8.1	– .3
Applications per 100,000 insured workers	5.1	–2.6
Disabled workers in current payment status	10.8	2.8
Disabled workers in current payment status per 100,000 insured workers	7.7	.1
Initial determinations	9.8	–1.2
Initial allowances	8.9	–7.7
Initial allowances per 100,000 insured workers	5.9	–8.4
Awards	11.1	–5.7
Awards per 100,000 insured workers	8.0	–6.9

SOURCE: Mordechai Lando, Alice Farley, and Mary Brown, "Recent Trends in the Social Security Disability Insurance Program," Social Security Bulletin 45(August 1982):5.

A Social Security Subcommittee staff member offered other explanations for the drop in awards. In testimony before the Ways and Means Committee in 1979, he stated that the decrease in beneficiaries could be traced to more direction from the Social Security Administration to the state agencies. He also cited the imposition of the Quality Assurance Program under Commissioner Robert Trachtenberg and the increased number of cases determined on medical factors as well as better documentation of medical evidence (which avoided giving the benefit of doubt to the claimant).[56]

Others have suggested that the reason for the decline in awards stems from stricter adjudicative standards imposed by the Social Security Administration.[57] In its report to Congress in 1982 (the Bellmon Report), SSA admitted "that a more stringent application of the subjective adjudicative standards has been in evidence in the last few years."[58]

Table 4.2
Disability Allowances after Initial Denial

Year	Total	Reconsideration*	ALJ Hearing**	Appeals Council***	Judicial Review****
1970	48,258	33,540	13,607	743	368
1975	120,962	72,948	46,101	1,143	770
1980	138,389	36,032	99,975	1,770	612

* Includes worker claim only.

** Includes worker and child claims.

*** After 1974, includes concurrent DI and SSI claims.

**** Includes worker, children and widow(er)s claims.

SOURCE: Mordechai Lando, Alice Farley, and Mary Brown, "Recent Trends in the Social Security Disability Insurance Program," Social Security Bulletin 45(August 1982):12.

Table 4.3
Disposition of SSDI and SSI Disability Claims

Decisional Level	1970		1975		1980	
	Total Number	Percent Reversed*	Total Number	Percent Reversed*	Total Number	Percent Reversed*
Initial Determination**	599,836	---	930,618	---	788,231	---
Reconsideration	96,046	34.9%	222,237	32.8%	245,341	14.7%
Hearing***	31,365	43.4%	95,234	48.4%	169,088	59.1%
AC Review****	8,223	9.0%	17,713	6.8%	38,242	4.6%
Court Action	1,111	33.1%	2,094	36.8%	3,081	19.9%
Total Allowances	370,848		615,165		392,444	

* Refers to percentage allowed at specified level by reversing denial

of claim at the earlier stage of consideration.

** Excludes denials on basis of non-insured status.

*** May include a few disabled children claims.

**** May include a few disabled children and disabled widow(er)

claims.

SOURCE: Mordechai Lando, Alice Farley, and Mary Brown, "Recent Trends

in the Social Security Disability Insurance Program," Social

Security Bulletin 45(August 1982):13.

State DDS Allowances

Aside from the general decline in awards, one of the leading indicators of a change in the character of the SSDI program during the latter part of the decade of the 1970s was the decrease in the *initial* allowance rates. (The initial allowance rate is equal to the number of initial allowances divided by the number of initial determinations.) The rate of 266 initial allowances per 100,000 insured workers in 1980 was the lowest on record. On a comparative dimension, 92 percent of all awards in 1970 were made at the initial determinations, 83 percent in 1975, and only 65 percent in 1980. Concomitant with the decrease in initial awards was an increase in benefits awarded after the initial determination—from 8 percent in 1970 to 35 percent in 1980.[59]

Reconsideration Allowances

Table 4.2 confirms the change in the program by demonstrating the growing number of claims allowed at the latter stages of the social security disability adjudication process over a ten-year period from 1970 to 1980.

Although there were increasing allowances at the reconsideration stage from 1970 to 1975, a decline set in after 1975. As it became more difficult to be awarded a period of disability at the state level, it became easier to receive benefits at the hearing stage from the federal administrative law judge.

ALJ Allowances

The percentage of claims allowed at the latter stages of the claims process that were denied at the level below, shown in Table 4.3, also illustrates the changing character of the adjudicative process from 1970 to 1980.

Table 4.3 shows that the total number of allowances was cut virtually in half from 1975 to 1980 and that ALJs were not acting in accordance with the other units within the Social Security Administration. The growing number of reversals at the ALJ stage augmented the tensions within the program and ultimately led to an "us and them" mentality that was exacerbated by the flood of cases following the implementation of the continuing review process in 1981.[60]

Administrative Hearings

As signals were sent to claimants that it would be profitable to appeal their initial denial to a higher level, not surprisingly, there was an increase in the number of administrative hearings requested. In 1970 only about one-third of claimants whose applications were initially denied asked for reconsideration; by 1980, this figure rose to almost 50 percent. Similarly, in 1970 about one-half of claimants denied at reconsideration went on to appeal to the next stage, but by 1980, as many as 80 percent were asking for a hearing by an ALJ.

The increase in administrative appeals was accompanied by a greater number of reversals at the ALJ stage: in 1970 the proportion of ALJ allowances of reconsideration denials was only about one-fifth, and in 1980, it rose to one-half. Finally, claimants denied by ALJs were similarly encouraged to pursue their claims further and the proportion of persons turned down by ALJs who sought judicial review from the courts rose from 46 percent in 1970 to 55 percent in 1980.[61]

The problems experienced by the Social Security Administration during the decade of the 1970s suggested the need for remedial action (either by Congress or the Agency) to resolve the conflict among the various levels of disability adjudicators and prescribe the proper standard for determining eligibility. The Bellmon Amendment had been one solution for resolving SSA's administrative tensions but it only served to exacerbate them. The legislative imposition of periodic review of disability recipients in 1980 resulted in even greater problems for the Agency and sent repercussions throughout the entire social security program.

NOTES

1. Charles Soule, *Disability Income Insurance* (Homewood, Ill.: Dow Jones-Irwin, 1984), p. 184.

2. Deborah Stone, *The Disabled State* (Philadelphia: Temple University Press, 1984), p. 140 and see chapters 2–5 generally.

3. Ibid. Robert Lehrer also suggested this notion of the disparity between disability beneficiaries and public assistance beneficiaries. Interview with Robert Lehrer, deputy director, Legal Assistance Foundation of Chicago, September 10, 1986.

4. The Social Security Administration is under the auspices of the Department of Health and Human Services. The Social Security Act grants the Secretary of Health and Human Services broad authority to "adopt reasonable and proper rules and regulations to regulate and provide for the nature and extent of the proofs and evidence and the method of taking and furnishing the same in order to establish the rights to benefits hereunder." 42 U.S.C. §405(a) (1984). The legislative or rule-making function of an administrative agency consists of filling in the interstices of legislation by devising standards of a general nature applicable to an entire category of persons. The adjudicatory or fact-finding role consists of exercising a quasi-judicial function by holding formal hearings designed to elicit specific facts pertaining to an individual and applying general rules to the case at hand.

5. The Social Security Disability Amendments of 1980, Pub. L. No. 96–265, §304(c)(2), 94 Stat. 441, 456 (1980). In 1956 the Secretary had been given authorization to reverse disability determinations by the state agencies. Until 1972, SSA reviewed most state allowances in a preadjudicative review and after 1972 the Agency moved to a sample postadjudicative review involving only about 5 percent of favorable decisions. Section 304(c)(3) of the 1980 Amendments prescribed a preeffectuation review of 15 percent of

all state allowances in 1981, 35 percent in 1982, and 65 percent in 1983. Other provisions of section 304 allowed the Secretary to take over the role of disability determinations from a state either because the Secretary was dissatisfied with the state operation or because the state desired to opt out of this part of the program.

6. The Virgin Islands Source Income—Social Security Disability Benefit Appeals Act, Pub. L. No. 97–455, §§4, 5, 96 Stat. 2497, 2499–501 (1983).

7. The Virgin Islands Source Income—Social Security Disability Benefit Appeals Act, Pub. L. No. 97–455, §2, 96 Stat. 2497, 2498–99 (1983). If the claimant elected to have payments continued through the ALJ review and the Secretary concluded that the claimant was not disabled, the Secretary could seek repayment of the benefits. If the claimant's appeal to the ALJ was filed in good faith, repayment could be waived by the Secretary.

8. Jeffrey Lubbers, "A Unified Corps of ALJs: A Proposal to Test the Idea at the Federal Level," in Howard Ball, ed., *Federal Administrative Agencies* (Englewood Cliffs, N.J.: Prentice-Hall, 1980), p. 80.

9. Subcommittee on Oversight of Government Management of the Senate Committee on Governmental Affairs, *The Role of the Administrative Law Judge in the Title II Social Security Disability Insurance Program*, 98th Cong., 1st Sess. (Comm. Print 1983), p. 6 (hereafter *The Role of the ALJ*).

10. 5 U.S.C. §§701–6 (1984). The Supreme Court stated in *Richardson v. Perales*, 402 U.S. 389, 409 (1971) that "the social security administrative procedure does not vary from that prescribed by the APA." See also *Wong Yang Sung v. McGrath*, 339 U.S. 33 (1950) for analysis of adjudicative hearings under Section 5 of the APA.

11. Ibid. Two cases in which the Supreme Court expressed concern for the independence of the adjudicators within federal agencies are *Butz v. Economou*, 438 U.S. 478 (1978) and *Ramspeck v. Federal Trial Examiners Conference*, 345 U.S. 128 (1953).

12. Lubbers, "A Unified Corps of ALJs," p. 84. Lubbers discusses the proposal that has been made to set up a unified corps of ALJs as a way of reducing dependence by the judge on the "employing" agency. See also Michael Levant, "A Unified Corps of Administrative Law Judges—The Transition from a Concept to an Eventual Reality," *Western New England Law Review* 6(1984):705–21; Norman Zankel, "A Unified Corps of Administrative Law Judges Is Not Needed," *Western New England Law Review* 6(1984):723–44.

13. See Donna Cofer, *Judges, Bureaucrats, and the Question of Independence* (Westport, Conn.: Greenwood Press, 1985) for an analysis of the Quality Assurance Program under Robert Trachtenberg.

14. The Social Security Disability Amendments of 1980, Pub. L. No. 96–265, §304(g), 94 Stat. 441, 456 (1980).

15. See H.R. Rep. No. 944, 96th Cong., 2d Sess. 57–58 (1980). See also Donna Cofer, "The Question of Independence Continues: Administrative Law Judges within the Social Security Administration," *Judicature* 69(December-January 1986):230–31.

16. *The Role of the ALJ*, p. 10.

17. "The Bellmon Report," Reprinted in *Social Security Bulletin* 5(May 1982):16.

18. Cofer, "The Question of Independence Continues," p. 231; see also Jerry Mashaw, "The Definition of Disability from the Perspective of Administration," in Edward Berkowitz, ed., *Disability Policies and Government Programs* (New York: Praeger Publishers, 1979), pp. 160–67.

19. Anthony Russo, "The Social Security Disability Programs: Representing Claimants under the Changing Law," *Stetson Law Review* 14(1984):139.

20. *The Role of the ALJ*, p. 9. See H.R. Rep. No. 944, 96th Cong., 2d Sess. 57–58 (1980) and 126 Cong. Rec. S719 (Jan. 31, 1980) (statement of Sen. Bellmon) for the legislative history of the Bellmon Amendment.

21. *Bono et al. v. United States of America Social Security Administration*, No. 77–0819-CV-W–4 (W.D. Mo. 1979) (settled on June 7, 1979) and *Association of Administrative Law Judges, Inc. v. Heckler*, 594 F.Supp. 1132 (D.D.C. 1984). A subsequent suit was filed against the Social Security Administration for instituting a production quota by an individual ALJ who had been brought before the Merit Systems Protection Board in the early part of 1984. See *Goodman v. Svahn*, 614 F.Supp. 726 (D.D.C. 1985). The district court held that the Administrative Procedure Act did not create a remedy in favor of ALJ Goodman against executive officers of the Social Security Administration for instituting a case production quota. For a discussion of the outlines of the "good cause" standard for reviewing ALJs, see generally Victor Rosenblum, "Contexts and Contents of 'For Good Cause' As Criterion for Removal of Administrative Law Judges: Legal and Policy Factors," *Western New England Law Review* 6(1984):593–642.

Hearings before the House Committee on Ways and Means in 1979 focused in part on the role of the ALJ and the conflict between ALJs and Robert Trachtenberg on the issues of productivity and allowance rates. Documents and letters presented to the Committee showed considerable unrest and dissension within the Office of Hearings and Appeals (then Bureau of Hearings and Appeals). See *Disability Insurance Legislation: Hearings before the Subcommittee on Social Security of the House Committee on Ways and Means*, 96th Cong., 1st Sess. (1979) (hereafter *Disability Insurance Legislation*).

22. *The Role of the ALJ*, p. 33.

23. Subcommittee on Oversight of Government Management of the Senate Committee on Governmental Affairs, *Oversight of the Social Security Administration Disability Reviews*, 97th Cong., 2d Sess. (Comm. Print 1982) (hereafter *Oversight of Disability Reviews*).

24. Stone, *The Disabled State*, chapter 5.

25. Jack Weinstein, "Equality and the Law: Social Security Disability Cases in the Federal Courts," *Syracuse Law Review* 35(1985):897–938. See also Robert Rabin, "Preclusion of Judicial Review in the Processing of Claims for Veterans' Benefits: A Preliminary Analysis," *Stanford Law Review* 27(1975):905–23. In *Johnson v. Robison*, 415 U.S. 361 (1974), the Supreme Court held that judicial review is precluded for administrative

decisions involving benefits but is permissible for constitutional attacks on the statute.

26. Interview with District Court Judge Susan Getzendanner, September 17, 1986.

27. Interview with District Court Judge Prentice Marshall, September 24, 1986.

28. 5 U.S.C. §706(2)(A-C) (1984). See Gary Bryner, *Bureaucratic Discretion: Law and Policy in Federal Regulatory Agencies* (New York: Pergamon Press, 1987), chapter 2.

29. *Schweiker v. Wilson*, 450 U.S. 221 (1981).

30. 541 F.2d 1018, 1026 (4th Cir. 1976), *aff'd in part, rev'd in part*, 430 U.S. 112 (1977).

31. 5 U.S.C. §706(2)(E) (1984). The Social Security Act provides that "the findings of the Secretary as to any fact, if supported by substantial evidence, shall be conclusive." 42 U.S.C. §405(g) (1984).

32. *Perales*, 402 U.S. at 401 quoting *Consolidated Edison v. National Labor Relations Board*, 305 U.S. 197, 229 (1938); see also *Universal Camera Corp. v. National Labor Relations Board*, 340 U.S. 474, 477–87 (1951).

33. 383 U.S. 607, 619–20 (1966).

34. Lance Liebman, "The Definition of Disability in Social Security and Supplemental Security Income: Drawing the Bounds of Social Welfare Estates," *Harvard Law Review* 89(1976):845. Deborah Stone, *The Disabled State*, pp. 154–55, also points out since courts can only act by granting benefits, if they wish to act at all, they are thrust in an expansionist posture.

35. Even though they often involve disputes about "genuine issues as to any material fact," disability appeals are decided as a summary judgment on the basis of affidavits, a transcript of the adjudication proceedings, and legal briefs. There is no oral argument before the district court in disability cases. See Rule 56 of the Federal Rules of Civil Procedure.

36. See Jerry Mashaw, *Bureaucratic Justice* (New Haven: Yale University Press, 1983); Jerry Mashaw, et al., *Social Security Hearings and Appeals* (Lexington, Mass.: Lexington Books, 1978).

37. Mashaw, et al., *Social Security Hearings and Appeals*, p. 136. The authors stated that judicial review promotes accuracy through two functions called the "corrective" ("correcting erroneous administrative decisions") and the "regulative" ("inducing more accurate decisionmaking at the administrative level in the great mass of cases that do not go to court"). The regulative function is served by fear of reversal which encourages the lower levels of adjudication to do a better job (the "in terrorem effect") or by forcing the lower levels to follow judicial rules of decisionmaking ("the precedential effect").

38. Ibid., p. 146.

39. Mashaw, *Bureaucratic Justice*, p. 2. Although he does not explicitly recommend eliminating judicial review in social security disability cases in his 1983 book, Mashaw seems more harshly disposed toward it in this later book than he was in the 1978 collaborated work; there is no explanation given for this apparent change of position. My impression of the subtle distinction between the two books is confirmed in Lance Liebman and Rich-

ard Stewart, "Book Review: Bureaucratic Justice," *Harvard Law Review* 96(1983):1958, n. 24.

40. Mashaw, *Bureaucratic Justice*, p. 222.

41. Liebman and Stewart, "Book Review," p. 1963.

42. Deborah Maranville, "Book Review: Bureaucratic Justice," *Minnesota Law Review* 69(1984):325–47.

43. Richard Posner, *The Federal Courts* (Cambridge: Harvard University Press, 1985), p. 155.

44. The establishment of an Article I Social Security Court, modeled after the United States Tax Court would eliminate problems of lack of judicial expertise. Proposed in 1982 by Congressman Pickle of Texas, chair of the Subcommittee on Social Security of the House Committee on Ways and Means, this court was to be a specialized one with jurisdiction over all OASDI issues. An earlier 1977 proposal would have restricted jurisdiction to disability issues only. For a debate over the desirability of a specialized social security court, see Frederick Arner, "The Social Security Court Proposal: An Answer to a Critique," *Journal of Legislation* 10(1983):324–50; and J. P. Ogilvy, "The Social Security Court Proposal: A Critique," *Journal of Legislation* 9(1982):229–51.

45. *Disability Insurance Legislation*, p. 79 (statement of Stanford Ross, commissioner, Social Security Administration).

46. The Administration-sponsored bill was H.R. 2854, 96th Cong. 1st Sess. (1979); see *Social Security Act Disability Program Amendments: Hearings before the Senate Committee on Finance*, 96th Cong., 1st Sess. (1979) (hereafter *Disability Program Amendments*).

47. H.R. Rep. No. 944, 96th Cong., 2d Sess. 61 (1980).

48. Robert Dixon, *Social Security Disability and Mass Justice* (New York: Praeger, 1973), p. 21.

49. Rulings are customarily derived from SSA regulations, case law and SSA interpretations of the law. The Social Security Rulings are binding on both state and federal levels of adjudication, that is, through the Appeals Council, but are not subject to the public notice and comment provisions of the APA as are regulations.

50. Cofer, *Judges, Bureaucrats*, p. 125.

51. *Oversight of Social Security Disability Benefits Terminations: Hearing before the Subcommittee on Oversight of Government Management of the Senate Committee on Governmental Affairs*, 97th Cong., 2d Sess. (1982), p. 129 (statement of Herbert Brown, administrator of the Tennessee DDS) (hereafter *Oversight of Disability Terminations*).

52. "The Bellmon Report," p. 12.

53. Mordechai Lando, Alice Farley, and Mary Brown, "Recent Trends in the Social Security Disability Insurance Program," *Social Security Bulletin* 45(August 1982):3–27.

54. Ibid., p. 5.

55. Ibid., p. 11.

56. *Disability Insurance Legislation*, p. 24 (statement of Frederick Arner, staff, House Committee on Ways and Means).

57. *Oversight Of Disability Terminations*, pp. 392–94 (statement of

Chester Shatz, New England director of the Association of Administrative Law Judges of the Department of Health and Human Services). See also Senate Committee on Finance, *Issues Related to Social Security Act Disability Programs*, 96th Cong., 1st Sess. (Comm. Print 1979) (hereafter *Issues Related to Disability Programs*).

58. "The Bellmon Report," p. 17.

59. Lando, Farley, and Brown, "Recent Trends in the Disability Program," pp. 5–6.

60. See *Oversight of Disability Terminations*.

61. Lando, Farley, and Brown, "Recent Trends in the Disability Program," p. 13.

5

A New Approach to Continuing Eligibility

Congress delegated its power to determine eligibility for disability benefits to the Department of Health and Human Services authorizing the Secretary "to regulate and provide for the nature and extent of the proofs to establish rights to benefits hereunder."[1] Congressional direction was largely limited to the admonition that "no payment . . . may be made to an individual who would not meet the definition of disability."[2] Because a beneficiary's right to receive benefits was conditioned upon a continued inability to perform substantial gainful activity, the Secretary's responsibility included a duty to verify the continuing disability of persons collecting benefits.

Prior to 1980 the Social Security Administration's policy of verification of eligibility, termed the continuing disability investigation process (CDI), could fairly be characterized as a rather haphazard attempt to maintain the integrity of the program by removing the nondisabled from the disability rolls. Also, until 1980, SSA's policy toward continuing eligibility of disability program beneficiaries had been neglected by Congress; Title II of the Social Security Act neither detailed nor restricted how disability was to be interpreted in the review process. The selection of recipients for review and the determination of the proper standards for continued eligibility was left to the discretion of the Social Security Administration whose regulations stipulated that an individual was no longer disabled when medical evidence showed that he or she was capable of performing substantial gainful activity.[3]

In the late 1970s an increasing concern with fiscal restraint and reports of the Agency's administrative inefficiency had prompted the Ninety-Sixth Congress to exercise its legislative prerogative and provide direction for SSA by prescribing a three-year review of the majority of current recipients. The legislation enacted in 1980 did not specify how SSA was to determine whether an individual was still entitled to benefits and it was not until 1984 that Congress finally stepped in to mandate the standards for the continuing disability investigation. Rather incredibly, Congress as a whole had not addressed the issue of the proper standard for determining continued eligibility of persons within the program until 1984—thirty years after SSA's disability program was initiated.

CONTINUING DISABILITY INVESTIGATIONS BEFORE 1980

The Agency's procedure for trimming current beneficiaries from the disability rolls was, as almost all administrative decisionmaking, subject to judicial review. The Supreme Court's commitment to judicial deference to administrative expertise meant that SSA's administrative procedure was relatively insulated from interferences by the federal courts, as long as SSA did not stray beyond the ill-defined constraints of due process. When challenged on constitutional grounds in 1976, SSA's policy on continuing disability investigations and the cessation of benefits received a stamp of approval from the Supreme Court.

The Supreme Court ruled in the 1976 case of *Mathews v. Eldridge*,[4] that disability beneficiaries were not entitled to a hearing prior to termination of benefits because due process was satisfied with a post-termination hearing before an administrative law judge. The Court distinguished social security disability benefits from public assistance or welfare aid. Because disability benefits, unlike welfare benefits, were not based on need, the Court held that a recipient's survival was not likely to be jeopardized with a disruption of disability benefits. (SSI beneficiaries continued to receive benefits through appeal to the ALJ level; they were also allowed to bypass the reconsideration stage and proceed directly to the administrative hearing stage.) Disability insurance program recipients whose benefits were terminated and who were later determined upon appeal to be proper beneficiaries were entitled to back benefits. Although the hiatus between the initial determination of ineligibility and the subsequent reinstatement of benefits often imposed severe economic hardship, it was not, according to the Supreme Court, beyond the bounds of due process.

While *Mathews* represented a retreat from the due process protections of the Warren court, because terminations were rather infrequent at the time, the decision did not have a major impact on current beneficiaries of the program. After 1980, when terminations assumed a major portion of disability adjudications, the *Mathews* ruling would begin to affect a great many individuals. *Mathews* was reversed in part by Congress when the 1983 legislation provided for face-to-face interviews at reconsideration with a continuation of benefits through the ALJ phase of the administrative review process.

A Change in the Adjudicative Climate

The decline in disability awards, discussed in the previous chapter, that became manifest during the latter part of the 1970s did not result from a legislative mandate, nor, with the exception of the "Grid" and the sequential evaluation, was it a product of changes in SSA regulations. The retrenchment that surfaced after 1975 was effected through a new "climate of adjudication" that was characterized by a philosophy coloring the interpretation of the rules and regulations that encouraged the denial of claims. In response to a survey from the Subcommittee on Social Security, a state administrator explained that:

the primary reason for the recent conservative approach to disability evaluation is a direct result of the activities of... [those] involved in evaluating the effectiveness of the program. The Administration has apparently... concluded that a "tightening up" is desired. This view may be somewhat of an oversimplification; but in the real world it is quite likely the root cause of the recent trends.[5]

Another simply wrote that "it has become easier to deny a claim."[6]

The Diary System

The harsher adjudicative climate within the Social Security Administration was accompanied by a growing concern with the costs of the program that prompted a reevaluation of the policy of monitoring current beneficiaries in the latter half of the 1970s. Prior to this upswing of interest, SSA's policy toward continuing eligibility of disabled individuals was essentially one of benign neglect with only a small number of recipients reviewed after the initial award of benefits. Although their continued eligibility for benefits had always been subject to review by Agency officials, in practice, the overwhelming majority of beneficiaries were allowed to maintain their benefit status despite potential or actual changes in their medical conditions.

Under procedures established by SSA, all persons receiving disability benefits were placed in one of the following three categories when awards were made: the permanently disabled, where little improvement could be expected in the impairment; the less severely disabled, where the medical impairment causing the disability was expected to change merely through the passage of time; and the nonpermanently disabled, with impairments that were not serious enough to be within the first group and possibilities of improvement were not certain enough to place them in the latter class.

Before 1981 only about 130,000 to 150,000 cases a year were actually reviewed by SSA because continuing disability investigations were focused on persons targeted for review on the basis of their expected improvement.[7] Only when diagnosed with one of a number of preselected impairments such as tuberculosis, infections, rheumatoid arthritis, obesity, certain kinds of fractures, or cases in which corrective surgery was contemplated were beneficiaries placed on a calendar or "diaried" status and given a predetermined date for review.

SSA's eligibility review activity was also triggered by volunteered information that a recipient's medical condition had improved, by earnings records that reflected work activity, or by notification that the individual had returned to work. Prior to passage of the 1980 Amendments, however, the primary focus of CDI was on the diaried cases.[8]

State DDS officials who were responsible for determining continued eligibility were discouraged from a vigorous pursuit of potential ineligibles. The agencies were cautioned in a Social Security Claims Manual that most disability awards involved "chronic, static, or progressive impairments subject to little or no medical improvement." In other cases they were told that, while some improvement may be anticipated, "the likelihood of finding objective medical evidence of 'recovery' has been shown by case experience to be so remote as not to justify establishing a medical reexamination diary."[9]

According to a report issued by the General Accounting Office, from 1973 to 1977 only about 18 to 26 percent of persons receiving initial disability awards were "diaried" cases, that is, scheduled for medical reexamination. Over three-fourths of the workers awarded disability benefits during this time were therefore not subject to reevaluation unless there was work activity or medical improvement that came to SSA's attention.[10]

The LaBonte Rule

Even when persons were selected for review, they were not often removed from the disability rolls. In judging the continued existence of the impairment and its effect upon the individual's ability to perform substantial gainful activity, SSA had utilized a medical improvement standard (the LaBonte rule) where the burden was on the Agency to show an improvement in the beneficiary's medical condition before benefits could be terminated.[11]

The LaBonte rule, named after disability beneficiary Frances LaBonte, was based upon the principle that cessations had to be supported by documentation of medical improvement. Subject of a continuing disability investigation, LaBonte was allowed to remain on the disability rolls because SSA was not able to produce evidence of a changed medical condition since the initial award.

The Social Security Administration's adoption of the LaBonte rule was formalized when, on March 13, 1969, the assistant director of SSA's Bureau of Disability Insurance sent a memorandum to the state agencies indicating that they should not rely on "substantially similar evidence" in the continuing eligibility investigation (as was used in the initial claim) to conclude that beneficiaries were no longer disabled. The instructions specified that benefits should be continued barring a "material change" in the beneficiary's medical condition.[12]

The 1980 Regulations

The medical improvement, or LaBonte, standard was in effect from 1969 until May 1976 when it was abolished by the Social Security Administration. Considering itself hamstrung by this procedural rule, SSA abandoned the LaBonte rule and replaced it with a "current medical evidence" standard for determining eligibility for those already on the disability rolls. The elimination of the medical improvement standard was accomplished internally with no formal announcement of a policy shift until 1980 when SSA published the following belated notice in the August 20, 1980 edition of the Federal Register:

At one time we would not find that disability or blindness had stopped unless the medical evidence showed that the person's condition had improved since we last determined that he or she was disabled. About three years ago we changed this policy and began to find that disability or blindness had stopped if we found, on the basis of new evidence, that the person was not disabled or blind as defined in the law.[13]

The 1980 regulations confirmed that the Social Security Administration was sending a "get tough" message to disability beneficiaries. Under the new policy, a finding would be made that a disability ceased when it was shown by "current medical or other evidence" that an individual was able to "do substantial gainful activity."[14] The Agency explained that the procedural shift was prompted because the old policy was thought by some to require a showing of medical improvement in addition to proof of the ability to engage in substantial gainful activity.

The Social Security Administration expressed concern that this interpretation of continuing eligibility had led to "the payment of benefits to persons who can engage in substantial gainful activity and who are no longer disabled or blind within the meaning of the law, but for whom actual 'improvement' cannot be shown. These recodified regulations make it clear that disability ends when current evidence shows that the individual is able to engage in SGA [substantial gainful activity] regardless of whether actual improvement can be demonstrated."[15]

When the Agency explicitly stated in a later ruling that "the determination or decision as to whether or not disability continues is not controlled by any prior determination or decision which established that the individual was disabled,"[16] the practical effect of the abandonment of the medical improvement standard was made clear. The adjudication of initial and continuing eligibility claims would now become virtually indistinguishable with no legal effect given to the earlier finding of disability in the continuing eligibility analysis. Publication of the 1980 regulations also clearly established that the sequential evaluation regulations, promulgated the year before, applied to termination cases as well as to initial claims.

Although the statutory definition of disability had not been legislatively altered, with the 1980 announcement, SSA confirmed that a new policy toward continuing eligibility had been in place for the last four years. It was also made apparent that the change in policy had been instituted without public notice as a proposed rule in the Federal Register.

Despite the change, disability recipients were not greatly affected by the stricter standards for judging continued eligibility because the Agency had not made a corresponding change in the selection criteria for review of cases. While there was an increase in the rate of terminations, the number of people being reviewed had not appreciably grown because, from 1976 to 1980, CDI was still primarily limited to a small number of diaried cases.[17]

A private attorney who had been involved in disability cases since 1977 noted that the abandonment of the medical improvement standard did not impact greatly upon recipients until 1980 because before then, there were "just a handful of terminations."[18] Another attorney, with disability experience dating back to 1974, commented that she had not been struck by the changes in the program in 1976 because terminated beneficiaries were not generally seeking legal counsel to appeal termination decisions before 1980. She added that the full impact of the demise of the medical improvement standard was not felt until 1981 when the implementation of periodic review led to a huge increase in the numbers of people under review.[19]

THE 1980 AMENDMENTS

Enactment of the Social Security Disability Amendments of 1980[20] was prompted by apprehension over rising costs, administrative inefficiency, and insufficient work incentives. Members of Congress contended that disabled workers were discouraged from returning to work when their disability benefits exceeded their predisability earnings.[21] The primary focus of the bill, H.R. 3236,[22] as explained by its congressional supporters, was to make disability less inviting for those capable of working.

Disability benefits are determined by applying a formula to the worker's average indexed monthly earnings (AIME) ending with the year before the onset of disability. The individual's primary insurance amount (PIA) is supplemented by his or her dependents' benefits with an overall limit on family benefits held to a certain percentage of the worker's benefits. Passage of the 1980 Amendments was partially motivated by reports that some recipients were drawing a higher income from their disability benefits than they drew from their employment earnings. The 1980 Amendments attempted to remedy this situation, beginning for workers who qualified for benefits after June 1980, by setting a limit on family benefits of the lesser of 85 percent of the worker's average indexed monthly earnings or 150 percent of the primary insurance amount.[23]

The method by which a worker's earnings in the prior years of employment were counted constituted another area of concern for some members of Congress. Prior to the 1980 Amendments, all workers were allowed to exclude five years of low earnings. H.R. 3236 limited the number of dropout years of low income earnings for workers under age forty-seven presumably to equalize their status with older workers.[24] As part of the emphasis on rehabilitation, the bill also extended the trial work period from nine months to 24 months, allowed a disabled worker's medicare benefits to continue for 36 months after a return to employment, and eliminated a second two-year medicare waiting period for those whose work attempts failed.

Periodic Review

Amid dispute about the need for such legislation and, over the protests of a variety of interests, including farm groups, unions, veterans, and the disabled, H.R. 3236 was enacted as the Social Security Disability Amendments of 1980.[25] Concerned also about SSA's rather lax policy toward continued eligibility, Congress included a provision in H.R. 3236 that required SSA to take a closer look at the kind of cases that had fallen through the administrative cracks: persons with impairments that were not serious enough to qualify as permanently disabled and not mild enough to be able to predict eventual recovery with any degree of certainty.

The House version of the bill proposed a three-year review of people in the largest category—the nonpermanent and nondiaried cases.[26] The message from Congress to the Agency was: straighten out your administrative procedure and start to pay attention to that vast group of disability recipients who are not currently under scrutiny for continuing eligibility and may be receiving benefits although recovered from their impairments.

The provision for periodic review of disability recipients with nonpermanent impairments was a relatively insignificant feature of the 1980 Amendments. Most of the discussion in the committee hearings was centered on the cap on benefits and the dropout years. In comparison with the other provisions in the bill, the hearings before the Subcommittee on Social Security of the House Committee on Ways and Means and the Senate Committee on Finance devoted very little attention to the new requirements for continuing disability review (CDR).

A reading of the transcripts of the committee hearings and the Congressional Record leaves the impression that the periodic review provision was approved quite perfunctorily and without much deliberation. It was clear only that Congress desired to put a stop to the practice of reviewing only diaried cases and wanted SSA to begin a triennial review of beneficiaries with nonpermanent impairments. The litigation over the disability terminations prompted by periodic review required the courts to ascertain the legislative intent behind this provision of the Amendments.

Legislative Intent

Congress assigned the implementation of the plan for review to the Social Security Administration's discretion under SSA's authority to "regulate and provide for the nature and extent of proofs to establish rights to benefits." The great unanswered question was whether Congress intended SSA to remove persons from the disability rolls whether or not they recovered from their illness. Also unresolved was the issue of which party bore the burden of showing the continued eligibility.

A 1982 report from the General Accounting Office (GAO) to the Senate Government Management Subcommittee stated that "the legislative history of the 1980 Amendments clearly indicates that the Congress was concerned about individuals who have medically improved and remain on the disability rolls. However," the report continued, "it is not clear what the Congress' view was toward those who have not medically improved [and] whether the Congress intended that all beneficiaries would be subjected to a 'new determination,' or whether it expected the earlier decisions to afford some presumptive weight. . . . "[27] Testimony before the Senate Finance Committee and the House Social Security Subcommittee expressed witnesses' certainty about the necessity of removing improved or recovered people who could perform substantial gainful activity from the disability rolls. But no opinions were offered about *how* the Agency should determine if persons were no longer disabled.[28]

Testimony on Periodic Review

The concept of periodic review was supported by Joseph Califano, then secretary of Health and Human Services, as well as by representatives of the National Association of Manufacturers, the American Council on Life Insurance, and the Health Insurance Association of America. In his testimony, Secretary Califano neither mentioned nor was asked about the standard SSA would use in the proposed continuing disability review process. Mr. Califano endorsed the imposition of a new CDR policy by simply agreeing with his questioner that periodic review had merit because it would enable SSA to determine "whether there has been a change in circumstances."[29]

Testimony by Robert Meyers, former chief actuary of the Social Security Administration and now consultant to the Social Security Subcommittee, expressed support for a periodic review process that would include face-to-face meetings with recipients. Mr. Meyers did not indicate a preferred method for judging continued eligibility but merely stated that the purpose of the review was to investigate whether "the disability is still continuing."[30] One of the key subcommittee witnesses, Wilbur Cohen, former secretary of Health, Education, and Welfare and current chair of a group called the Coalition to Save Our Security, stated emphatic disapproval of the proposed cap on benefits and the dropout rate provision but did not even comment on the advantages or disadvantages of periodic review, nor was he asked to do so.[31]

The Social Security Administration itself seemed unclear about the procedure it would follow in implementing the provision for continuing disability review and did not even propose a set of rules for determining continued eligibility. In response to a set of inquiries from the Subcommittee on Social Security, Stanford Ross, commissioner of Social Security, stated that SSA felt it was "desirable to avoid the rigidity of putting a mandatory reexamination procedure in the law, and [that it] would prefer the flexibility to develop the most cost-effective program for reexamining cases where improvement seems likely."[32]

In questioning a group of ALJs, Subcommittee Chair Jake Pickle discussed the issue of periodic review by asking whether recovery could be predicted within a certain time and whether that kind of specificity should be written into the Act. One fact stood out in the midst of the ambiguity surrounding the quest for ineligible recipients. Members of Congress envisioned periodic review of continuing eligibility as an attempt to streamline the administrative procedure for determining whether beneficiaries had recovered, that is, whether their medical conditions had improved so that they were no longer disabled.[33]

Legislative Debate over Periodic Review

Periodic review was similarly given short shrift during the Senate and House debate over H.R. 3236. Congressional attention was focused almost entirely on the effectiveness of the benefits cap as a work incentive measure and the equity of changing the dropout years policy. There was some debate on the floor of Congress over whether the primary purpose of the bill was to save money for the program. And while the bill's opponents charged that its enactment was motivated by a desire to save money at the expense of "those most dependent on Federal help—the disabled, those who cannot work,"[34] its proponents claimed financial considerations were secondary or even nonexistent. Three years after enactment of the new continuing disability review policy, Representative Pickle reiterated that Congress was "not trying to save money, [that] that was not the objective of the Congress"; he felt that only "inadvertently and indirectly . . . the question of a saving does come about. . . . "[35]

In explaining the Subcommittee version of the bill before the full House on September 6, 1979, Mr. Pickle deplored the fact that the debate over H.R. 3236 had gotten "hung up on the caps" and attempted to stress the positive features of the bill. He pointed out that H.R. 3236 also included a provision for a preadjudicative review of a gradually increasing sample of state allowances as well as the provision for review of the individuals currently receiving disability benefits.

Representative Pickle cited periodic review as part of the package of administrative reforms designed to assure greater control of loose administrative procedures and to strengthen the work incentives of the program. He defended his position by pointing out that there was virtually no review of current beneficiaries and that "an individual can get on disability now and he can ride it through, 5, 10, 15 years, and he stays on the rolls and he does not have to say he is either able or not able to go to work. We are trying," he stated, "to say to the recipient that we believe the average person wants to go to work, and we are giving him the incentive to do it, and that is really what the bill does."[36]

Later in the debate Mr. Pickle described periodic review as a "provision . . . that says that every three years each person not determined permanently disabled will be reviewed again to see whether they are disabled and should they be continued."[37] He explained that the goal of periodic review was to ensure "that a person would not be left on the rolls long after he or she may have recovered."[38]

These three references were the sum total of stated legislative intent on the meaning of periodic review out of six days of debate in both houses of Congress.[39] The remarks by Mr. Pickle, one of the chief sponsors of the bill and an important figure in assessing legislative intent, make it clear that periodic review was an attempt to respond to the problem of the inadequacy of review under the current diary system that was reported during the committee and subcommittee hearings.[40] The inclusion of periodic review as part of the administrative reform package strongly suggests that the majority of Congress was persuaded that better controls were needed to remove nondisabled persons from the disability rolls and maintain the integrity of the program.

The congressional consensus over periodic review did not include an agreement about the implementation of CDR—primarily because the consensus was reached without an adequate exploration of the proper standards for judging eligibility of the beneficiaries under review. According to a report by the Congressional Research Service, "what is not really clear from the legislative history is how Congress expected section 311 to be implemented and what it expected its impact to be."[41]

The legislative history of periodic review suggests that members of Congress were unfamiliar with SSA's standards for determining continued eligibility, that is, were unaware of the status of the medical improvement standard in termination cases. Although the Social Security Administration had replaced the medical improvement standard with the current medical evidence standard in 1976, the change was not publicly announced until August 1980, three months after the 1980 Amendments were passed. The legislative history does not indicate that members of Congress were told of the change in standards, nor does it reflect congressional awareness of the change. There is also no evidence that Congress appreciated the extent to which periodic review would affect beneficiaries currently on the disability rolls.

IMPLEMENTATION OF PERIODIC REVIEW

The new continuing disability review policy had been ordered into effect in January 1982—two years after passage of the 1980 Amendments. The estimates of savings presented in the committee reports indicated that while SSA would immediately begin to reduce expenditures on benefits, these early savings would be more than offset by increased administrative costs. Overall savings to the program would only be realized after three or four years of operation of periodic review depending upon assumptions about when the legislation would be enacted and the process begun.[42]

The 1980 Amendments did not specify the scope of the periodic reviews nor the method by which the reviews were to be conducted.[43] The Congressional Research Service report on congressional intent stated that the legislative history of the new continuing disability review policy was similarly unhelpful in providing answers to questions about the implementation of periodic review. This inattention to detail by the framers of the legislation not surprisingly resulted in an substantial exercise of discretion by SSA program administrators.

Periodic Review Is Accelerated

Although Congress had clearly expressed its disapproval of nondisabled persons remaining on the disability rolls, it did not appear that during the debate over passage of the bill members of Congress were given estimates of how many eligible persons were actually collecting benefits.[44] The sub-stance of the committee testimony and the floor debate focused on the vaguely-stated goal of monitoring eligibility rather than on a concern over a specific number of ineligibles. Perhaps in response to this perceived in-formation gap, in March 1981, the General Accounting Office released a report entitled "More Diligent Followup Needed to Weed Out Ineligible SSA Disability Beneficiaries."[45] The report was critical of the Social Security Administration's previous continuing eligibility policy and indicated that about 20 percent of the 2.9 million primary beneficiaries of the DI program, representing as many as 584,000 persons, were not currently disabled and yet were receiving disability benefits.

The GAO's estimate of a $2 billion annual loss resulting from this slippage was calculated on the basis of an SSA study of a random sample of cases that indicated that almost 20 percent of disability beneficiaries did not meet current eligibility standards.[46] The General Accounting Office report used this 20 percent figure, which included diaried workers who had been ex-pected to improve, to arrive at the estimate of 548,000 current ineligibles on the disability rolls; based upon these conclusions, the GAO urged the Social Security Administration to "give more priority to identifying the non-disabled currently on the rolls and terminating their benefits."[47]

Largely on the basis of the GAO report and another SSA study suggesting an even greater number of ineligibles, the Social Security Administration justified an early beginning for CDR (under its preexisting authority to review the disability status of beneficiaries) in March 1981—ten months before its originally scheduled starting date of January 1982.[48] As indicated by an Agency spokesperson, the primary justification for the early onset of periodic review was the "huge sums of benefits [that] were being paid in-correctly" and that by starting early, SSA "had 18 months in which to spread this workload."[49]

The Profiling System

The Social Security Administration estimated that 2.3 million of the 4.8 million DI and SSI beneficiaries would be subject to periodic review over a three-year cycle.[50] Because of the enormity of the task, SSA devised a system, called "profiling," for selecting beneficiaries from the Master Beneficiary Re-cord. Individuals were more likely to be selected for review if they were younger, were more recently awarded benefits, and were at higher benefit lev-els. After the cases were chosen on the basis of the profile, the individual's impairment was considered to allow elimination of the "permanently dis-abled" from the CDR process.[51] This method of selection was questioned by Senator Cohen in the Oversight Subcommittee hearings when he asked Dep-uty Commissioner Paul Simmons why SSA did not look at the disability first: "It seems to me if you really want to get the cases, you should look at injury, the type of injury. . . . "[52] According to Simmons, however, "profiling . . . was required by commonsense administration of the amendments."[53]

SSA justified its use of a targeted population in the CDR process by point-ing to two studies that revealed that recipients in certain categories were more likely to be considered "ineligible" for benefits during a continuing disability review.[54] Because of the concentration on these factors, the cessation rate that had been predicted at 18 to 20 percent (based upon the GAO report on ineligibles) was actually almost 50 percent.

While the profiling approach was an efficient method for removing "ineligibles" quickly, its success was a mixed blessing because it led to an overwhelming number of terminations as well as an enormous backlog of appeals.[55] The numerous problems created by the profiling system led Margaret Heckler, secretary of the Department of Health and Human Services, to announce in June 1983 that profiling would no longer be utilized and that henceforth recipients subject to the continuing disability review process would be selected on a random basis.[56] The decision to end profiling stemmed from a need to ameliorate the devastating effects of the continuing review process on state agencies that were unprepared for it, on ALJs who came under increasing pressure to improve their productivity and the "quality" of their decisions, and on the hundreds of thousands of disability recipients who were shocked to discover that their benefits were not as secure as they had been led to believe.[57]

Processing the Reviews

The continuing disability review process required that the state agencies process an additional 30,000 disability cases a month (almost a threefold increase over the pre–1981 rate). In fiscal year 1981 about 180,000 cases were reviewed; in fiscal year 1982, almost 500,000 cases were reviewed with approximately 850,000 cases scheduled for review in 1983. Although the expectation for 1983 was not met, by May 1983, about 340,000 reviews had been carried out.[58] Between March 1981 and November 1983, over one million CDRs were conducted by SSA. With the concentration on "profiled" cases, the rate of terminations was a good deal higher than had been anticipated; about 45 percent of the individuals investigated (approximately 470,000 people) were sent cessation notices. Two-thirds of the beneficiaries who appealed their termination to an ALJ were subsequently reinstated.[59] The effectiveness of appealing benefit cessation was soon made apparent to beneficiaries and their attorneys. Initially (at the inception of CDR), 70 percent of those terminated by the state agencies were asking for an administrative hearing. By the end of 1983, over 90 percent requested such a hearing.[60]

The early onset of periodic reviews and the massive number of terminations soon had an unsettling effect on social security policymakers as evidenced by the following statement appearing in an appendix to a congressional hearing on the "human costs" of CDRs:

Not long after the CDIs were implemented in March 1981, widespread concern arose about the quality, accuracy, and fairness of the reviews. Press accounts of severly disabled individuals who had been terminated from the rolls began to proliferate; and constituent reports to Members of Congress established an alarming pattern of questionable terminations. It became clear that close to half of all DI beneficiaries subjected to a CDI were terminated at the initial decision level, often without much warning, and in many instances without much evidence that the individual was not disabled.[61]

CONTROVERSY OVER PERIODIC REVIEW

The early years of social security disability policymaking had been characterized by political and ideological controversy. Once in place, however, there was relatively little dispute about the direction of the disability program—including the enactment of the 1980 Amendments. Under the Carter administration, anxiety about the growth of the disability insurance program precipitated such belt-tightening measures as the "Grid" and the new pain regulations. Periodic review was the manifestation of this concern for persons already on the disability rolls and it too had bipartisan support. The Social Security Administration's vigorous pursuit of its campaign to cease benefits for ineligibles through the continuing disability review process, however, ended the spirit of bipartisanship and transformed social security policymaking into a political football over the next four years.

Friction within Congress

The Social Security Administration's implementation of periodic review created friction within Congress and between the legislative and executive branches of government. Partisan conflict over social security policymaking resurfaced as the consensus over periodic review began to disintegrate. Many congressional Democrats charged that the Reagan administration was motivated by more than a mere desire to "weed out" disability ineligibles. They accused SSA of subverting the intent of Congress in the implementation of periodic review by changing the primary goal of CDR from administrative efficiency to program austerity.

Among the more vocal critics was James Shannon, representative from New York, who told Deputy Commissioner Simmons that, "from the very beginning of this administration you have gone beyond what was required by the law and projected savings way beyond what anybody thought you could save from the review of these cases."[62] Representative Pickle, "godfather" of the 1980 Amendments, characterized the implementation of periodic review as "a hasty and harsh implementation . . . [that] has magnified problems in the program a thousandfold and caused much pain for beneficiaries and much dislocation among agency personnel."[63]

In his opening statement before the Senate Budget Committee hearings in 1984, Tennessee Senator Jim Sasser also chastized the Social Security Administration for "abandon[ing] its commitment to compassion and fairness for the disabled in an all out attempt to identify those cases where individuals did not belong on the Disability rolls." He added that "such callousness for the truly eligible goes beyond the bounds of economic or political efficiency."[64]

Although most denunciations of SSA's implementation of periodic review emanated from Democrats in Congress, criticism of, as well as support for, CDR came from both sides of the aisle. One of the strongest proponents of a vigorous CDR campaign was Senator Russell Long, (D-La.). On the opposite side, a leader in the move to slow down the CDR process was Senator William Cohen, (R-Maine). Senator Cohen defended his Democratic colleagues who criticized periodic review by denying that they "sought to exploit [this] issue because of political advantage."[65]

Partisan Debate over Periodic Review

Criticism of the CDR process arose from other sources as well. In his testimony before the Social Security Subcommittee, John Harris, president of the National Council of SSA Field Office Locals, a union representing social security employees in district and branch offices, stated "we are witnessing a savage purge of the rolls, with mean applications of self-serving rules, and without heart or mind to the consequences."[66] Some laid the blame directly on the newly elected Republican president and argued that the Reagan administration took advantage of the "flaccid definition of disability" and seized upon the opportunity presented by the 1980 Amendments and the mandate of periodic review to carry out cutbacks in federal social welfare spending.[67]

The Importance of Cost Savings

Because Congress had not clearly specified the objectives and methods of periodic review, the focus of political debate over the next few years was whether SSA was prompted by the desire for budget cuts or was merely being faithful to the congressional intent behind the 1980 Amendments. The source of controversy between the Social Security Administration and the Congress revolved around the emphasis SSA gave to savings above all other considerations.

Defenders of the Carter administration have argued that the administrative changes "were intended to be implemented in an orderly, unhurried, and careful manner . . . [and] while it was expected to result in cost savings eventually (roughly five years hence), it was abundantly clear that the new procedures would initially cost more than they would save."[68] The events surrounding passage of the 1980 Amendments suggest, however, that Congress and the Democrats cannot escape culpability so easily. While Congress had been informed that periodic review would not achieve immediate savings, passage of the 1980 Amendments was prompted by a concern for increased administrative efficiency accompanied by a desire to reduce program costs.

An internal memorandum from the Associate Commissioner for Operational Policy and Procedure addressed to all regional commissioners suggests that savings, rather than efficiency, was SSA's top priority. The memorandum, written in 1981 even before periodic review was scheduled to begin, stated that "in recent weeks it has become clear that one of our most important goals for FY 1982 and following is to save disability dollars, particularly Title II dollars."[69]

Within the next few years, the codewords, "excessive" and "overzealous" were invoked—for the most part by Democratic critics of the Reagan administration, perhaps motivated in part by a desire to defuse criticism of their complicity in creating periodic review—to describe SSA's termination policy. A typical statement came from Missouri Representative Ike Skelton who referred "to the overzealous and irresponsible actions of the Social Security Administration in conducting their reviews of continuing disability insurance claims."[70]

Another observer of periodic review, the medical director of the American Psychiatric Association, charged that the "current approach, in an excess of fervor to reduce Federal expenditures, is contrary to both the letter and the spirit of the careful review that was mandated by Congress in the Social Security Disability Amendments of 1980."[71] SSA Commissioner Jack Svahn dismissed these charges as "political diatribe" and denied that budgetary considerations motivated the Agency's actions.[72]

Although Commissioner Svahn denied that the continuing disability review process was part of the president's economic recovery program, congressional critics further attributed SSA's enthusiasm for CDR to encouragement from the Office of Management and Budget (OMB) which, they argued, relied on trimming the disability rolls to reduce the federal deficit.

Representative Pickle claimed that the Social Security Administration exceeded congressional estimates of savings from the review policy by a multiple of ten. He pointed out that savings of $168 million by the *fifth* year of operation had been anticipated when the bill mandating periodic review was passed. Now, he said, the administration was projecting savings of over one and one-half billion dollars by its fifth year. Pickle charged that the "Administration, in order to get immediate budget savings, began the continuing disability reviews a year before they were required, and greatly accelerated the number of reviews." He characterized the administration's CDR process as a "too hasty and harsh implementation of a sensible legislative requirement [that] has proven disastrous."[73]

Adding his voice to the criticism, Senator Donald Riegle of Michigan stated in a House Ways and Means Committee hearing that he felt that "part of what is going on here is an attitude within OMB and other agencies within the executive branch designed to wring out savings." He continued, "we all want to reduce the deficit, but I think there is undue pressure being focused in certain areas where the constituency groups are the least able to fight back. So that there is the appearance that you can go get a quick, easy savings in budget terms by squeezing down these outlays."[74] In his opening statement in the Senate Oversight Subcommittee hearings, Senator Carl Levin of Michigan also attributed the acceleration of the CDR process by almost a year to OMB's "urging . . . in an attempt to save some $200 million for fiscal year 1982."[75]

The Reagan Administration Position

Statements by President Reagan and administration spokespersons throughout 1981 provided support for these charges. They revealed that the accelerated reviews were part of the Reagan administration's fiscal year 1982 budget initiative and involved a strong desire to realize deficit reduction from CDR. The administration's intention had been signaled in early 1981 when the White House released a document entitled "America's New Beginning: A Program For Economic Recovery"; it contained a section on "Tightening Eligibility for Disability Insurance."[76]

A 1983 Congressional Research Service report to the Social Security Subcommittee explained that the "expanded use of section 311 [periodic review]... was one of a number of initiatives taken by the Administration as part of its Fiscal Year 1982 Budget reduction package"; achievement of this goal was to be accomplished in part by administrative measures which "consisted primarily of an effort to 'intensively review' the existing DI caseload."[77]

The basis of the Congressional Research report was an administration budget report promising that "under the direction of this Administration, the SSA will begin to intensively review cases to insure that only the truly disabled receive disability benefits."[78] The administration report also predicted a decrease in "rapidly growing disability insurance costs through ending misdirected benefits."[79] Following up on these initiatives in the latter part of 1981, President Reagan decried the "widespread abuse" of the disability program "which should not be allowed to continue."[80]

In one of a series of articles in *Newsday*, a Long Island, New York newspaper, a representative of the Office of Management and Budget admitted that the White House wanted to achieve cuts in the disability program as part of a plan for huge savings. He acknowledged that OMB planned over $200 million saved in fiscal year 1982 (beginning in October 1981) with a gross annual savings of over $1.7 billion projected by fiscal year 1986.[81]

Shortly after periodic review was implemented, a *New York Times* article contended that the Reagan administration "has singled out disability payments, one of the fastest growing areas of Government spending, as a primary target for budget cutting."[82] In this analysis (fourth in a series on "key programs that President Reagan wants to cut"), Edwin Dale, Jr., spokesperson for OMB, was quoted as saying that "there are simply too many people getting disability insurance who don't deserve or need it." He added that the program "was a very subjective program [and] sometimes it seems that nobody ever gets turned down or taken off the rolls."[83]

The furor over the "correct" interpretation of legislative intent of periodic review was, of course, exacerbated by the absence of legislative direction in the 1980 Amendments. Because statutory guidelines for CDR were virtually nonexistent, implementation of periodic review was left largely to the Social Security Administration's discretion. While the Agency's CDR policy was generally consistent with congressional concern over monitoring ineligibility, it was clear that Congress had not foreseen the thoroughness and fervor with which SSA would carry out the mandate of section 311, nor had Congress anticipated the extent of the devastation on current beneficiaries.

The political fallout from periodic review eventually motivated Congress to hold hearings and ultimately propose some ameliorative measures. Unwilling to wait for the political process to alleviate the harsh effects of periodic review, beneficiaries turned to the federal courts for relief. When disability recipients sought judicial review of the decision to terminate their benefits, the courts were drawn into the debate and were charged with the task of determining legislative intent of the periodic review provision and judging the propriety of the methods by which the executive branch implemented the continuing eligibility policy. Such challenges to bureaucratic discretion soon led to heavy judicial involvement in the social security policymaking process.

The years following March 1981 illustrate the problems that arise when implementation of legislative policy becomes a source of contention between the executive branch and the courts. Typifying the increasingly bitter interaction between the courts and the Agency over legislative intent, New York's District Court Judge Jack Weinstein depicted the Social Security Administration's continuing eligibility policy as the action of "a zealous administration that believed it had congressional sanction to cut costs at the expense of what some believed was an impotent constituency."[84]

NOTES

1. 42 U.S.C. §405(a) (1984).
2. 42 U.S.C. §423(a)(1)(D) (1984).
3. These regulations are no longer in effect.
4. 424 U.S. 319 (1976). In 1970, in *Goldberg v. Kelly*, 397 U.S. 254 (1970), the Supreme Court had ruled that the due process clause required that public assistance or welfare recipients must be given a hearing prior to termination of benefits. The *Mathews* decision was a defeat for those wishing to expand procedural due process rights in entitlement programs but it left intact the Social Security Act's mandate of a due process hearing after termination of benefits as well as judicial review by the federal courts after final administrative appeal.
5. Subcommittee on Social Security of the House Committee on Ways and Means, *Subcommittee Survey of State Disability Agencies: Adjudicative Climate*, 96th Cong., 1st Sess. (Comm. Print 1979), p. 12 (hereafter *Survey of State Agencies*). For additional discussion of the adjudicative climate after 1975 see Senate Committee on Finance, *Issues Related to Social Security Act Disability Programs*, 96th Cong., 1st Sess. (Comm. Print 1979), p. 113 (hereafter *Issues Related to Disability Programs*); *Oversight of Social Security Disability Benefits Terminations: Hearing before the Subcommittee on Oversight of Government Management of the Senate Committee on Governmental Affairs*, 97th Cong., 2d Sess. (1982), pp. 245–46 (statement of Gregory Ahart, director, Human Resources Division, General Accounting Office) (hereafter *Oversight of Disability Terminations*);

"The Bellmon Report," Reprinted in *Social Security Bulletin* 5(May 1982): 3–27.

6. *Survey of State Agencies*, p. 13.

7. Subcommittee on Oversight of Government Management of the Senate Committee on Governmental Affairs, *Oversight of the Social Security Administration Disability Reviews*, 97th Cong., 2d Sess. (Comm. Print 1982), p. 13 (hereafter *Oversight of Disability Reviews*).

8. *Oversight of Disability Reviews*, p. 13; see also Katherine Collins and Anne Erfle, "Social Security Disability Benefits Reform Act of 1984: Legislative History and Summary of Provisions," *Social Security Bulletin* 48(April 1985):11.

9. *Issues Related to Disability Programs*, p. 31.

10. General Accounting Office, "More Diligent Followup Needed to Weed Out Ineligible SSA Disability Beneficiaries," HRD–81–48 (March 3, 1981), p. 6.

11. 20 CFR §404.1539(a); see Donald Chambers, "Policy Weaknesses and Political Opportunities," *Social Service Review* 59(March 1985):8.

12. The memorandum stated:

If at the time of the initial decision, the inferences from the evidence reasonably supported a favorable decision, substantially similar evidence in a later continuing disability investigation should not be used to find current cessation based solely on different inferences. Unless current evidence at the time of the continuing disability investigation shows a material change in the claimant's situation, the period of disability established by the hearing examiner should administratively be held to be continuing. Material change in this context involves either medical improvement to a point consistent with substantial gainful work, or an actual return to substantial gainful activity.

Social Security Disability Insurance: Hearing before the Subcommittee on Social Security of the House Committee on Ways and Means, 98th Cong., 1st Sess. (1983), p. 120 (cited by Peter McGough, associate director, Human Resources Division, General Accounting Office) (hereafter *Disability Insurance*).

13. 45 Fed. Reg. 55568 (1980); this regulation was subsequently published as SSR 81–6 (1981) which reads in relevant part:

Where the evidence obtained at the time of a continuing disability investigation (CDI) establishes that the individual is not currently disabled or blind, a finding of cessation is appropriate. It will not be necessary to determine whether or how much the individual's condition has medically improved since the prior favorable determination.

14. 20 C.F.R. §404.1594(b)(1) (no longer in effect).

15. 45 Fed. Reg. 55583 (1980).

16. SSR 82–64 (1982).

17. In 1975 31.2 percent of the continuing disability investigations conducted led to termination of benefits while 50.8 percent of the CDIs resulted in lost benefits by 1978; see *Issues Related to Disability Programs*, p. 117.

18. Interview with Deborah Spector, disability attorney, September 24, 1986.

19. Interview with Barbara Samuels, disability attorney, September 19, 1986.

20. Social Security Disability Amendments of 1980, Pub. L. No. 96–265, 94 Stat. 441 (1980).

21. See *Disability Insurance Legislation: Hearings before the Subcommittee on Social Security of the House Committee on Ways and Means*, 96th Cong., 1st Sess. (1979) (hereafter *Disability Insurance Legislation*); *Subcommittee on Social Security of the House Committee on Ways and Means, Disability Amendments of 1980—H.R. 3236*, 96th Cong., 2d Sess. (Comm. Print 1980) (hereafter *Disability Amendments of 1980*); *Issues Related to Disability Programs*.

22. H.R. 3236, 96th Cong., 2d Sess. (1980).

23. This provision was a compromise between the House proposal of 80 percent of the AIME or 150 percent of the PIA and the Senate proposal of 85 percent of the AIME or 160 percent of the PIA.

24. There was an initial disparity between the Senate and the House proposals on calculation of the permissible number of dropout years for workers under thirty-two years of age.

25. Confronted with inadequate funding in the disability program Congress had enacted legislation in 1977 (Pub. L. 95–216) in which money was reallocated to the disability insurance fund from the retirement and survivor's OASI fund in 1977 and from the health insurance fund in 1978; presumably the disability insurance fund had become solvent as a result of this influx of money. By 1981 "both disability and Medicare [trust funds] were doing well." Paul Light, *Artful Work: The Politics of Social Security Reform* (New York: Random House, 1985), p. 106.

Unions such as the American Federation of State, County, and Municipal Employees opposed the 1980 Amendments in part because of their view that the DI trust fund was not in financial crisis. They deplored the effect that the dropout years provision would have on younger workers as well as the toll that the reduced benefits would take on families. Opponents of the bill argued that only a very small percentage of recipients received more income from disability benefits than from predisability employment and that these were at the low end of the income scale.

Other groups opposing the bill included the National Farmers Union, the National Multiple Sclerosis Society, and the American Council of the Blind. The National Association of Manufacturers and the Health Insurance Association of America were in favor of the bill but most of the written and oral testimony before the Senate Finance Committee was opposed to H.R. 3236. See *Social Security Act Disability Program Amendments: Hearings before the Senate Committee on Finance*, 96th Cong., 1st Sess. (1979) (hereafter *Disability Program Amendments*) for this testimony.

26. Section 311 of the 1980 Disability Amendments provides that:

In any case where an individual is or has been determined to be under a disability, the case shall be reviewed by the applicable State agency or the Secretary . . . for purposes of continuing eligibility, at least once every three years, except that where a finding has been made that such disability is permanent, such reviews shall be made at such times as the Secretary determines to be appropriate. 42 U.S.C. §421(i) (1984).

The House bill proposed to review beneficiaries with nonpermanent disabilities every three years. The Senate version concurred but added a provision that allowed the Secretary to review cases with a probability of permanence at his discretion; the Conference Committee adopted the Senate language.

27. *Oversight of Disability Terminations*, p. 251 (statement of Gregory Ahart).

28. See *Disability Insurance Legislation: Disability Program Amendments*.

29. *Disability Insurance Legislation*, p. 55 (statement of Joseph Califano, secretary, Department of Health and Human Services, responding affirmatively to the words quoted in a question from Rep. Mikva).

30. Ibid., p. 19 (statement of Robert Meyers, consultant to the Subcommittee on Social Security).

31. Ibid., p. 405 (statement of Wilbur Cohen, chair, Coalition for Save Our Security).

32. Ibid., p. 78 (statement by Stanford Ross, commissioner, Social Security Administration).

33. See *Disability Insurance Legislation*.

34. 126 Cong. Rec. S621 (Jan. 30, 1980) (statement of Sen. Moynihan).

35. *Disability Insurance*, p. 15 (statement of Rep. Pickle).

36. 125 Cong. Rec. H23380 (Sept. 6, 1979) (statement of Rep. Pickle).

37. Ibid., p. H23383.

38. Ibid., p. H23385.

39. The debate in the House took place on September 6, 1979; the Senate debate covered three days: December 5, 1979 and January 30 and 31, 1980. The bill went to conference on March 26, 1980 and was reported out of conference and agreed to in the House on May 22, 1980 and in the Senate on May 29, 1980.

40. Interview with Patricia Dilley, professional assistant, Subcommittee on Social Security of the House Committee on Ways and Means, May 8, 1986. The primary purpose of periodic review was to achieve administrative reform; the bill's supporters in Congress had not anticipated that the review process would net an early savings because of the initial expenditures in administrative costs.

41. *Disability Insurance*, p. 60 (statement of David Koitz, specialist in Social Legislation, Education and Public Welfare Division, Congressional Research Service).

42. The Senate Finance and House Ways and Means Committee reports each presented estimates of administrative costs of periodic review and savings in benefit payments; the variations among the estimates were attributable to different assumptions about the effective date of the reviews and whether the savings pertained to disability benefits alone or also included savings of medicare payments. Both reports indicated that periodic review would add to the costs of the disability program during the first two

or three years and that substantial savings would begin only after that time. All estimates agreed on an ultimate savings of $-.03$ percent as the long-range (75-year) effect on OASDI expenditures as to the percentage of taxable income. See S. Rep. No. 408, 96th Cong., 1st Sess. (1979); H.R. Rep. No. 100, 96th Cong., 1st Sess. (1979); see also *Issues Related to Disability Programs; Disability Amendments of 1980.*

43. See *Disability Insurance,* pp. 58–61 (statement of David Koitz).

44. Ibid., p. 61.

45. "More Diligent Followup Needed."

46. Ibid., p. 8. The GAO later acknowledged that it never checked SSA's figures and that the accuracy of the report was questionable. See Bob Wyrick and Patrick Owens, "The Disability Nightmare," Special Reprint, *Newsday* (March 21, 1983), p. R9.

47. "More Diligent Followup Needed," p. 5.

48. See *Oversight Of Disability Terminations;* see also Collins and Erfle, "Disability Benefits Reform Act."

49. *Oversight of Disability Terminations,* p. 47 (statement of Paul Simmons, deputy commissioner for Programs and Policy, Social Security Administration). See also *Disability Insurance,* p. 54 (statement of Paul Simmons).

50. *Oversight of Disability Terminations,* p. 152 (Memorandum from Sandy Crank, associate commissioner for Operational Policy and Procedures, Social Security Administration, March 6, 1981).

51. Profiling was based on a computer analysis at SSA headquarters in Baltimore and then files were sent to the states which notified individuals that a review had been undertaken. The notices sent by the state DDSs required individuals to report on their current work capability and their recent medical treatment. When the medical evidence was deemed insufficient, beneficiaries were sent for medical evaluation by consulting physicians at SSA's expense. When it was determined that the individual was no longer disabled, another notice was sent stating that benefits would be terminated two months from the date of the notice unless additional evidence of disability was submitted within ten days. The file was then sent back to Baltimore which sent out official notification of the termination and advised the recipient of his or her right to appeal. Claimants were then given sixty days to ask for reconsideration.

52. *Oversight of Disability Terminations,* p. 20 (statement of Sen. Cohen).

53. *Disability Insurance,* p. 53 (statement of Paul Simmons).

54. The findings of these studies were used to select cases for periodic review in 1981 and 1982. A SSA study of 3,154 recipients in 1979 produced a list of most likely error-prone cases. On the basis of this study, a total of 537,021 cases were selected for review from March 1981 through April 1982; see *Oversight of Disability Terminations,* p. 177 (Memorandum from Sandy Crank). State DDSs selected 405,000 of these cases for review and nearly half (191,000) were terminated; see *Oversight of Disability Reviews,* p. 19.

A new formula was devised for the remainder of 1982 (after April) in which beneficiaries were targeted based on the results of a study using a sample of 25,000 cases. This analysis revealed that the following persons were the most likely to be ineligible: those with auxiliary beneficiaries; those between 31 and 55; those awarded benefits between 1973 and 1976; those receiving worker's compensation; those initially denied benefits and later awarded them on appeal at an administrative hearing or at the reconsideration stage; and those receiving less than $200 or more than $599 in monthly benefits. *Oversight of Disability Terminations*, p. 174 (Memorandum from Sandy Crank).

55. *Disability Insurance*, p. 31 (statement of Paul Simmons).

56. *Social Security Disability Reviews: A Federally Created State Problem: Hearing before the House Select Committee on Aging*, 98th Cong., 1st Sess. (1983), p. 126 (statement of Paul Simmons) (hereafter *A Federally Created Problem*).

57. See *Oversight of Disability Terminations*, p. 120 (statement of Herbert Brown, administrator of the Tennessee DDS) for a reaction by a state DDS official and p. 137 (statement of Francis O'Byrne, Administrative Law Judge) for the views of an administrative law judge. For a statement confirming the vulnerability of beneficiaries see Chambers, "Policy Weaknesses and Political Opportunities," p. 7: "Beneficiaries with extremely severe disabilities have been led to believe that they can count on DI benefits in one year, only to be informed some years later that despite the fact that their condition has not changed, benefits will be terminated."

58. *A Federally Created Problem*, p. 122 (statement of Paul Simmons); *Oversight of Disability Terminations*, p. 3 (statement of Sen. Levin).

59. *Social Security Disability Reviews: The Human Costs: Hearing before the Senate Special Committee on Aging*: Part 1, 98th Cong., 2d Sess. (1984), p. 75 (Appendix) (hereafter *The Human Costs*).

60. Ibid., p. 74.

61. Ibid., p. 75.

62. *Disability Insurance*, p. 57 (statement of Rep. Shannon).

63. Ibid., p. 3 (statement of Rep. Pickle).

64. *Social Security Disability Program Reform: Hearings before the Senate Committee on the Budget*, 98th Cong., 2d Sess. (1984), p. 3 (statement of Sen. Sasser).

65. *Oversight of Disability Terminations*, p. 41 (statement of Sen. Cohen).

66. *Disability Amendments of 1982: Hearings before the Subcommittee on Social Security of the House Committee on Ways and Means*, 97th Cong., 2d Sess. (1982), p. 136 (statement of John Harris, president, National Council of Social Security Field Office Locals) (hereafter *Disability Amendments of 1982*).

67. Chambers, "Policy Weaknesses and Political Opportunities," p. 6; see also Donald Chambers, "The Reagan Administration's Welfare Retrenchment Policy: Terminating Social Security Benefits for the Disabled," *Policy Studies Review* 5(November 1985):230–40.

68. Chambers, "Policy Weaknesses and Political Opportunities," p. 7.

69. *Oversight of Disability Terminations*, p. 152 (Memorandum from Sandy Crank).

70. *Disability Amendments of 1982*, p. 139 (statement of Rep. Skelton).

71. *New York Times*, May 9, 1982, p. 22.

72. Ibid.

73. *Status of Continuing Disability Reviews: Hearings before the Sub-committee on Social Security of the House Committee on Ways and Means*, 98th Cong., 2d Sess. (1982), p. 4 (statement of Rep. Pickle) (hereafter *Status of Disability Reviews*).

74. *Disability Amendments of 1982*, p. 25 (statement of Sen. Riegle).

75. *Oversight of Disability Terminations*, p. 4 (statement of Sen. Levin).

76. Wyrick and Owens, "The Disability Nightmare," p. R8.

77. *Disability Insurance*, p. 58 (statement of David Koitz).

78. This quote was cited in Chambers, "The Reagan Administration's Welfare Retrenchment Policy," p. 231. In furtherance of this goal, the administration proposed several legislative changes in the social security disability program that would have eliminated consideration of vocational factors and relied entirely upon medical factors, would have required a finding that the impairment would be disabling for twenty-four months instead of twelve months, and would have raised the number of qualifying months of employment; see *New York Times*, September 28, 1981, p. B2.

79. Wyrick and Owens, "The Disability Nightmare," p. R8.

80. *New York Times*, September 28, 1981, p. B2.

81. Wyrick and Owens, "The Disability Nightmare," p. R9.

82. *New York Times*, April 7, 1981, p. B9.

83. Ibid.

84. Jack Weinstein, "Equality and the Law: Social Security Disability Cases in the Federal Courts," *Syracuse Law Review* 35(1985):913.

6

The Judiciary's Role in Continuing Eligibility Policymaking

The judiciary's power over the Social Security Administration is defined by the Social Security Act which dictates that Agency determinations must be submitted for judicial approval upon proper presentation by a dissatisfied claimant.[1] The scope of judicial review of the Agency's determination in an adjudicatory hearing is narrow; the Act precludes the courts from engaging in fact-finding by stating that the Secretary's findings of fact "if supported by substantial evidence, shall be conclusive."[2]

Most appeals of Agency benefit denials are heard at the lower court level; the majority are inappropriate for Supreme Court consideration because they arise from a claimant's disagreement with SSA over a factual appraisal of a medical condition. Although the lower courts are the major arena for the disability litigation, because they take their cues on interpretation of the Social Security Act from the Supreme Court, this next section will focus on the high court's disability opinions.

THE SUPREME COURT AND DISABILITY LAW

From the inception of the program through the Supreme Court's 1986–1987 term, the high court has only ruled on 21 disability cases. In these 21 cases, the Court only wrote fifteen opinions—thirteen on the merits and two limited to jurisdictional questions. In the six remaining cases, after initially granting certiorari, the Supreme Court did not issue an opinion as the cases were either remanded to the lower courts or dismissed because the statutory provision had been amended.[3] Most of the Supreme Court cases arising under the social security disability laws were brought by the Social Security Administration asking the Court to sanction its procedures and regulations. Of the other cases, two originated as equal protection challenges to the constitutionality of statutory provisions, two turned on issues of judicial review only, and three merely concerned requests to the Court for a stay of a lower court order pending appeal. In two disability cases, one a clash between a state and a disability recipient and the other, a dispute between a client and an attorney, it appeared that the result did not affect the Agency.

Table 6.1 summarizes the Supreme Court's actions in the disability program cases and illustrates the Court's deference to SSA in upholding its procedures and regulations.

The Supreme Court's deference to SSA stems in part from its view that the Social Security Act "is among the most intricate ever drafted by Congress" and that "perhaps appreciating the complexity of what it had wrought, Congress conferred on the Secretary exceptionally broad authority to prescribe standards for applying certain sections of the Act."[4] As Table 6.1 demonstrates, SSA's only major judicial defeat at the Supreme Court level occurred in *Bowen v. City of New York*,[5] a case appealed by SSA only on jurisdictional grounds and therefore not decided on the merits. In almost all substantive issues in which the Supreme Court sat in judgment of the Social Security Administration's implementation of the Act, the Court concluded that the Agency was operating within statutory and constitutional parameters.

JURISDICTIONAL REQUISITES OF THE ACT

The initial inquiry of any legal action must be directed toward the question of whether the plaintiff is properly invoking the power of the court, that is, whether the court has jurisdiction over the case. No matter how great the alleged injustice, before relief can be granted, plaintiffs must clear the jurisdictional hurdles or persuade the courts to waive them.

The jurisdictional requirements of the Social Security Act—spelled out in section 405(g)—encompass all social security programs; the language and legislative history of the Act make it clear that Congress intended administrative exhaustion as a precondition to judicial review in all cases arising under the Social Security Act. Problems appear when plaintiffs fail to comply with the prerequisites of the Act by proceeding in a timely fashion through the four steps of the administrative process and securing a "final" agency decision. In such situations courts must decide whether to allow them to deviate from the statutory requirements. The cases indicate that the Supreme Court has generally concurred with lower court decisions to create judicial exceptions to allow litigants access to the federal courts to challenge SSA interpretations of the Act.

Exhaustion of Remedies

The Supreme Court explained in *Weinberger v. Salfi* in 1975 that the exhaustion of remedies doctrine was established to prevent "premature interference with agency processes, so that the agency may function efficiently and so that it may have an opportunity to correct its own errors, to afford the parties and the courts the benefits of its experience and expertise, and to compile a record which is adequate for judicial review."[6]

Table 6.1
U.S. Supreme Court Disability-Related Cases (1954–1987)

Case*	Major Issue	Disposition
Yuckert	Validity of "severity" regulation	SSA wins/regulation upheld
City of New York	Exhaustion of remedies and time limit for appeal	SSA loses/judicial review allowed
Kilpatrick	Validity of termination without medical improvement	No decision/case remanded
Caraballo	Validity of termination without medical improvement	No decision/case remanded
Lopez**	Validity of termination without medical improvement	No decision/case remanded
Kuehner	Validity of termination without medical improvement	No decision/case remanded
Day	Mandatory deadline for administrative review	SSA wins/no deadlines permitted
Blankenship	Application for stay of mandatory deadline	SSA wins/stay granted: per O'Connor
Lopez**	Application to vacate stay granted by Rehnquist	SSA wins/ stay continued
Lopez**	Application for stay of interim benefits	SSA wins/stay granted: per Rehnquist
Campbell	Validity of regulations creating "Grid"	SSA wins/regulations upheld
Yamasaki***	Due process challenge on prerecoupment hearing	SSA wins in part/ procedure modified

Table 6.1 (continued)

Case*	Major Issue	Disposition
Jobst	Equal protection challenge to marriage provision	SSA wins/statute constitutional
Sanders	Judicial review of SSA refusal to reopen decision	SSA wins/procedure upheld
Eldridge	Due process challenge to post-termination hearing	SSA wins/procedure upheld
Morris	Statutory interpretation of adoption provision	No decision/writ of certiorari dismissed
Philpott	Dispute between claimant and state agency	Dispute not affecting SSA
Wright	Due process challenge to termination procedure	No decision/case vacated and remanded
Belcher	Equal protection challenge to offset benefits provision	SSA wins/statute constitutional
Perales	Requirements of substantial evidence	SSA wins/procedure upheld
Hopkins	Statutory interpretation of attorney fee provision	Dispute not affecting SSA

* See below for citations.

** This case appeared before the Supreme Court on three successive occasions.

*** Although the named plaintiffs in the class were attempting to avoid recoupment of survivors' and old age benefits, the class included all old age, survivor, and disability recipients. SSA won in part because the Court ruled that requests for reconsideration of overpayment determinations did not require a hearing while requests for waiver of repayment did.

SOURCE: Computer Word Search "Social Security and Disability after 1954."

Table 6.1 (continued)

Citations

Bowen v. Yuckert, 107 S.Ct. 2287 (1987)

Bowen v. City of New York, 106 S.Ct. 2022 (1986).

Kilpatrick v. Heckler, 472 U.S. 1004 (1985).

Caraballo v. Heckler, 471 U.S. 1113 (1985).

Heckler v. Lopez, 469 U.S. 1082 (1984).

Heckler v. Kuehner, 469 U.S. 977 (1984).

Heckler v. Day, 467 U.S. 104 (1984).

Heckler v. Blankenship, 465 U.S. 1301 (1984).

Heckler v. Lopez, 464 U.S. 879 (1983).

Heckler v. Lopez, 463 U.S. 1328 (1983).

Heckler v. Campbell, 461 U.S. 458 (1983).

Califano v. Yamasaki, 442 U.S. 682 (1979).

Califano v. Jobst, 434 U.S. 47 (1977).

Califano v. Sanders, 430 U.S. 99 (1977).

Mathews v. Eldridge, 424 U.S. 319 (1976).

Morris v. Weinberger, 410 U.S. 422 (1973).

Philpott v. Essex County Welfare Board, 409 U.S. 413 (1973).

Richardson v. Wright, 405 U.S. 208 (1972).

Richardson v. Belcher, 404 U.S. 78 (1971).

Richardson v. Perales, 402 U.S. 389 (1971).

Hopkins v. Cohen, 390 U.S. 530 (1968).

Salfi was one of the first Social Security Act cases to spell out the exhaustion requirements of section 405(g). The case arose when plaintiff filed an action against the Social Security Administration after his claim for survivor's benefits at both the initial and reconsideration stages of the administrative process was denied. The complaint, filed in the Northern District of California, asserted the unconstitutionality of a duration of relationship requirement in the Act. Plaintiffs argued that because their claim raised a constitutional question, it was properly within the scope of judicial power even though they had bypassed the latter stages of the administrative process.

The Supreme Court reasoned that because Congress had granted the Secretary authority to specify requirements for exhaustion, the Secretary may, in a particular case, decide that "full exhaustion of internal review procedures is not necessary for a decision to be 'final' within the language of §405(g)."[7] The Court inferred that the Secretary's failure to object to the plaintiff's premature legal action was an admission that the reconsideration stage had been a "final" decision and to demand further exhaustion would not only be futile but detrimental to the interests of efficiency as well.

The Court explained a year later in *Mathews v. Eldridge*[8] that the exhaustion requirement of section 405(g) contained two elements: a waivable rule of exhaustion of administrative remedies and a nonwaivable prerequisite of presentment of a claim for benefits.[9] Although the decision to waive exhaustion was within the Secretary's discretion, the Court held that a refusal to waive may be overridden by a court "where a claimant's interest in having a particular issue resolved promptly is so great that deference to the agency's judgment is inappropriate."[10] Though plaintiff Eldridge had not exhausted his administrative remedies, his interest in expediency was sufficiently great to warrant a wavier of exhaustion and to treat the Secretary's initial decision to terminate benefits as "final" within the meaning of section 405(g).

The Court also indicated that, in *Mathews*, as in *Salfi*, the plaintiff need not have presented his constitutional claim to the Secretary because the Secretary had no power to amend the statute to cure its unconstitutionality; presentment is satisfied by merely making a claim for entitlement to benefits. Eldridge's complaint alleged that his injury could not be remedied by retroactive benefits awarded in a post-termination hearing; moreover, because the constitutional question could not have been resolved at such a hearing, his constitutional challenge was "entirely collateral to his substantive claim of entitlement."[11]

In 1977 the Supreme Court decided *Califano v. Sanders*[12] under the Administrative Procedure Act as well as the Social Security Act. Here, the Court restricted the court's power over disability determinations by denying judicial review of the Secretary's refusal to reopen a previously adjudicated disallowance of a claim. The Social Security Act provides that a claim for benefits, denied by the Agency, may be reopened for a number of reasons; if, however, a second claim is brought on the same evidence, the later claim may be denied on the basis of a principle called administrative res judicata.[13] When the administrative law judge determined that the applicant, Sanders, was not covered by any of the provisions for reopening, Sanders sued in federal court alleging that, in light of *Salfi* and *Mathews*, section 405(g) of the Act gave courts the power to review the Agency's decision against reopening his benefit denial.

The Supreme Court held in *Sanders* that section 405(g) of the Social Security Act did not authorize judicial review of a refusal to reopen. Distinguishing *Salfi* and *Mathews*, the Court held that "those cases merely adhered to the well-established principle that when constitutional questions are in issue, the availability of judicial review is presumed."[14] The plaintiff in *Sanders*, said the Court, was not alleging a constitutional violation of the Act but was merely seeking another opportunity to establish his entitlement to disability benefits.

Class Relief under Section 405(g)

In *Califano v. Yamasaki*,[15] two years later, the Court partially amended SSA procedure for collecting unearned benefits but, even more importantly, made it clear that a class action suit was permissible under section 405(g). The case arose under the Act's provision that beneficiaries of the old-age, survivors' and disability program were not obligated to repay mistaken overpayments if they were "without fault" and if such overpayment "would defeat the purpose" of the Act or "would be against equity and good conscience."[16] Under SSA rules, after notification of the receipt of overpayments, beneficiaries were able to seek reconsideration of the decision that they had been incorrectly awarded benefits and to ask for a waiver of recovery of benefits; they were not permitted an oral hearing to argue their case for waiver.

Plaintiffs brought suit claiming they were entitled to an oral hearing to challenge the Agency's demand for a return of unearned benefits. They asked the court to enjoin the Secretary from ordering recoupment without providing an opportunity for such a hearing. The Supreme Court held that SSA must allow a prerecoupment oral hearing when waiver is requested but not when the Agency is simply reconsidering the accuracy of the overpayment decision.

The Supreme Court also determined in *Yamasaki* that class relief is permissible under section 405(g).[17] The Secretary argued that the statutory language of section 405(g), referring to suit brought by "any individual," indicates congressional intent to restrict relief to a "case-by-case adjudication of claims."[18] The Secretary supported his claim by pointing to the *Weinberger* holding in which class relief had been denied. Ironically, in light of SSA's practice of nonacquiescence, the Secretary also argued that class relief was unnecessary because "he will appeal adverse decisions or abide them within the jurisdiction of the courts rendering them [and] there is thus no need for repetitious litigation in order to establish legal principles beyond the confines of a particular case, and no need to afford class relief in cases brought under section [405(g)]."[19]

The Supreme Court disagreed with the Agency's interpretation of the Act and the rules for class action suits. Speaking for the Court, Justice Blackmun pointed out that there was no evidence that Congress intended to exempt actions brought under the Social Security Act from the rules established for all civil suits. He noted that other jurisdictional statutes are written "in terms of an individual plaintiff, since the Rule 23 class-action device was designed to allow an exception to the usual rule that litigation is conducted by and on behalf of the individual named parties only."[20] Concluding that such suits are especially appropriate for class actions as long as members of the class conform to the jurisdictional requirements of section 405(g), Justice Blackmun also upheld the certification of the nationwide class "since the scope of injunctive relief is dictated by the extent of the violation established, not by the geographical extent of the plaintiff class."[21]

Statute of Limitations

One of the latest cases interpreting section 405(g), *Bowen v. New York*,[22] was brought as a class action suit challenging the Secretary's policies on mental impairments. The complaint alleged that the Secretary "had adopted an unlawful unpublished policy" and was misapplying the regulations by utilizing a presumption that mentally impaired persons could perform unskilled labor if they did not meet the Listings.

Judge Jack Weinstein of the Eastern District of New York had certified a class that included plaintiffs who had not exhausted their administrative remedies, holding that here, as in *Mathews*, it would be inappropriate to defer to the Secretary regarding exhaustion. For the same reason the judge also included as class members plaintiffs who had not filed their claims for judicial review within the required 60-day time limit. The judge also ordered interim relief to terminated beneficiaries until their entitlement could be properly assessed. The Second Circuit affirmed the district court's ruling.

Having lost at both levels below, the Secretary's appeal did not challenge the lower court's ruling on the procedure for assessing mental impairments nor the remedy prescribed by the district court—reopening the claims of class members to redetermine eligibility. Rather SSA's appeal was addressed solely to the lower court's decision to allow the class to include individuals who had exceeded the 60-day deadline for judicial review and had not exhausted their administrative remedies.

The Supreme Court reasoned that the 60-day limit was merely a statute of limitations and therefore subject to equitable tolling or waiver. Concluding that "on these facts the equities in favor of tolling are compelling," the Court affirmed Judge Weinstein's decision to permit persons who had not complied with the statutory requirement to be included in the class.[23]

The Court utilized the *Mathews* test to determine whether to defer to the Agency's judgment on administrative exhaustion. Justice Powell, speaking for a unanimous Court, ruled that in this case, as in *Mathews*, because plaintiffs were objecting to the Secretary's failure to follow his own regulations, their challenge was collateral to their claim for benefits and exhaustion was not required. The exhaustion decision, said Justice Powell, "should not be made solely by mechanical application of the [*Mathews v.*] *Eldridge* factors, but should also be guided by the policies underlying the exhaustion requirement."[24]

Pointing to the lower court finding "that a systemwide, unrevealed policy that was inconsistent in critically important ways with established regulations" had deprived these claimants of benefits, he held that exhaustion would have been futile under these circumstances and plaintiffs were excused from conforming to the requirements of the Act for purposes of judicial review.[25]

APPROVAL OF ADMINISTRATIVE PROCEDURE

Notwithstanding the Court's rulings on jurisdictional questions, its decisions generally reflected the view that "in the context of a comprehensive complex administrative program, the administrative process must have a reasonable opportunity to evolve procedures to meet needs as they arise."[26] Consequently, when reaching decisions on the merits, the Court consistently demonstrated a willingness to defer to administrative interpretations of the enabling statute and to restrict judicial interference with administrative procedures.

Beginning in 1971, litigants raised a number of challenges to SSA's procedures for determining eligibility. In one of the first disability cases, *Richardson v. Perales*,[27] the Court upheld the Agency's reliance on a written medical report from an absent doctor despite its hearsay character and the claimant's inability to subject the writer of the report to cross-examination at the hearing. The Court's reasoning was based, in part, on the fact that the claimant could have exercised his subpoena powers to compel the doctor to appear at the hearing and present his findings in person.

Although plaintiff had prevailed on the jurisdictional issue in *Mathews v. Eldridge*, the Court decided for SSA on the merits in that case by affirming the Agency's policy of granting only a post-termination hearing. Holding that the constitutional guarantee of due process did not mandate a rigid timetable for the opportunity to be heard, the Court declined to extend its ruling on pretermination hearings for public welfare benefits to disability cessation cases.[28] Establishing a three-part balancing test for evaluating the requirements of due process, the Supreme Court carefully pointed to the numerous "carefully structured procedures," in the administration of social security disability claims and concluded that SSA's present policy showed adequate regard for due process.[29]

Time Limits on SSA Procedure

The Court's policy of allowing SSA wide latitude for determining proper procedure was also apparent in *Heckler v. Day*,[30] a class action suit arising in district court in 1978. In *Day*, plaintiffs had challenged the "unreasonable" delay in SSA processing of administrative review in termination decisions. Finding for plaintiffs, a Vermont District Court had required the Secretary to issue reconsideration decisions within 90 days and to hold administrative hearings within 90 days after requests for hearings were made. The district court judgment, applying to a statewide class of plaintiffs, also ordered payment of interim benefits when these deadlines were not met. When the Second Circuit affirmed the lower court decision, the Secretary appealed to the Supreme Court arguing that a mandatory deadline was contrary to congressional intent and that the district court had abused its equitable powers in imposing one.

The Supreme Court agreed that the district court had overstepped its bounds and reversed. Analyzing the legislative intent, the Court found that Congress had consistently refused to impose mandatory deadlines for adjudication of social security claims. The Secretary had also argued that the district court's order constituted judicial interference with the Secretary's discretion to adopt rules and procedure in claims adjudication. The Supreme Court declined to reach this issue, noting however, as a possible

warning to the lower courts that the congressional intent on this matter
was clear and "it would be an unwarranted judicial intrusion into this
pervasively regulated area for federal courts to issue injunctions imposing
deadlines with respect to future disability claims."[31] In a footnote the Court
added, "we understand that the courts below were moved by long delays
that may well have caused serious deprivations" but reiterated that "this
does not justify imposing absolute periods of limitations applicable to all
claims—limitations that Congress repeatedly has declined to enact."[32]

SSA's Rule-Making Authority

The most important aspect of judicial interpretation of SSA's administrative process arises from the Court's ability to oversee the Agency's rule-
making authority. Two recent cases upheld the Secretary's regulatory authority to formulate procedures to implement the Social Security Act; the
last one, however, evoked some sharp criticism from several members of
the Court.

A case testing the validity of the Secretary's rule-making for the disability
program arose in the Second Circuit when the appellate court reversed a
lower court judgment that Carmen Campbell was not disabled. The ALJ had
determined that Campbell's back condition and hypertension prevented her
from returning to her former hotel maid job but that she was capable of
doing light work. Basing his decision upon the medical-vocational guidelines, the "Grid," the ALJ found that she was not disabled. The district court
affirmed.

The Second Circuit ruled that the Secretary's finding of no disability was
not supported by substantial evidence because the Secretary had not produced evidence of alternative jobs in the national economy that she could
perform.

On appeal, the Supreme Court unanimously overruled the Second Circuit.
Relying upon its statement in the *Gray Panthers* case that the Secretary
has "exceptionally broad authority to prescribe standards for applying certain sections of the Act,"[33] the Supreme Court reaffirmed that a court's role
in reviewing SSA regulations is narrow and must be limited to deciding
only whether the regulations exceed the scope of the Secretary's authority
under the Act. Using these criteria, the Supreme Court held that they did
not.

The Supreme Court also upheld the Agency in its most recent decision,
Bowen v. Yuckert,[34] a case arising out of the Western District of Washington.
The issue in *Yuckert* was whether the second step of the sequential evaluation, the so-called severity requirement, was consistent with the language
and history of the Social Security Act. Under Agency regulations, applicants
must satisfy this step of the claims process by proving that they have an
impairment "that significantly limits" their capacity for performing "basic
work activities."[35]

Janet Yuckert was denied disability insurance benefits and SSI benefits
by the Washington State Agency at the severity stage of the administrative
process, and according to regulations, the Agency did not complete the

evaluation to consider the vocational factors. Yuckert filed suit in district court alleging that her inner ear dysfunction, dizzy spells, and headaches entitled her to disability benefits. The district court affirmed that the Secretary's finding of no disability was supported by substantial evidence. The Ninth Circuit reversed and remanded, and joining four other circuits, invalidated the severity regulation as facially inconsistent with the statute. Unlike the medical improvement issue, on which the circuits were unanimous, four appellate courts had upheld the severity step of the sequential evaluation—at least to some extent.

Citing *Campbell*, a majority of Supreme Court Justices reaffirmed the Court's deferential posture toward SSA. The Court's view, stated Justice Powell, must be limited to affirming that the regulations were within statutory authority and were neither arbitrary nor capricious. The Justice described the severity standard as a logical threshold determination for disability eligibility and not inconsistent with the Social Security Act. Justice Powell also looked to the legislative history of the Act, including reports accompanying the 1984 Reform Bill, to confirm that Congress approved of SSA's interpretation of the severity regulation as an early qualifying step in the adjudication process.

This case aroused some passion on the Court as Justice O'Connor, joined by Justice Stevens, concurred in the judgment but wrote separately to express concern that SSA might have been using this regulation "systematically to deny benefits to claimants who *do* meet the statutory definition of disability" (emphasis in the original).[36] Justice O'Connor reminded her brethren that all eleven circuits had either invalidated the regulation or weakened it by requiring only a "de minimis" showing of an impairment; she also expressed sympathy for the "frustration" of the appellate courts for having to contend "with the Secretary's application of step 2."[37] She appeared satisfied, however, that a newly-adopted Social Security Ruling would solve the problem by creating a minimum severity standard that would prevent premature findings of nondisability.[38]

A strong dissent by Justice Blackmun, joined by Justices Brennan and Marshall, argued that the regulation directly contradicted the plain language of the Act that mandates a severity determination based upon a consideration of age, education, and work experience. Additionally, the dissent drew upon the legislative history of the Act to support its conclusion that the regulation was invalid. The dissenting Justices criticized the majority for incorrectly relying on the 1984 Amendments as endorsement of its position. They refused to accept Justice O'Connor's assumption that the regulation, if validated by the Court, would no longer be used to obstruct legitimate disability entitlement.

Thus, in this case, a majority of justices explicitly criticized the Agency for enforcing the regulations in a way that denied benefits to persons properly entitled to them. Although the regulation was upheld and the Supreme Court expressed deference toward Agency rule-making, perhaps SSA was being placed on notice, for the first time, that henceforth its adjudication policy would be more closely scrutinized.

Judging by the small number of disability cases decided by the Supreme

Court, it is clear that most of the disability action was played out in the lower courts. Moreover, considering the deference shown to SSA by the highest court, it is also clear that charges of judicial activism in disability policymaking cannot be leveled at the Supreme Court. Since the major battles have been fought in the trial and appellate courts, charges of judicial activism must be assessed by evidence of lower court involvement in social security disability policy. It should not be surprising to learn that in disability policymaking, as in other areas of the law, the lower court judges were more activist than their colleagues on the Supreme Court.[39]

THE LOWER FEDERAL COURTS AND THE DISABILITY PROGRAM

The federal court's role of judicial oversight in disability claims is ostensibly limited to ascertaining whether the Secretary's finding of no disability is supported by substantial evidence—not a difficult standard for the Agency to meet. Given the strictures of the substantial evidence rule, as well as the example set by the deferential posture of the Supreme Court, it is not surprising that the Social Security Administration has traditionally received favorable treatment from the federal courts. Emphasizing SSA's successful litigation record, the Fifth Circuit cited "the strict requirements for showing disability and the limited scope of judicial review [as reasons why] reversals of the Secretary are quite rare while affirmances abound."[40]

Despite the constraints of the substantial evidence rule, the federal courts have managed of late to exert strong influence over social security disability policymaking. The part played by the lower courts in the security disability litigation gave rise to accusations of improper judicial intervention into administrative prerogatives as the courts found themselves in conflict with the bureaucracy over the proper interpretation of the legislative mandate.

Litigation prompted by the Social Security Administration's continuing disability review policy ushered in a more conflictual relationship between SSA and the lower courts and raised disturbing questions about whether the judiciary was acting properly in reversing the Agency's findings that plaintiffs were no longer disabled. The litigation also posed questions about whether the courts were "legitimately scrutiniz[ing] administrative action for excesses that violate legally-established limits, [or whether these were] . . . cases of judicial lawmaking, where judges go beyond the written law to resolve matters on the basis of policy considerations or their own political theories."[41] The situation was further complicated by the fact that the appellate courts lacked guidance from the Supreme Court because the highest court never ruled on the proper standards for adjudication of disability termination cases.[42]

PROCEDURAL RULINGS

Plaintiffs' claims of continuing eligibility most frequently began with legal arguments over the preliminary issues of presumptions and burdens of proof; the strategic importance of these procedural claims cannot be over-emphasized because, while allocation of the burden of proof does not pre-destine a case, it gives the court an opportunity to exercise more control over the outcome of the case. Moreover, the debate over procedural issues allowed the courts to sidestep the more troubling and controversial matter of the deference owed to Agency procedure and to defuse accusations of interference with administrative decisionmaking.

As Angus MacIntyre pointed out in his study of environmental litigation, manipulation of procedural devices such as the burden of proof allows "en-terprising judges [to] inconspicuously accomplish desired policy out-comes."[43] Similarly, the determination of the burden of proof issue played a significant role in the outcome of the disability litigation. For when the preliminary round was over and the dust had settled, it was obvious that resolution of the procedural debate had tipped the odds in plaintiffs' favor. At this point in order to present an accurate picture of the judiciary's role in the disability policymaking process, it is necessary to explain some basic rules of civil procedure.[44]

Burden of Proof

The popular expression, "burden of proof," actually consists of two legally distinct parts. The first, the burden of persuasion, requires the party who bears it to convince the factfinder, usually by a preponderance of the evi-dence in civil cases, to accept the truth of a fact or issue. The second com-ponent, more properly called the burden of production, or going forward with evidence, initially belongs to the plaintiff but may be shifted to the defendant after the plaintiff's presentation of evidence.

Presumptions

Plaintiffs' struggles to persuade the courts to grant them a presumption of continuing disability proved to be even more significant to their judicial success than allocation of the burden of proof. A presumption is a legal device arising from an inference; when granted to one side, it is incumbent upon the other to offer countervailing evidence to negate the acceptance of the presumed fact.[45]

Allocating the Burden of Proof

In *Mathews v. Eldridge*, the Supreme Court proclaimed that claimants bear a "continuing burden of showing ... a physical or mental impairment" to prove their disability.[46] The Court added later in its opinion that "to *remain eligible* for benefits the disabled worker must demonstrate ... that he is unable 'to engage in any substantial gainful activity'...." (emphasis added).[47]

Based on these two statements, lower courts have required the disability plaintiffs to prove the existence of their disability. In initial disability claims, it is well established in all circuits that a claimant must first show an inability to return to a former occupation; following this, the burden of proof shifts to the Secretary to show that there is alternative work that the individual can perform.[48] It was not as clear how the burden of proof should be allocated in continuing disability cases: lower courts were faced with the problem of reconciling the Supreme Court's statement in *Mathews* with the logical dictates of accounting for SSA's prior determination of eligibility.

There are three alternative approaches for resolution of the burden of proof issue in continuing eligibility cases.[49] The first eliminates the distinction between a claim for initial benefits and one for continued benefits and simply requires the plaintiff to prove that the disability still exists. This approach attaches no presumption, that is, gives no significance, to the initial award of disability. The second alternative shifts the entire burden of proof onto the Secretary by requiring a showing that plaintiff is no longer disabled. This position has been rejected by most courts because it conflicts with the apparent direction of the Supreme Court's statement in *Mathews*. Lastly, there is a compromise solution that, by utilizing a presumption, conforms to *Mathews* and still accords weight to the original classification of disability. Here, the burden of proof remains with the plaintiff, yet the court acknowledges that the original award of benefits entitles plaintiff to a presumption of continuing disability.[50]

With some variation, the circuits adopted the latter, compromise, position. Under this scheme while the plaintiff continually bore the *burden of persuasion*, the original finding of disability gave rise to a presumption that shifted the *burden of production* to the Secretary to come forward with evidence that the impairment had improved to the point that the plaintiff could now engage in substantial gainful activity. Unless the Secretary could successfully rebut the presumption of continuing disability with evidence of medical improvement, the plaintiff was entitled to remain on the disability rolls.

Most appellate courts adopted the reasoning of the Ninth Circuit's decision in *Patti v. Schweiker*.[51] The court held that the plaintiff's burden of proof "does not cease or shift after an initial ruling of disability has been had. In an appropriate case, however, a prior ruling of disability can give rise to a presumption that the disability still exists." The Fourth Circuit agreed with this approach because "to conclude otherwise would permit the Secretary to submit the same medical evidence to different physicians time and time again until the Secretary obtains a favorable result."[52]

ASSESSING CONTINUING ELIGIBILITY

With the preliminary skirmish over the presumption and burden of proof issues over, litigants and the Social Security Administration proceeded to do battle over the kind of evidence the Secretary must offer to rebut the presumption of continuing eligibility.

The Substantial Evidence Rule

The social security disability litigation tested the boundaries of the substantial evidence rule when the court substituted its determination of disability for the Secretary's in order to reverse the termination decision. The problem was heightened because, while the vast majority of cases simply alleged that the Secretary's finding of nondisability was not supported by substantial evidence, plaintiffs were actually requesting the courts to curtail the Secretary's authority to apply "certain sections of the Act." Requiring the Secretary to produce evidence of medical improvement precluded SSA from evaluating the plaintiff's ability to engage in substantial gainful activity solely on the basis of current medical evidence. Therefore, by asking the courts to include a medical improvement component in continuing disability review cases, litigants were really urging the courts to override SSA's interpretation of the 1980 regulations.

The Current Medical Evidence Standard

Litigants argued that their benefits could not be terminated without substantial evidence of improvement in their medical condition. SSA claimed that it "need only measure the claimant's current medical status against the relevant standards for determining disability in the first instance."[53] When SSA abandoned the medical improvement standard in 1976, it was able to ignore the earlier finding of disability when making its termination decision and simply judge whether the individual could currently engage in substantial gainful activity. By limiting its assessment to the plaintiff's present physical capabilities, the Social Security Administration could avoid confronting the problem that the beneficiary's medical condition had not changed for the better.

Most courts, however, interpreted the current medical evidence rule as requiring the Secretary to come forward with *new* evidence, gathered since the original award of disability, showing that the plaintiff's medical condition had improved or that there had been an erroneous determination in the original adjudication. To do otherwise, ruled the courts, would mean that the "termination would of necessity be based on whim or caprice or would constitute an impermissible relitigation of facts and determinations already finally decided."[54] In the opinion of the Fourth Circuit, the procedure urged by the Secretary would allow SSA "as many bites of the apple" as necessary to get a favorable determination.[55]

SSA argued that it was given statutory authority to establish rules and procedures for entitlement, including the "nature and extent of proofs" required to demonstrate disability. Under the applicable regulations, the Secretary would find that the beneficiary was no longer disabled when, despite the earlier determination of disability, current medical evidence showed an ability to engage in substantial gainful activity. This posture permitted the Agency to remove individuals from the disability rolls even when the medical evidence presented in the termination hearing was similar or identical to the evidence presented in the initial claim. SSA's focus on current disability and its refusal to accord weight to the original determination of disability meant that it was logically possible for a claimant to be disabled under the old rules and not disabled under the new rules—without a positive change in medical condition.

New Evidence Required

In seeking reversal of the Agency's termination decisions, plaintiffs complained that the current medical evidence test allowed the Social Security Administration to terminate their benefits on the basis of evidence that was virtually or actually identical to the evidence used in making the initial award of eligibility. The Eighth Circuit was especially receptive to their argument and noted that "although she does not say so explicitly, we understand the Secretary's position to be that she is free to terminate benefits even if the current evidence about the claimant's condition is substantially identical to the evidence considered in the prior disability determination."[56] Continuing this reasoning, the Eleventh Circuit feared that termination without a showing by SSA of medical improvement might "often depend not on a finding of changed condition, but simply on the whim of a changed ALJ."[57]

Plaintiffs appeared to hold the logical, if not the legal, high ground in this dispute. Logic suggests that if an impairment initially precludes performing gainful activity, and the impairment has not improved, the beneficiary should remain unable to engage in gainful activity. The Ninth Circuit articulated this position well when it announced that it was "unable to discern any reason why the familiar principle that a condition, once proved to exist, is presumed to continue to exist, should not be applied when disability benefits are at stake."[58]

Analysis of the statute did not shed much light on the problem for neither the statutory definition of disability nor a distillation of the legislative intent of periodic review provided much support for plaintiffs' efforts to halt the Agency's rush of terminations. Plaintiffs' were basing their claim in part upon the Agency's adoption of the current medical evidence standard in 1980 when SSA guaranteed that "the decision that a person's disability or blindness has ended will not be used on a reexamination of old evidence but will be based on new evidence which will have to reasonably show that the person is able to perform substantial gainful activity . . ."[59] The Social Security Administration, however, argued that it could relitigate the issue of plaintiff's disability by producing new medical evidence—even if this evidence showed that the medical condition remained essentially unchanged.

Plaintiffs countered by charging that the use of the current medical evidence standard allowed SSA simply to reevaluate the same medical condition under different standards of eligibility. The difficulty stemmed in part from the fact that the initial award of benefits had often been made under a more liberal evaluation process and the new "current medical evidence" was being evaluated under the harsher adjudicative climate of the post–1976 era.[60]

The lines of battle on these issues were drawn in the early part of the

1980s as the courts were thrust into the fray between terminated beneficiaries and the Agency. The events surrounding the social security disability
litigation suggest that the atmosphere was favorable for judicial policymaking: litigants clamoring for judicial redress, a vague and nondirective statute, a still silent Congress, and a problematic implementation of the statute
by the bureaucracy.

Amid charges of judicial policymaking, the courts expressed their disagreement with SSA's standards for judging eligibility for benefits and, by
reversing SSA decisions, appeared to question the Agency's authority to
implement the statute. Because the judiciary was statutorily enpowered to
review only the Secretary's findings of fact and review was narrowly defined
by the substantial evidence rule, it was not surprising that conflict between
the two institutions was generated.

THE COURTS ADOPT A MEDICAL IMPROVEMENT
STANDARD

Within a few years, all courts ruling on this issue adopted a medical
improvement standard and enforced it by granting a presumption of continuing disability to the plaintiff. Some courts also simply held, without
using presumption language, that absent evidence of medical improvement,
the Secretary's finding of fact that plaintiff was no longer disabled was not
supported by substantial evidence. These two positions were reconciled in
a thoughtful explanation by Judge John Kane of the Colorado District Court
in *Trujillo v. Heckler*.[61] The judge felt that "the presumption of disability
approach ... accomplishes the same thing as an improvement standard.
More to the point, it typically incorporates an improvement standard."
Judge Kane continued, "under either standard, benefits may not be terminated without showing that the recipient's medical condition has improved. Accordingly, I decline to adopt the presumption theory because I
find it duplicative."[62]

The cessation cases that appeared in the circuit courts before 1982 had
been adjudicated by the Agency under the LaBonte rule. Consequently,
because the ALJs had found medical improvement in determining that
plaintiffs were no longer disabled, the dispute primarily centered around
the evidence used to demonstrate the improvement. Although SSA was not
bound by the medical improvement standard after the promulgation of the
1980 regulations, later cases, however, continued to cite the earlier cases
for the proposition that SSA needed to show medical improvement.

The medical improvement standard ultimately became the rule of law in
the circuits. Because the courts were statutorily mandated to affirm the
Secretary's findings if supported by substantial evidence, much of the judicial response to the termination cases was obfuscated by burden of proof
and presumption language; many opinions, however, evidenced the judiciary's displeasure with the Agency's implementation of the continuing eligibility review process.

The Early Cases

A First Circuit opinion decided in 1975, *Miranda v. Secretary of Health, Education, and Welfare*,[63] was one of the first disability cases making explicit mention of the concept of medical improvement. In *Miranda*, expressing concern that the district courts had exceeded the limits of the substantial evidence rule, the circuit court reversed the lower court opinion that had continued benefits to Manuel Miranda.

Miranda suffered a back injury on the job while lifting a heavy beam. He had been awarded disability benefits in 1969 for severe back pain and numbness in the leg and arm which, he claimed, prevented him from returning to his old job. In deciding to terminate his benefits in 1971, the ALJ found that Miranda's impairments had improved sufficiently for him to be able to return to a job that did not involve stooping or heavy lifting. The administrative law judge had based his finding on the 1969 medical reports as well as the 1971 medical records; the latter reports "reflect[ing] a detailed examination with essentially negative findings except as to bending and pain."[64]

Reasoning that the Secretary's decision to terminate benefits would normally be based upon "current evidence showing that a claimant has improved to the point of being able to engage in substantial gainful activity . . . ," the court rejected the district court's ruling that the Secretary was precluded from also considering medical evidence offered at the initial award.

The appellate court explained that judgments on continuing eligibility may also be based on "evidence that claimant's condition is not as serious as was at first supposed."[65] Indeed, Mr. Miranda's cessation hearing had concluded with the ALJ's finding that his disabling back condition was not as serious as it was originally thought to be. Finally, although the appellate court was willing to accept the rationale of the ALJ's conclusion, it balked at the determination that Miranda was no longer disabled because the ALJ appeared to dismiss Miranda's testimony on his back pain. The court remanded the case to the Secretary with instructions to elicit specific evidence on the disabling effect of Miranda's pain on his ability to work.

A 1981 case, *Weber v. Harris*,[66] was presented to the Eighth Circuit following the ALJ's decision that Mary Weber's medical condition had improved. Despite the absence of specific evidence of improvement, the district court affirmed after concluding that the Secretary's determination was supported by substantial evidence.

Mary Weber had been awarded disability benefits for a condition of low back degenerative arthritis in 1975. At a hearing to review her disability status in 1979, the ALJ incorporated the evidence of the first hearing and reviewed the new evidence primarily consisting of hospitalization in 1977 to remove a tumor on her nose. Although Weber testified that her pain had increased, the evidence showed that she took almost no medication beyond aspirin for relief. Giving credence to a consulting physician's report that "the lower back pain was chronic postural strain caused by her obesity, which is a remedial condition which cannot be the basis for a finding of disability,"[67] the ALJ found that her impairments had improved and that she had regained her ability to engage in substantial gainful activity as of 1978.

Alleging that the evidence of her impairment had not changed since her initial award and, relying on *Miranda*, Mrs. Weber argued that the Secretary was required to give a res judicata effect to the earlier disability determination unless evidence of improvement were presented. The Eighth Circuit rejected this restrictive reading of Miranda by pointing out that although the Secretary was barred from simply reappraising the earlier evidence, it was immaterial whether the Secretary's "conclusion that Weber's condition had improved to a point of being able to engage in substantial gainful activity is based solely on evidence of improvement from the first hearing or instead is also based on evidence that Weber's condition was not as serious as first supposed."[68]

Even though the court affirmed the cessation of benefits in *Weber*, the case ultimately became known as the Eighth Circuit case that established the medical improvement standard. It was not until 1984 in *Rush v. Secretary of Health and Human Services*,[69] that the Eighth Circuit explicitly announced that *Weber* had imposed a medical improvement standard. In *Rush*, the court enforced this requirement by imposing a burden-shifting presumption.

Freddie Rush's original award of disability in 1975 was based on gastrointestinal pain and related symptoms caused by previous stomach surgery to correct a duodenal ulcer. His file was reviewed in 1977 and his benefits were continued by an administrative law judge following a hearing. Another review in 1981 became the subject of the present lawsuit when the ALJ denied his claim for continuing disability. Rush argued that the similarity between his earlier medical records and his current medical records showed that he was disabled and urged the court "to apply the so-called medical-improvement standard, enforced by a burden-shifting presumption. Specifically, he argue[d] that he should be entitled to a presumption of disability and that to overcome the presumption the Secretary should be required to present some evidence that his condition has improved or that his condition, when evaluated in the light of current evidence, is not so serious as first believed."[70]

The Eighth Circuit agreed with the Secretary that the 1980 regulations meant that SSA was not necessarily required to show medical improvement prior to a cessation of benefits. The court added, however, that the regulations must be interpreted to include a res judicata effect that precluded the Secretary from simply disregarding the earlier disability determination. Because the current medical "reports clearly demonstrate[d] that Rush's condition was substantially the same as it was in 1977 when [Administrative Law] Judge Hubbard determined that he was still disabled," the court held that the Secretary had not come forward with evidence of improvement or other acceptable means of overcoming the presumption.[71]

It was a few years before the impact of the courts' adoption of a medical improvement standard was widely felt. Because *Weber* and *Miranda* had been decided with no real debate over the Social Security Administration's need to show improvement, it was not immediately clear that the Secretary was headed for confrontation with the courts over a medical improvement standard; in other cases, it was not readily apparent that the circuit was adopting a medical improvement standard.[72]

The escape clause offered by *Miranda's* "not as serious" phrase allowed SSA to avoid an immediate clash with the courts on the medical improvement issue. By merely gathering new evidence and creating an inference that the condition "was not as serious as first supposed," the Secretary was able to argue successfully that plaintiff was not currently disabled. Gradually, as the number of cases increased, the courts lost patience with SSA's attempts to terminate benefits for so many persons formerly considered disabled and were more insistent on showing a medical improvement.

The Later Cases

The first obvious setback for the Secretary came in 1982 in *Patti v. Schweiker*[73] when the Court of Appeals for the Ninth Circuit flatly stated that a "prior ruling of disability can give rise to a presumption that the disability still exists" and that the presumption forces the Secretary to come forward with evidence that the condition has changed.

Plaintiff Juanita Patti had received SSI benefits for a disability established in 1976 on the basis of severe back pain and hypertension. When reviewed in 1977, her benefits were terminated but that decision was reversed following a hearing before an ALJ one year later. Her benefits were again terminated by SSA as of April 1979. When the district court affirmed the Secretary, Patti's appeal to the Ninth Circuit followed.

Patti claimed that the medical evidence was not sufficient to support the ALJ's finding that her disability had ceased. After combing through the medical testimony, the appeals court concluded that "it does not comprise substantial evidence of any change in the claimant's condition since the 1978 hearing and determination of disability."[74] The court added that the Secretary's own regulations provide that an ALJ's decision is binding on all parties unless appeal is taken. The court effectively imposed a medical improvement standard by simply characterizing the question for review as "whether that [1978] determination gave rise to a presumption at the time of the 1979 hearing that the claimant was still disabled—a presumption which the Secretary was required to 'meet or rebut' with evidence that her condition had improved in the interim."[75]

Other circuits with slight variation soon associated themselves with these decisions and gradually, over the next two years, the remainder of appellate courts made it clear that the Secretary must present evidence of an improved medical condition or a reason to cast doubt upon the original finding of disability.[76]

Although the controversy in the disability termination cases centered on administrative interpretation of the Social Security Act, most cases did not directly address the legitimacy of the current medical evidence regulations. The opinions glossed over the contradiction between the presumption of continuing disability that required the Secretary to show medical improvement and the 1980 regulations that only required the Secretary to show that plaintiff was not currently disabled. The judiciary also preferred not to address the issue of whether SSA's administrative review process was in accord with the statutory requirement of periodic review, or any other statutory mandate for terminating benefits.[77]

Despite the persistence of judicial rulings in favor of plaintiffs, SSA's policy of terminating benefits without showing medical improvement remained unchanged. Consequently, each beneficiary appealing a termination decision to the district court was obligated to reargue the medical improvement issue. The Social Security Administration's rejection of the judiciary's authority over its administrative procedure, that is, its nonacquiescence, obviously diluted the impact of the judicial victories.

Forced to carry the fight beyond the courthouse doors, litigants attempted to offset the power of the administrative agency by appealing to the political arena. And because the disability litigation also raised questions about the relationship between the states and federal government, as well as the growing conflict between the bureaucracy and the judiciary, congressional attention became focused on the demands of terminated disability beneficiaries. The limitations of judicial review of bureaucratic policy sharply illustrated the courts' inability to force an executive agency's compliance with its rulings in the face of a policy of nonacquiescence.

NOTES

1. 42 U.S.C. §405(g) authorizes judicial review of the Social Security Administration's actions by providing that:

any individual, after any final decision of the Secretary made after a hearing to which he was a party, irrespective of the amount in controversy, may obtain a review of such decision by a civil action commenced within sixty days after the mailing to him of notice of such decision or within such further time as the Secretary may allow. Such action shall be brought in the district court of the United States for the judicial district in which the plaintiff resides, or has his principal place of business. . . . The court shall have power to enter upon the pleadings and transcript of the record, a judgment affirming, modifying, or reversing the decision of the Secretary, with or without remanding the cause for a rehearing.

2. The Administrative Procedure Act also imposes a narrow scope of judicial review; see *Citizens to Preserve Overton Park, Inc. v. Volpe*, 401 U.S. 402 (1971).

3. A computer search of the words "social security and disability after 1954" conducted in the latter part of August 1987 revealed 99 cases. Because a word search only indicates that the requested words appear in a case, it was necessary to examine the cases more closely to determine which were relevant to the subject matter of the search; most of these cases did not include disability law issues.

4. *Schweiker v. Gray Panthers*, 453 U.S. 34, 43 (1981).

5. 106 S.Ct. 2022 (1986).

6. 422 U.S. 749, 764 (1975).

7. *Salfi*, 422 U.S. at 767.

8. 424 U.S. 319 (1976).

9. The Court explained that the latter condition had been implicit in *Salfi*; the failure to satisfy the "presentment" requirement explained the dismissal of the unnamed members of the class who had not alleged that they had filed applications with the Secretary. The exhaustion rules in class action suits allow the class to consist of plaintiffs who had not exhausted all their remedies as long as they had originally made a claim to the Secretary for benefits.

10. *Mathews*, 424 U.S. at 330.

11. *Mathews*, 424 U.S. at 330.

12. 430 U.S. 99 (1977).

13. Res judicata, a Latin phrase meaning "the matter already decided" or the "judgment made," is designed to avoid repeated litigation on the same issue once a judgment has been made by a court, or in this case, by an administrative agency. 20 C.F.R. §404.960 (1986) provides that an administrative law judge may dismiss a hearing request when SSA has "made a previous determination or decision . . . about your rights on the same issue or issues, and this previous determination has become final by either administrative or judicial action."

14. *Sanders*, 430 U.S. at 109.

15. 442 U.S. 682 (1979).

16. 42 U.S.C. § 404(b) (1984).

17. Certification of a class is governed by Rule 23 of the Federal Rules of Civil Procedure. In *Yamasaki*, a class was certified under Rule 23(b)(2). Ironically, the Secretary had argued against the availability of class relief under section 205(g) of the Social Security Act asserting that it was not necessary because the Agency would follow the law of the circuit with respect to future plaintiffs, that is, it promised that it would acquiesce in circuit court decisions.

18. *Yamasaki*, 442 U.S. at 699.

19. *Yamasaki*, 442 U.S. at 699.

20. *Yamasaki*, 442 U.S. at 700–01.

21. *Yamasaki*, 442 U.S. at 702.

22. *City of New York*, 106 S.Ct. at 2022.

23. *City of New York*, 106 S.Ct. at 2030.

24. *City of New York*, 106 S.Ct. at 2032.

25. *City of New York*, 106 S.Ct. at 2032.

26. *Richardson v. Wright*, 405 U.S. 208, 209 (1972).

27. 402 U.S. 389 (1971).

28. The Court's decision in *Goldberg v. Kelly*, 397 U.S. 254 (1970), mandated a pretermination hearing for public aid recipients.

29. *Mathews*, 424 U.S. at 346. For a discussion of the effects of Quality Assurance programs as substitutes for, or additions to, the requirements of due process in achieving better adjudication of welfare entitlement, see Jerry Mashaw, "The Management Side of Due Process: Some Theoretical and Litigation Notes on the Assurance of Accuracy, Fairness, and Timeliness

in the Adjudication of Welfare Claims," *Cornell Law Review* 59(1974):773–824 and Deborah Chassman and Howard Rolston "Social Security Disability Hearings: A Case Study in Quality Assurance and Due Process," *Cornell Law Review* 65(1980):801–22.

30. 467 U.S. 104(1984).
31. *Day*, 467 U.S. at 119.
32. *Day*, 467 U.S. at 120, n. 33.
33. *Gray Panthers*, 453 U.S. at 43.
34. 107 S.Ct. 2287 (1987).
35. 20 C.F.R. §§404.1520(c), 416.920(c) (1986).
36. *Yuckert*, 107 S.Ct. at 2298.
37. *Yuckert*, 107 S.Ct. at 2299.
38. SSR 85–28 (1985) reads in relevant part:

Great care should be exercised in applying the not severe impairment concept. If an adjudicator is unable to determine clearly the effect of an impairment or combination of impairments on the individual's ability to do basic work activities, the sequential evaluation process should not end with the not severe evaluation step. Rather, it should be continued.

39. Marvin Schick, "Judicial Activism on the Supreme Court," in Stephen Halpern and Charles Lamb, eds., *Supreme Court Activism and Restraint* (Lexington, Mass.: Lexington Books, 1982), pp. 37–38.
40. *Mims v. Califano*, 581 F.2d 1211, 1213 (5th Cir. 1978).
41. Angus MacIntyre, "A Court Quietly Rewrote the Federal Pesticide Statute: How Prevalent is Judicial Statutory Revision?" *Law and Policy* 7(April 1985):265–66.
42. Of the five cases in which the primary purpose of appeal was to ask for a judicial statement on the Social Security Administration's continuing eligibility review policy, three, *Kilpatrick v. Heckler*, 472 U.S. 1004 (1985), *Carabello v. Heckler*, 471 U.S. 1113 (1985), and *Heckler v. Kuehner*, 469 U.S. 977 (1984), were remanded to the lower courts following enactment of the 1984 disability legislature. Another, *Heckler v. Lopez*, 469 U.S. 1082 (1984), 464 U.S. 879 (1983), and 463 U.S. 1328 (1983), appeared before the Court three times but was never decided on the merits. The last case, *City of New York*, 106 S.Ct. at 2022, was decided entirely on jurisdictional grounds.
43. MacIntyre, "A Court Rewrote the Federal Pesticide Statute," p. 267.
44. See Graham Lilly, *An Introduction to the Law of Evidence* (St. Paul: West, 1978), chapter 3, for additional information on presumptions and burdens of proof.
45. Federal Rule of Evidence 301 explains that "a presumption imposes on the party against whom it is directed the burden of going forward with evidence, but does not shift to such party the burden of proof in the sense of the risk of nonpersuasion, which remains throughout the trial upon the party on whom it was originally cast."
46. *Mathews*, 424 U.S. at 336. Although these words are often described as dicta, that is, words not necessary to reach the result of the decision,

the lower courts nevertheless continually cite this phrase as controlling on the allocation of the burden of proof in continuing disability cases.

47. *Mathews*, 424 U.S. at 343.

48. SSR 63–11c (1963); see, for example, *Torres v. Schweiker*, 682 F.2d 109 (3d Cir. 1982), *cert. denied*, 459 U.S. 1174 (1983).

49. See Beth Glassman, "Terminating Social Security Disability Benefits: Another Burden for the Disabled," *Fordham Urban Law Journal* 12 (1983):195–217.

50. It is also said that the initial award of disability signifies that plaintiff has made a prima facie case of disability.

51. 669 F.2d 582, 586 (9th Cir. 1982).

52. *Dotson v. Schweiker*, 719 F.2d 80, 82 (4th Cir. 1983). Although most courts granted the presumption solely on the basis of the prior determination of disability, others, such as the Third Circuit, required the plaintiff to produce some current evidence of disability before granting the presumption to plaintiff. In *Kuzmin v. Schweiker*, 714 F.2d 1233, 1237 (3d Cir. 1983), the appellate court held that "a prior finding of eligibility does not, of itself, establish a *prima facie* case of continuing eligibility. . . . " The court continued, however, that "basic principles of fairness as well as the need to provide both the appearance and fact of consistency in the administrative process lead us to conclude that in a termination proceeding, once the claimant has introduced evidence that his or her condition remains essentially the same as it was at the time of the earlier determination, the claimant is entitled to the benefit of a presumption that his or her condition remains disabling." An exception to this approach appeared in the Seventh Circuit case of *Cassiday v. Schweiker*, 663 F.2d 745, 749 (7th Cir. 1981), in which the appellate court rather ambiguously referred to the Secretary as "the burdened party, [who] did not make his proof. . . . "

53. *Rush v. Secretary of Health and Human Services*, 738 F.2d 909, 912 (8th Cir. 1984).

54. *Simpson v. Schweiker*, 691 F.2d 966, 969, n. 2 (11th Cir. 1982), citing *Shaw v. Schweiker*, 536 F.Supp 79, 83 (E.D.Pa. 1982).

55. *Dotson*, 719 F.2d at 81.

56. *Rush*, 738 F.2d at 912.

57. *Simpson*, 691 F.2d at 969.

58. *Patti*, 669 F.2d at 587.

59. 45 Fed. Reg. 55583 (1980).

60. Katherine Collins and Anne Erfle, "Social Security Disability Benefits Reform Act of 1984: Legislative History and Summary of Provisions," *Social Security Bulletin* 48(April 1985):16.

61. *Trujillo v. Heckler*, 569 F.Supp. 631, 635 (D. Col. 1983).

62. *Trujillo*, 569 F.Supp. at 636.

63. 514 F.2d 996 (1st Cir. 1975).

64. *Miranda*, 514 F.2d at 999.

65. *Miranda*, 514 F.2d at 998.

66. 640 F.2d 176 (8th Cir. 1981).

67. *Weber*, 640 F.2d at 178.

68. *Weber*, 640 F.2d at 179, citing *Miranda*, 514 F.2d at 998.

69. *Rush*, 738 F.2d at 909.

70. *Rush*, 738 F.2d at 912.

71. *Rush*, 738 F.2d at 911.

72. In *Cassiday*, 663 F.2d at 749, the court did not explicitly announce the adoption of the improvement standard. Relying on *Miranda*, the court reversed Mrs. Cassiday's termination because "the evidence continued to show the existence of the same condition and given that there was no question of improvement but only disagreement about how totally disabling the condition had ever been. . . . "

Similarly, in *Hayes v. Secretary of Health, Education and Welfare*, 656 F.2d 204, 206 (6th Cir. 1981), without citing any cases, the Sixth Circuit reversed Deborah Hayes' termination because "the evidence does not support the conclusion that termination of Hayes' benefits was proper because her condition had improved."

73. *Patti*, 669 F.2d at 586. An earlier case in the Ninth Circuit, *Finnegan v. Mathews*, 641 F.2d 1340 (9th Cir. 1981), concerned medical improvement but involved a narrow fact situation in which a beneficiary of an approved state disability program had been "grandfathered" into the Supplemental Security Income Program. When SSA tried to terminate his benefits, the court refused to allow it unless the Agency could show that there was error in the original determination or sufficient improvement in his condition so that he was no longer disabled.

74. *Patti*, 669 F.2d at 586.

75. *Patti*, 669 F.2d at 587.

76. Although it is difficult to pinpoint the specific case within each circuit in which a medical improvement standard was adopted, there appears to be a consensus that the following cases were responsible for imposing a medical improvement requirement: First Circuit: *Miranda*, 514 F.2d at 996; Second Circuit: *De Leon v. Secretary of Health and Human Services*, 734 F.2d 930 (2d Cir. 1984); Third Circuit: *Kuzmin*, 714 F.2d at 1233; Fourth Circuit: *Dotson*, 719 F.2d at 80; Fifth Circuit: *Buckley v. Schweiker*, 739 F.2d 1047 (5th Cir. 1984); Sixth Circuit: *Hayes*, 656 F.2d at 204; Seventh Circuit: *Cassiday*, 663 F.2d at 745; Eighth Circuit: *Weber*, 640 F.2d at 176; Ninth Circuit: *Patti*, 669 F.2d at 582; Tenth Circuit: *Van Natter v. Secretary of Health, Education, and Welfare*, No. 79–1439 (10th Cir. 1981) (Not For Routine Publication); Eleventh Circuit: *Simpson*, 691 F.2d at 966.

77. As indicated in the previous chapter, neither the language nor legislative intent of the periodic review amendment provided guidance for the courts in reviewing SSA's continuing eligibility policy. The Act as a whole did not help much either as the only reference to cessation of benefits appears in 42 U.S.C. §425(a) (1984) which states that "if the Secretary . . . believes that an individual entitled to benefits . . . may have ceased to be under a disability, the Secretary may suspend the payment of benefits . . . until it is determined . . . whether or not such individual's disability has ceased or until the Secretary believes that such disability has not ceased."

The Second Circuit pointed out that the statute's "reference to a disability 'ceas[ing]' suggests that the Congress intended the Secretary to compare an applicant's condition at the time of review with his or her condition at the time benefits were initially granted." The court also pointed to the references in 20 C.F.R. §§404.1590(a) and 404.1594(a) (1983) to "whether a claimant's disability 'continues' or 'has ended' " to support its interpretation that the regulations also indicate that a "comparative" dimension of disability must be applied. *De Leon*, 734 F.2d at 936.

7

Conflict between the Executive and the Judiciary

The Social Security Administration's shift from the medical improvement standard to the current medical evidence standard in 1976, in concert with the acceleration of the continuing disability review process, created an avalanche of cases in the federal courts in the early 1980s. Tens of thousands of terminated beneficiaries turned to the federal courts to undo Agency decisions revoking their disability benefits. While it was certainly foreseeable that SSA's continuing disability review policy would cause distress to beneficiaries under review, there was also an unanticipated fallout from the review procedure. Aside from the turmoil and trauma for the individuals involved in this now-you-see-it, now-you-don't benefit program, SSA's implementation of periodic review precipitated a near constitutional crisis between the Social Security Administration and the federal judiciary over SSA's policy of nonacquiescence.

Between 1980 and 1985, as the drama of CDR unfolded, the federal courts were faced with a substantial increase in social security disability cases and, were confronted as well, because of nonacquiescence, with a challenge to their judicial authority. The effect of nonacquiescence was to reduce the power of judicial rulings over agency decisions to a case-by-case approach. Because the litigation over the termination of benefits did not cause SSA to change its adjudicatory standards, litigation activity increased as beneficiaries were forced to go to court to obtain reversal of their administrative denials.

DISABILITY CASES IN THE LOWER FEDERAL COURTS

Judicial awareness of the increased caseload was evidenced by District Court Judge Milton Shadur's comment in a 1984 opinion that "the new spate of social security cases represents a highly significant component of the total workload."[1] Similarly, Judge John Nordberg, also of the Northern District of Illinois, noted in a personal interview that "the sheer magnitude [of cases] was staggering."[2] The infusion of disability cases, with an approximately 50 percent reversal rate by the federal courts, indicates that the judiciary played a significant part in the disability review process.[3] By the beginning of 1985, the *New York Times* reported that the federal courts had ordered the Social Security Administration to restore benefits to more than 200,000 persons.[4] The heavy volume of cases, with so many leading to reversal, exacerbated the friction between the two branches of government because they were a continual reminder to the courts of the Agency's refusal to accept judicial interpretation of the Social Security Act.

Social Security Act Claims

Disability claimants represented the majority of Social Security Act cases in federal court in 1980 and, as periodic review progressed, disability cases assumed an ever increasing proportion of Social Security Act claims. As Table 7.1 shows, while demands for judicial review of all Social Security claims multiplied by a factor of three between 1980 and 1985, the number of cases involving disability claims grew fivefold. Disability claims continued to predominate until, by 1984, only 5 percent of all cases involving claims for benefits under the Social Security Act were *not* disability claims.

Disability Cases Commenced

In the fifteen years between 1955 and 1970, a *total* of slightly under 10,000 disability claims were filed in federal district courts.[5] As evidence of the dramatic increase in social security disability cases following the onset of periodic review, in 1982 *alone* over 10,000 requests for judicial review of disability claims were filed. The effect of these increases on the judiciary's workload is demonstrated in Table 7.2, indicating the number of cases commenced under the Social Security Act from 1980 to 1985 as a percentage of the total number of civil suits commenced during these years.

Disability Cases Pending

Similarly, as Table 7.3 shows, cases arising under the Social Security Act consumed a steadily rising share of the total number of cases pending before the district courts after 1981. The greater increase in cases pending compared with the increase in cases filed shows that the courts were unable to keep pace with the number of disability cases filed.

Disability Appeals

To complete the statistical picture, Table 7.4 demonstrates the increase in Social Security Act appeals from district court decisions from 1980 to 1985. Appeals, of course, rose during these years but the relatively few number of cases appealed compared to the number of cases commenced in district courts suggests that a large majority of cases were not appealed to

Table 7.1
Disability Cases as a Percentage of All Social Security Act Cases Filed in District Court during Twelve-Month Periods Ending June 30

Year	Number SS Act Cases Filed*	Number Disability Cases Filed**	Percentage Disability Cases
1980	9,043	5,771	64%
1981	9,780	7,167	73%
1982	12,812	10,380	81%
1983	20,315	18,764	92%
1984	29,985	28,710	95%
1985	19,771	18,747	95%

* Includes claims for Health Insurance Benefits, Black Lung Benefits, and Retirement and Survivors Benefits; also includes claims based on disability for Insured Worker's Benefits, Child's Insurance Benefits, Widow(er)'s Insurance Benefits, and Supplemental Security Income Benefits and Other Miscellaneous Claims.

** Includes claims based on disability for Insured Worker's Benefits, Child's Insurance Benefits, Widow(er)'s Insurance Benefits, and Supplemental Security Income Benefits.

SOURCE: Annual Reports of the Director of the Administrative Office of the United States Courts.

a higher court—probably because so many plaintiffs were successful in the lower courts under the judicially imposed medical improvement standard.

While the policy of nonacquiescence made it necessary for each terminated beneficiary to seek judicial review of the administrative decision, once the appellate court imposed a medical improvement standard within the circuit and SSA did not present substantial evidence of improvement, the lower courts were able to remand the case back to the Secretary or simply reverse the termination. Thus, thousands of plaintiffs were forced to appeal their terminations to the lower courts but were spared the necessity of appealing to a higher court.

THE POLICY OF ADMINISTRATIVE NONACQUIESCENCE

The legal and political problems arising from administrative nonacquiescence are not amenable to easy resolution. Although the lower federal courts

Table 7.2
Social Security Act Cases as a Percentage of All Civil Cases Commenced in District Court during Twelve-Month Periods Ending June 30

Year	Number Civil Cases Commenced	Number SS Act Cases Commenced	Percentage SS Act Cases
1980	168,789	9,043	5.4%
1981	180,576	9,780	5.4%
1982	206,193	12,812	6.2%
1983	241,842	20,315	8.4%
1984	261,485	29,985	11.5%
1985	273,670	19,771	7.2%

SOURCE: Annual Reports of the Director of the Administrative Office of the United States Courts.

Table 7.3
Social Security Act Cases as a Percentage of All Civil Cases Pending in District Court during Twelve-Month Periods Ending June 30

Year	Number Civil Cases Pending	Number SS Act Cases Pending	Percentage SS Act Cases
1980	186,113	13,154	7.1%
1981	188,714	12,119	6.4%
1982	205,434	14,757	7.2%
1983	231,920	21,661	9.3%
1984	250,292	29,900	11.9%
1985	254,114	20,302	8.0%

SOURCE: Annual Reports of the Director of the Administrative Office of the United States Courts.

refuse to recognize the legitimacy of nonacquiescence and declaim it as unconstitutional and illegal, the dispute between the administrative and judicial branches of government persists, in part, because neither Congress nor the Supreme Court has spoken out definitively on it.

Nonacquiescence poses fundamental questions about the relative positions of executive agencies and courts within the American legal system and where the final authority resides when conflict between the two arises.[6]

Table 7.4
Social Security Act Appeals Arising from the District Courts during Twelve-Month Periods Ending June 30

Year	Number of Appeals	Percent Change Over Previous Year
1980	627	——
1981	642	+ 2.4%
1982	779	+21.3%
1983	992	+27.3%
1984	1,204	+21.4%
1985	1,188	- 1.3%

SOURCE: Annual Reports of the Director of the Administrative Office of the United States Courts.

It challenges many long-standing principles of the American judicial system and raises questions about the validity of the common law principle of stare decisis and the supremacy of the rule of law over the decisions of administrative agencies. In a legal system which prides itself on these principles, "an agency's outright refusal to abide by circuit court precedent, at least in subsequent cases arising within the same circuit, undermines Americans' belief in the rule of law."[7]

The controversy over nonacquiescence is primarily generated by the practice of *intracircuit* nonacquiescence which must be distinguished from *intercircuit* nonacquiescence. The former challenges the basic principles of American jurisprudence. The latter arises from the geographically compartmentalized structure of the federal court system into twelve regional circuits.

Intercircuit Nonacquiescence

Each judicial circuit develops its own "rule of the circuit" and only district courts and future appellate panels *within the circuit* are bound.[8] There is little argument when an agency refuses to change its administrative policy in one circuit because another circuit has ruled against that policy; "virtually all circuits, and the Supreme Court, accept the right of an agency to lose in one circuit yet argue the same points when a similar case arises elsewhere."[9]

In the normal course of events, this dispersal of judicial authority produces intercircuit conflict which, if perceived as sufficiently serious, will be resolved by the Supreme Court. Moreover, some even suggest that intercircuit "nonacquiescence is desirable where it allows administrative agencies to contribute to the well-reasoned development of the law. By relitigating complex legal issues in several courts of appeals, an agency ensures that these issues are sufficiently analyzed. "This percolation process," it is argued, "not only allows for multiple consideration of a particular legal issue, but where it produces intercircuit conflict, it ripens the issue for Supreme Court review."[10]

This benevolent image of intercircuit nonacquiescence is not universally shared and some judges have expressed their impatience with agencies that seek judicial endorsement of their position in a multiplicity of circuits— even when the courts consistently reject the agency's legal posture. There has been at least one suggestion that *intercircuit* nonacquiescence should not be tolerated and should be eliminated by forcing a government agency into "accepting the first decision by a court of appeals in a statutory interpretation case ... or securing reversal by the Supreme Court or by Congress."[11]

Intracircuit Nonacquiescence

An agency practices intracircuit nonacquiescence when it rejects judicial supremacy over administrative policy *within* the circuit. It arises "when a circuit court interprets a statute contrary to the agency's interpretation of the statute, [and] the agency will only abide by that decision as to the parties in the particular case that generated the ruling."[12] Challenging the judiciary's authority of statutory interpretation, the agency simply "continue[s] to administer its programs according to the agency's own interpretation of the applicable statute."[13] While agencies accept a Supreme Court ruling as authoritative, often they do not seek judicial review of unfavorable decisions, and until the highest court rules, the agency's view prevails within the circuit. In following an intracircuit nonacquiescence policy, an agency continues to argue, or relitigate, the correctness of its interpretation in later cases in the same circuit.

Despite the almost unanimous disapproval of the federal courts, at least two other executive agencies, the National Labor Relations Board (NLRB) and the Internal Revenue Service (IRS), have utilized intracircuit nonacquiescence. They claim that agencies with national responsibilities require uniform program administration and that relitigation is necessary to disseminate the agency interpretation nationwide. This is especially important, they insist, when there is conflict among the circuits and agencies would be required to conform their administrative procedure to the law of each circuit. It is far preferable, they say, to allow the agency to determine the proper administrative procedure and apply it throughout the nation.[14]

The lower federal courts view nonacquiescence as a challenge to the legitimacy of the rule of law and they argue that agencies have other methods of convincing the courts of the correctness of their administrative policy. Like other losing parties, agencies may petition the court for a rehearing en banc, petition for a writ of certiorari from the Supreme Court, or ask for a stay of the lower court order pending appeal; moreover, unlike other losing parties, agencies have the resources to argue their position in other circuits in an attempt to persuade them to support their interpretation of the law.

Judicial Supremacy

The judiciary claims that nonacquiescence is antithetical to the principle of judicial supremacy established in *Marbury v. Madison*; they denounce it because they believe that an agency's refusal to accept the court's authority on matters of statutory interpretation is a usurpation of the judicial role within the constitutional framework. Judges assert that agencies are delegated enormous power under the condition, as it were, that they accept the restraints of judicial review and when agencies refuse to accept judicial statutory interpretation, "this conception of agency power allows an agency to define its own powers."[15]

Prior to the Social Security Administration's highly publicized reliance on nonacquiescence, the major proponent of this doctrine was the National Labor Relations Board and thus the judicial response to nonacquiescence primarily arose out of NLRB cases. The Third Circuit's position in *Allegheny General Hospital v. the National Labor Relations Board*[16] exemplified judicial disapproval of nonacquiescence when it pointedly reminded the NLRB that it "is not a court nor is it equal to this court in matters of statutory interpretation. Thus, a disagreement by the NLRB with a decision of this court is simply an academic exercise that possesses no authoritative effect. . . . Congress has not given to the NLRB the power or authority to disagree, respectfully or otherwise, with decisions of this court." Citing *Marbury*, the appellate court stated that "a decision by this court, not overruled by the Supreme Court, is a decision of the court of last resort in this federal judicial circuit. Thus our judgments . . . are binding on all inferior courts and litigants in the Third Judicial Circuit, and also on administrative agencies when they deal with matters pertaining thereto."[17]

A year later, the Second Circuit also remonstrated with the NLRB for its cavalier attitude toward judicial precedent by pointing out that "the Board cannot, as it did here, choose to ignore the decision as if it had no force or effect. Absent reversal, that decision is the law which the Board must follow. The Board cites no contrary authority except its own consistent practice of refusing to follow the law of the circuit unless it coincides with the Board's views. This is intolerable if the rule of law is to prevail."[18]

Agency Authority

Agencies question the legitimacy of the judicial supremacy argument and claim that because Congress created both executive agencies and lower courts, they are coequal branches of government. They stress that agencies must have freedom to relitigate issues and while they acknowledge that the judiciary can determine what the law is in the courtroom, they insist that judicial rulings are restricted to the litigants before the court. They claim that only Supreme Court opinions have binding authority beyond the immediate litigants.[19]

The agency view has received indirect support from the Supreme Court's insistence on judicial deference to bureaucratic judgments as typified by its statement in a 1978 case involving a dispute over the power of the Atomic Energy Commission: "this Court has for more than four decades emphasized that the formulation of procedures was basically to be left within the discretion of the agencies to which Congress had confided the responsibility for substantive judgments."[20]

The Supreme Court has stressed the need for deference to agencies, such as SSA, particularly where "Congress entrusts to the Secretary, rather than to the courts, the primary responsibility for interpreting the statutory term. In exercising that responsibility, the Secretary adopts regulations with legislative effect. A reviewing court," added the Supreme Court, "is not free to set aside those regulations simply because it would have interpreted the statute in a different manner."[21]

THE GOVERNMENT AS LITIGATOR

Government agencies, seeking to distinguish themselves from private litigants appearing before the lower courts, cite the recent Supreme Court opinion of *United States v. Mendoza*[22] to argue that nonacquiescence has been approved by the Supreme Court. "According to the agencies, under *Mendoza*, even though courts may eventually determine that their prior decisions should be given precedential effect in a particular case, agencies are not bound to follow a court's ruling at the administrative level or in subsequent litigation where different claimants are involved."[23]

U.S. v. Mendoza

The *Mendoza* case raised complex questions about the government's role as litigant and about the status of the doctrines of collateral estoppel and stare decisis.[24] The case arose when Sergio Elejar Mendoza, a Filipino national residing in the United States, sued to become a naturalized U.S. citizen pursuant to a treaty between the United States and the Philippines. Mendoza invoked collateral estoppel against the government on a due process issue which the government had lost in a district court case brought by other Filipino nationals about ten years ago.

The California district court granted Mendoza's petition for citizenship without argument because of this earlier unappealed district court decision against the government and held that the government was collaterally estopped from relitigating the due process argument in Mr. Mendoza's case. The Ninth Circuit affirmed but, on appeal, the Supreme Court unanimously reversed.

Pointing out that the government should not be held to the same standards as a private litigant, the Supreme Court ruled that "nonmutual collateral estoppel simply does not apply against the government in such a way as to preclude relitigation of issues such as those involved in this case."[25] The decision was based on three considerations: first, the desirability of developing legal doctrine by allowing litigation in a number of forums; second, the value in permitting the Solicitor General to exercise discretion in seeking appeal of an unfavorable decision; and third, the freedom necessary to successive administrations in conducting governmental litigation. The Court rejected the lower court's expansive interpretation of collateral estoppel because it would retard the percolation of legal doctrine and would unduly restrict the government's flexibility over relitigation of issues by virtually setting in concrete the first unappealed decision against the government.

Collateral Estoppel and Stare Decisis

Mendoza was quickly seized upon by administrative agencies to justify their stance on relitigation within the circuit, that is, they have relied on *Mendoza* as a "shield" against judicial attacks on nonacquiescence.[26] Their reliance, however, misperceives the Supreme Court's rationale in *Mendoza* and blurs the distinction between the doctrine of stare decisis and the doctrine of offensive nonmutual collateral estoppel.

The Supreme Court's reasoning behind the prohibition of nonmutual offensive collateral estoppel against the government was based upon policy considerations arising from "the interjurisdictional nature of offensive nonmutual collateral estoppel; any decision in any court throughout the country could potentially estop any agency. Stare decisis, in contrast, only creates binding law within a jurisdiction."[27]

Stare decisis should not be equated with collateral estoppel as the effects of these two doctrines upon government agencies are distinguishable. Stare decisis is more limited in scope and does not raise the same policy concerns as collateral estoppel. It is geographically bounded because only litigants and lower courts *within* the appellate jurisdiction are held to the appellate court's ruling. Collateral estoppel is not as self-limiting and, carried out to its logical conclusion, could bind every court in the country on the basis of a determination of an issue by a single court in the country—even a state court. Although stare decisis, like collateral estoppel, can prevent an agency from relitigating on a particular issue within that circuit, it does not preclude the agency from relitigating the issue in another circuit and would not force the agency to appeal every adverse decision to the Supreme Court.[28] Thus, the potential reach of collateral estoppel against the government is virtually boundless and, along with other problems, its unlimited use would impede the percolation process by preventing the creation of intercircuit conflict which the Supreme Court has stressed is essential to the full development of the law.

In testimony before a House Judiciary subcommittee, Professor Lea Brilmayer of Yale University Law School criticized the government's reliance on *Mendoza* to support nonacquiescence and warned against carrying the *Mendoza* argument too far. She suggested that, at the extremes, the case cited could be used to justify nonadherence to a Supreme Court ruling because of the government's need to relitigate an issue. She pointed out that *Mendoza* only narrowed the reach of collateral estoppel against the government; it did not limit the precedential effects of appellate court rulings based on stare decisis. Because a district court had originally determined the immigration due process issue, and district court opinions have no precedential effect, the doctrine of stare decisis was not even at issue in *Mendoza*.

According to Brilmayer, *Mendoza* rejected the extreme position that the government should never have an opportunity to relitigate. But, she felt, it should not be interpreted to mean that the government should have constant opportunities to relitigate. She added that she thought "the proper reading of *Mendoza* is one that falls some place between those two extremes. There have to be some kind of reasonable opportunities to relitigate, but they receive neither every opportunity nor no opportunity at all."[29]

The Need for a Uniform Policy

Putting aside the legal arguments, which appear to be inconclusive, the resolution of the nonacquiescence debate must ultimately be resolved by public policy considerations. Pursuing this reasoning, Jerry Mashaw and his collaborators have asked "to what extent is a national administrative agency bound, legally or morally, to follow the holdings of regional federal courts. Must it try to harmonize court law and agency law within each judicial jurisdiction, even at the price of regional variation in the administration of its program? Or must national uniformity at the administrative level be maintained, even at the expense of prolonged discordance between agency law and court law within judicial districts or circuits?"[30]

Most agencies ultimately resort to the argument of nationwide uniformity of administration; they "point out that Congress gave federal courts only regional jurisdiction, but gave agencies nationwide jurisdiction."[31] Agencies warn that if they are forced to comply with the decisions of each of the twelve circuit courts, agency policy will be based upon geographic rather than legal considerations, and administrative procedure will vary from circuit to circuit.

Ironically, the appeal to national uniformity is also made by opponents of nonacquiescence who argue that nonacquiescence creates disparities among individuals within a jurisdiction. The foes of nonacquiescence claim that intercircuit variation is a fact of life in a legal system with fifty state jurisdictions and twelve regional circuits and that a program is perceived as more inequitable when next-door neighbors are judged by different standards than when persons of different states or regional circuits are judged differently.

Critics of nonacquiescence, such as Brilmayer, say that nonuniformity more realistically stems from circuits adopting different legal positions—a practice that nonacquiescence does not prevent or cure; she attacks proponents of nonacquiescence for falsely presenting it as a solution for nonuniformity. In her view, "nonacquiescence functions to achieve consistency and reconcile intercircuit conflicts only to the extent that claimants do not assert their rights in court." When litigants appear in court, "the illusory uniformity achieved by disregarding established circuit law evaporates." She stressed that uniformity is preserved only as long as litigants do not claim their rights by seeking judicial review of Agency decisions.[32]

The disruptive effects of nonacquiescence are heightened when an agency does not appeal an adverse ruling to the Supreme Court and, at the same time, refuses to conform to the rule of law within the circuit. When the Social Security Administration pursued this policy during the disability review crisis, it raised the debate over nonacquiescence to a new level of conflict and provoked a bitter response from many federal court judges.[33]

SSA's NONACQUIESCENCE POLICY

The Social Security Administration is charged by statute to "promulgate regulations ... and procedures to be followed in performing the disability determination function in order to assure effective and *uniform administration of the disability insurance program throughout the United States*" (emphasis added).[34] Program administrators argue that individuals should not be treated differently according to the circuit in which they live and that "the only way that a national program can be administered so that claimants and beneficiaries are treated essentially equally, regardless of what particular State they happen to reside in around the country, is to follow the policy stated in the law and the regulations rather than individual court decisions around the country."[35]

When appellate courts issued a decree contrary to SSA policy, the Agency at times responded with a formal nonacquiescence ruling.[36] More frequently, however, SSA reacted to unfavorable court decisions by simply taking no heed of them in conducting its adjudicative hearings.[37] This left ALJs in the unenviable position of acting contrary to the rule of law within the circuit.

The Social Security Administration's instructions to its Administrative Law Judges attempted to clarify the parameters of their legal responsibility; the ALJs were told to "make every reasonable effort to follow the district or circuit court's views regarding procedural or evidentiary matters when handling similar cases in that particular district or court." However, when Agency rules and regulations were "inconsistent with the Secretary's interpretations, the ALJs should not consider such decisions binding on future cases simply because the case is not appealed." The instructions concluded by informing ALJs that they would "be promptly advised" if SSA decided to acquiesce in a judicial decision and change its rulings and regulations.[38]

Judicial Reaction to Nonacquiescence

While nonacquiescence did not originate with the Social Security Administration, the Social Security Administration clearly extended the limits of its use. As the Second Circuit pointed out, SSA has "failed to uncover any example of intra-circuit agency nonacquiescence in which an agency has repeatedly and routinely ignored circuit court rulings despite the absence of any reasonable likelihood of obtaining reconsideration of the unfavorable decisions, and where the agency has also failed to pursue either congressional remediation or Supreme Court review."[39]

Although he felt that a nonacquiescence policy was not totally indefensible, Judge Milton Shadur of the Illinois District Court suggested that SSA's reliance on nonacquiescence caused concern for federal judges because, despite the near unanimity of the courts on the medical improvement issue, SSA persisted in looking for a court to agree with its formula for judging disability. He added that the judicial response arose because "it turns the law on its head to allow an administrative agency to follow its own view of law in a system of laws" and "because there was a universal sense that what they [SSA] were doing was outrageous."[40] In another interview, District Court Judge James Moran humorously asked "when is SSA going to stop playing games and do what the courts tell them to?"[41]

The Effect of Nonacquiescence on Disability Claimants

SSA's nonacquiescence policy has been frequently attacked because it places an unfair burden upon disability beneficiaries. Claimants who appeal to the courts will have their benefits restored while those who do not because of scarce resources, lack of education, or, not surprisingly given the nature of the program, debilitating illnesses, will be denied.[42] Nonacquiescence "can be cruelly unfair to those parties . . . who stand to benefit from the unheeded court decisions, giving them a hard choice between burdensome litigation and the forfeiture of their court-declared rights."[43]

Because of the nature of the client population, the furor created by the Social Security Administration's nonacquiescence was qualitatively different from that occasioned by other agencies. While the nonacquiescence pursued by the IRS and the NLRB also created disparities among claimants and forces litigants to go to court to secure their rights, the typical plaintiff in such cases is the employer, the union, or the relatively affluent taxpayer who is most often represented by private counsel.[44]

Judge William Gray of the California District Court attacked nonacquiescence for its disproportionate impact by pointing out that "a claimant [who] has the determination and the financial and physical strength and lives long enough to make it through the administrative process . . . can turn to the courts and ultimately expect them to apply the law. . . . If exhaustion overtakes him and he falls somewhere along the road leading to such ultimate relief, the nonacquiescence and the resulting termination stand. Particularly with respect to the types of individuals here concerned, whose resources, health and prospective longevity are, by definition, relatively limited, such a dual system of law is prejudicial and unfair."[45]

Even more forcefully, Judge Leonard Sand of the Southern District of New York maintained that "nothing tests more acutely the sincerity of our nation's commitment to the concept of 'Equal Justice Under the Law' than the manner in which our government agencies respect the legal rights of its poorest and least influential citizens."[46]

The Effect of Nonacquiescence on ALJs

Aside from its effects on beneficiaries, the Secretary's policy of nonacquiescence also had a detrimental effect on the administrative law judges assigned to the Agency. In a brief to the district court in 1985, the Justice Department had argued that ALJs were "subordinate officers of the executive branch" and were not part of the "judicial hierarchy."[47] As the Secretary discovered, however, the ALJs could not be so easily dismissed as subordinates of the Social Security Administration.

When questioned by Tennessee Senator Jim Sasser about how Congress could improve the social security disability hearing system, ALJ Robert Laws replied that he felt that "the most critical area" requiring legislative attention was "the conflict that seems to be in existence between the Social Security Administration and the Federal court system." He related the struggle within himself as a "past practicing attorney and one who has studied the law" who would like to "follow these court interpretations" but is "mandated to do otherwise."[48] Moreover, as the Senate Oversight Subcommittee report concluded: "this [nonacquiescence] situation is demoralizing to the ALJs who know that their judicial efforts may be meaningless. If they adhere to SSA's non-acquiescence ruling, their decisions may be overturned in Federal court because they failed to follow precedent; and if they adhere to the courts' decisions, their decisions may be overturned by the SSA through the Appeals Council. To say the least, this practice creates a professional and judicial quandry [sic] for the ALJ."[49] ALJs were doubly affected because reversal by the Appeals Council also subjected them to scrutiny under Bellmon Review and to possible professional sanctions.

The Effect of Nonacquiescence on U.S. Attorneys

The Social Security Administration's nonacquiescence similarly put U.S. Government Attorneys in a difficult position because their dubious legal posture placed them in jeopardy of receiving sanctions from federal judges under the Federal Rules of Civil Procedure.[50] In *Jones v. Heckler*, Judge Shadur upbraided government attorneys for their participation in a case that he asserted was characterized by "poor lawyering by the government in an effort to support an insupportable administrative decision."[51] Citing the Code of Professional Responsibility, Judge Shadur noted that "counsel for the United States has a special responsibility to the justice system." He added that "given the wholly untenable position of the government (which should never have forced Jones to go to court in the first place), the professionally responsible answer to this lawsuit would have been a confession of error by government counsel."[52] Judge Shadur's assessment of the government's case was so negative that he virtually invited plaintiff to seek legal fees from the government under the Equal Access to Justice Act.

In a later case, a Seventh Circuit panel found that the Secretary had adhered, albeit minimally, to the medical improvement standard announced in *Cassiday v. Schweiker*,[53] but "remind[ed] counsel for the Secretary that they have professional obligations as officers of this court and may not, in presenting their position, simply ignore circuit precedent with which they or their client disagree."[54] Although judges did not readily impose Rule Eleven sanctions, some U.S. Attorneys (specifically those in New York and New Jersey) responded to the pressure by refusing to defend cases in which "there is not a defense available that we can assert in good faith."[55]

PERCEPTIONS OF SSA NONACQUIESCENCE

Defending itself againt charges of lawlessness, the Social Security Administration has attempted to justify its nonacquiescence policy on the basis of *Mendoza*. The Agency argues that the *Mendoza* decision implicitly approves of nonacquiescence by supporting the position that agencies are not bound by a previous judicial ruling in subsequent litigation with a different party.

The Government's Reliance on *Mendoza*

In her testimony before the Senate Finance Committee, Carolyn Kuhl, deputy assistant attorney general, spoke against the proposed restriction on nonacquiescence in the 1984 Disability Reform Act and warned of the problems that would be caused by limiting the Agency's nonacquiescence policy. She pointed out that a blanket rule of acquiescence would adversely affect the government's litigating posture by forcing a government agency to seek review of all unfavorable decisions.[56]

The government's claims for *Mendoza* have been rejected by the vast majority of courts that have considered the question. Fourth Circuit plaintiffs brought a class action suit against the Secretary of Health and Human Services challenging the Secretary's refusal to follow circuit precedent on a number of issues, including termination of benefits. Dismissing the relevancy of *Mendoza*, Judge James McMillan, of the District of North Carolina, said it was "not in point." The pertinent holding of *Mendoza*, he stated in *Hyatt v. Heckler*, was only that the government must be allowed to challenge a law in court on its merits, *not* that an officer of the government may disobey court decisions with which he or she disagrees" (emphasis in the original).[57]

The Social Security Administration argued in *Hyatt* that it had followed the Fourth Circuit's ruling in *Dotson* with respect to the plaintiffs in that case (one of whom had died after being declared nondisabled by SSA) and that it was currently appealing another Fourth Circuit decision raising the same issues as *Dotson*. The court ruled that the Secretary's position was untenable; it pointed out that the Agency cannot justify nonacquiescence in a circuit court's ruling on the grounds that an appeal is pending, in another case, on the issues already decided in *Dotson*. Such a policy "would allow the Secretary forever to escape the mandates of the law by abandoning appeals *before* a case reaches the Supreme Court for decision, but continuing to assert that she is litigating the issue by defending claims that have only freshly entered the federal court system" (emphasis in the original).[58]

Similarly, Judge Sand also rejected SSA's reliance on *Mendoza*, saying that it did not authorize the Secretary "to refuse to apply the legal rules enumerated in a *circuit court decision* in subsequent cases *within the same circuit*" (emphasis in the original).[59] He maintained that the principles underlying *Mendoza* would not be jeopardized by mandating Agency compliance with appellate court decisions. The judge added that it was important to distinguish between the *Mendoza* holding that allowed the government to relitigate adversely-decided issues under certain circumstances and SSA's assertion that it can "regularly disregard circuit court decisions with which it disagrees by refusing to apply them in subsequent cases within the same circuit."[60]

Judicial Sanctions against SSA

Other courts around the nation also took strong exception to the Secretary's "violation" of the rule of law within the circuit and warned of impending sanctions against her. One of the most stinging remarks came from Judge Harry Pregerson of the Ninth Circuit, in his concurring opinion in *Lopez v. Heckler*.[61] He condemned the Secretary's "ill-advised policy" which he likened "to the repudiated pre–Civil War doctrine of nullification whereby rebellious states refused to recognize certain federal laws within their boundaries." The Secretary's nonacquiescence, he added, "not only scoffs at the law of this circuit," but also ignores some of the fundamental beliefs of the American system including separation of powers and the principle of judicial supremacy articulated in *Marbury v. Madison*." The judge concluded by reminding the Secretary that "the government expects its citizens to abide by the law [and] no less is expected of those charged with the duty to faithfully administer the law."[62]

The magnitude of the judiciary's disapproval of SSA's policy became apparent as several judges attempted to secure Agency compliance by threatening to cite the Secretary for contempt of court.[63] *Valdez v. Schweiker*[64] was a 1983 Colorado District Court case in which the Secretary had refused to obey the court's earlier directive to reevaluate Mr. Gilbert Valdez's termination decision in light of Ninth Circuit precedent. When the plaintiff reappeared before him, Judge Kane bluntly stated that the Secretary's "obduracy" forced him to reverse the termination. He emphatically reminded the Secretary that "she cannot refuse to obey the orders of this court" and that her "obstinance will not be tolerated" and that "if there is a next one, contempt powers will be invoked." In a footnote, the judge added that "the defendant is fortunate that this court is only reversing her decision and not initiating contempt proceedings."[65]

Similarly, in the Eighth Circuit in *Hillhouse v. Harris*,[66] while the three-judge panel affirmed the lower court's denial of benefits to the claimant, it noted disapprovingly that the Secretary "continues to operate under the belief that she is not bound by district or circuit court decisions." Judge Theodore McMillian concurred in the panel's judgment and added that he has "no wish to invite a confrontation with the Secretary; yet, if the Secretary persists in pursuing her nonacquiescence in this circuit's decisions, I will seek to bring contempt proceedings against the Secretary both in her official and individual capacities."[67]

Congressional Testimony on Nonacquiescence

Opposition to the Social Security Administration's nonacquiescence policy arose from other quarters as well despite the Agency's protestations that it remained within the rule of law by adhering to the decision in the case and restoring benefits to the terminated beneficiary. Criticism became intensified as members of Congress also contributed to the rising chorus against nonacquiescence.

Senator Sasser announced that he was "astounded" when he was informed of SSA's policy and that he "couldn't believe that [it] was happening."[68] Even more strongly, Representative Barney Frank of Massachusetts indicated that he was "intrigued by the word 'nonacquiescence.' " He added that "it seems to be one of the great euphemisms of our time. Other words which suggest themselves are 'contempt of court' or 'disobedience to the law,' which it seems to me private parties would find themselves called if they were doing this."[69]

When Dr. Arthur Flemming, former secretary of Health, Education, and Welfare, testified before a House Judiciary subcommittee, he expressed astonishment at the notion that he "had the option of deciding whether or not to follow the opinion of the circuit court of appeals within that circuit."[70] In later testimony he added that "this idea that you have to, in effect, disobey within the circuit the decision of the circuit court of appeals because you're kind of unhappy about that decision, and that you have no remedy and there is nothing else that you can do, just doesn't make sense to me."[71] A spokesperson for the American Bar Association testifying before the same subcommittee also condemned the Social Security Administration's nonacquiescence because it "flouts the rule of law."[72]

A CASE STUDY OF NONACQUIESCENCE

The prevailing view within the Social Security Administration was that "the federal courts do not rule SSA's programs."[73] Arguing that the Ninth Circuit had not addressed the impact of the 1980 Regulations on the continuing review process and therefore did "not provide a judicial interpretation of the disability regulations which should be followed," the Social Security Administration issued two nonacquiescence rulings in 1982, following the *Patti* and *Finnegan* cases.[74] The Secretary's defiance of the rule of law within the Ninth Circuit precipitated the most carefully orchestrated and systematic attack on SSA's nonacquiescence policy.

Lopez in District Court

In February 1983 plaintiffs brought a class action suit against the Agency asking for an injunction to prohibit the Secretary from terminating disability benefits without finding that the individual's medical condition had improved. Plaintiffs also alleged that nonacquiescence was a violation of separation of powers, due process, and equal protection, as well as the principle of stare decisis.

On June 16, 1983, District Court Judge William Gray of the Central District of California issued a ruling denying SSA's motion for dismissal on jurisdictional grounds. He held that plaintiffs' constitutional challenges satisfied the exhaustion requirements of *Weinberger v. Salfi* and that, given the Secretary's formal nonacquiescence in *Patti* and *Finnegan*, exhaustion would be futile. Finding that plaintiffs met the criteria for injunctive relief, the judge credited them with "demonstrat[ing] probable success on the merits by making a strong argument that agencies are bound by the laws of the circuit."[75]

The judge certified a circuitwide class of terminated SSI and SSDI program beneficiaries, estimated at 72,000 people, and granted plaintiffs a preliminary injunction enjoining the Secretary from implementing its nonacquiescence policy, that is, from failing to follow the precedent set by the Ninth Circuit's medical improvement rulings. The most controversial part of Judge Gray's order was Section 4(c), ordering SSA to notify, within sixty days, all persons who had been terminated after the *Patti* and *Finnegan* decisions without a finding of medical improvement. The order provided that individuals who believed that their condition had not improved since their initial awards could apply for reinstatement of benefits. Upon receipt of application for reinstatement, SSA must restore benefits until, upon reinvestigation, they are able to show medical improvement.[76]

Lopez Is Appealed

Two months later the Ninth Circuit denied the Secretary's application for an emergency stay of Judge Gray's order; after mailing the requisite notifications, the Secretary then requested a stay of the remainder of Section 4(c) pending appeal of the preliminary injunction. The appellate court denied the latter stay also, in part because "the physical and emotional suffering shown by plaintiffs in the record before us is far more compelling than the possibility of some administrative inconvenience or monetary loss to the government." The court further held that the injury to plaintiffs would be irreparable because "retroactive restoration of benefits would be inadequate to remedy these hardships."[77]

Rejecting the Secretary's argument that the district court did not have proper jurisdiction over all members of the class, the appellate court upheld the district court's decision to waive the administrative exhaustion requirements for members of the plaintiff class who had not received a final administrative decision. The court also rejected the Secretary's contention that she would prevail on the merits of the nonacquiescence and jurisdictional arguments.

Justice Rehnquist's Stay Order

SSA immediately appealed the Ninth Circuit's denial of the stay order to Justice Rehnquist sitting as Circuit Justice. About two weeks after the appellate court's ruling, while accepting the district court's finding that the balance of equities were in favor of the disability beneficiaries, Justice Rehnquist granted the Secretary a stay of the order granting interim benefits—pending appeal of the preliminary injunction.[78]

Justice Rehnquist's decision was based in large part on his belief that the district court's order had overstepped the bounds of proper judicial review of administrative actions. He expressed concern that Judge Gray's injunction "significantly interfere[d] with the distribution between administrative and judicial responsibility for enforcement of the Social Security Act which Congress has established."[79]

The Justice noted that some members of the plaintiff class had not presented their claims for benefits to the Secretary as required by *Mathews*. Quoting *Salfi*, he also reminded the lower court that a court was not permitted to "substitute its [own] conclusion as to futility for the contrary conclusion of the Secretary."[80] He reasoned that the Secretary was likely to prevail on the merits of the jurisdictional argument because the district court order allowed benefits to be paid to claimants merely upon their application. Even more importantly, he felt, many members of the class had not exhausted their administrative remedies and were therefore not legitimately before the court. Additionally, distinguishing this claim from the constitutional claim in *Mathews*, Justice Rehnquist noted that "respondents' unlawful termination claim could benefit from further factual development and refinement through the administrative process."[81]

The Supreme Court Affirms the Stay

One month later, the full Court, without opinion, and with four justices dissenting, denied the claimants' emergency application to vacate the stay granted by Justice Rehnquist. Justice Stevens, speaking for himself and Justice Blackmun, dissented in part from the Court's ruling, on the grounds that Judge Gray's order should have been upheld for persons who had properly complied with the exhaustion requirements of the Act.

More fundamentally, Justice Brennan, joined by Justice Marshall, dissented and voted to vacate the stay. Justice Brennan was less persuaded of the Secretary's likelihood of success on the merits of the claim than Justice Rehnquist because he found "the overwhelming hardships imposed on the recipients to be determinative."[82] Justice Brennan also disagreed with Justice Rehnquist's characterization of the lower court's posture as "judicial interference in the administrative process." He pointedly remarked that it was the Secretary who had "not paid due respect to a coordinate branch of government by expressly refusing to implement the binding decisions of the Ninth Circuit."[83]

Back to the Ninth Circuit

Following the affirmation of the stay by the Supreme Court, the Ninth Circuit reviewed Judge Gray's preliminary injunction on appeal. Because the Secretary's appeal had not questioned the validity of the *Patti* and *Finnegan* decisions, the appellate court was able to decide the relatively narrow question of the legitimacy of the preliminary injunction under an abuse of discretion standard. The Ninth Circuit ruled that the lower court judge had not abused his discretion in granting preliminary injunctive relief; the court, however, restricted the scope of the lower court's injunction to require the Secretary only to reinstate benefits for those terminated after the *Patti* and *Finnegan* decisions.

Agreeing with plaintiffs that exhaustion would have been futile, the Ninth Circuit ruled that plaintiffs would likely prevail on the jurisdictional arguments and affirmed the lower court on the exhaustion issues. While upholding the district court's ban on nonacquiescence within the circuit, the appellate court did not take up the lower court's constitutional attack on nonacquiescence. Although the Ninth Circuit remonstrated with the Secretary for "flouting the procedures she is required by law to follow," it did not declare nonacquiescence unconstitutional. The court simply stated that "the Secretary, as a member of the executive, is required to apply federal law as interpreted by the federal courts. . . . "[84]

The Final Round

In December 1984 the *Lopez* case made its last appearance before the Supreme Court. The Court granted the petition for the writ of certiorari and vacated the Ninth Circuit judgment; the case was remanded to the appellate court to be sent back to the district court in light of the 1984 Disability Reform Act.[85]

When Congress at last responded to disability beneficiaries by enacting the eagerly-awaited Reform Act, it calmed, at least temporarily, the furor over the medical improvement standard. But because of disagreement within Congress over the boundaries of nonacquiescence, the legislature refused to mediate the conflict between the Agency and the judiciary even though an impartial referee was clearly required; the Act merely expressed disapproval of nonacquiescence but drew back from a blanket prohibition. And although the Social Security Administration devised a new nonacquiescence policy in June 1985, it is not clear that the new policy greatly differed from the one it replaced.

NOTES

1. *Jones v. Heckler*, 583 F.Supp. 1250, 1252 n.4 (N.D. Ill. 1984).

2. Interview with District Court Judge John Nordberg, September 10, 1986. All the federal court judges interviewed in the Northern District of

Illinois reported their growing awareness of the flood of cases arising from challenges to the disability program.

3. *New York Times*, June 8, 1984, p. B5.

4. *New York Times*, March 10, 1985, p. 33.

5. *Issues Related to Social Security Act Disability Programs.* Senate Committee on Finance, 96th Cong., 1st Sess. (Comm. Print 1979), p. 54 (hereafter *Issues Related to Disability Programs*).

6. Note, "Administrative Agency Intracircuit Nonacquiescence," *Columbia Law Review* 85(1985):598.

7. Deborah Maranville, "Book Review: Bureaucratic Justice," *Minnesota Law Review* 69(1984):341.

8. Most decisions at the appellate level are made by three-judge panels. If a majority of the circuit judges within the circuit agree, a hearing or rehearing may be held before the court en banc (the entire complement of judges within the circuit). The latter has the advantage "of avoiding conflicts of view within a circuit and promoting finality of decision in the courts of appeals." Charles A. Wright, *Law of Federal Courts* (St. Paul: West, 1979), p. 9.

9. Note, "Intracircuit Nonacquiescence," p. 583.

10. Steven Eichel, " 'Respectful Disagreement': Nonacquiescence by Federal Administrative Agencies in United States Courts of Appeals Precedents," *Columbia Journal of Law and Social Problems*, 18(1985):503.

11. *Goodman's Furniture Company v. United States Postal Service*, 561 F.2d 462, 466 (3d Cir. 1977) (Weis, J., concurring).

12. Note, "Judicial Supervision of Agency Action: Administrative Nonacquiescence in Judicial Decisions," *George Washington Law Review* 53(November 1984-January 1985):147.

13. Ibid.

14. Other agencies such as the Occupational Safety & Health Review Commission (OSHA) and the Federal Communications Commission (FCC) have occasionally attempted to use nonacquiescence also; see *S & H Riggers & Erectors, Inc. v. Occupational Safety & Health Review Commission*, 659 F.2d 1273 (5th Cir. 1981); *ITT World Communications Inc. v. Federal Communications Commission*, 635 F.2d 32 (2d Cir. 1980); *Goodman's Furniture*, 561 F.2d at 462.

Although the Internal Revenue Service's administrative procedure relies heavily upon intercircuit nonacquiescence, it has also occasionally used intracircuit nonacquiescence. It has not, however, practiced the latter with great regularity and may have even abandoned it. The National Labor Relations Board's practice of intracircuit nonacquiescence is justified by the NLRB on a number of grounds: the National Labor Relations Act prescribes that the NLRB can be sued in the District of Columbia, in the circuit in which the unfair labor practice occurred, or in any circuit where the party "transacts business." The NLRB argues, therefore, that it is unfair to force them to follow the law of a particular circuit since the venue of the lawsuit could not have been predicted when the agency action occurred. Moreover, the NLRB frequently seeks Supreme Court review and, even when it does not, suit may be brought by the losing party. See Note, "Intracircuit Nonacquiescence"; and Jerry Mashaw, et al., *Social Security Hearings and Appeals* (Lexington, Mass.: Lexington Books, 1978), pp. 110–11 for discussions of nonacquiescence by these two agencies.

15. Note, "Intracircuit Nonacquiescence," p. 601.

16. 608 F.2d 965, 970 (3d Cir. 1979).

17. *Allegheny Hospital*, 608 F.2d at 970.

18. *Ithaca College v. the National Labor Relations Board*, 623 F.2d 224, 228 (2d Cir.) *cert. denied*, 449 U.S. 975 (1980).

19. Note, "Judicial Supervision of Agency Action," p. 161.

20. *Vermont Yankee Nuclear Power Corporation v. Natural Resources Defense Council, Inc.*, 435 U.S. 519, 524 (1978).

21. *Batterton v. Francis*, 432 U.S. 416, 425 (1977); see also *Schweiker v. Gray Panthers*, 453 U.S. 34 (1981).

22. 464 U.S. 154 (1984).

23. Note, "Judicial Supervision of Agency Action," p. 160.

24. Stare decisis preserves the hierarchy of judicial rule. Under this principle, lower courts are bound by the rule of law established by higher courts within the jurisdiction. Collateral estoppel is a rule designed to promote judicial economy by preventing duplicative litigation; it restricts a litigant to only one bite of the apple, that is, to one full and fair opportunity to litigate an issue in a court of law. "Under the judicially-developed doctrine of collateral estoppel, once a court has decided an issue of fact or law necessary to its judgment, that decision is conclusive in a subsequent suit based on a different cause of action involving a party to the prior litigation." *Mendoza*, 464 U.S. at 158.

Collateral estoppel precludes litigants from relitigating an issue decided by another court—whether district court, appellate court, or even a state court. Although the common law doctrine of collateral estoppel was originally restricted by the requirement of mutuality of parties, this rule was eliminated in 1971 and collateral estoppel could be used even when only one of the litigants in the later case was a party in the first case; see *Blonder-Tongue Laboratories, Inc. v. University of Illinois Foundation*, 402 U.S. 313 (1971). Originally, only available for defendants (and known as defensive collateral estoppel), the doctrine was gradually broadened to allow either defensive or offensive (invoked by the plaintiff) use. Thus, in a civil suit involving the government, nonmutual collateral estoppel would prohibit the government from relitigating an issue if it had lost on that issue in any court anywhere in the country—even when the party opposing the government in the second suit was not the same party as in the suit in which government originally lost.

The Supreme Court conditionally struck down the limitation on offensive nonmutual collateral estoppel in *Parklane Hoisery Company v. Shore*, 439 U.S. 322 (1979) but in *Mendoza* the Court made it clear that *Parklane's* approval of offensive nonmutual collateral estoppel did not extend to use against the government.

25. *Mendoza*, 464 U.S. at 162.

26. Note, "Collateral Estoppel and Nonacquiescence: Precluding Govern-

ment Relitigation in the Pursuit of Litigant Equality," *Harvard Law Review* 99(1986):847.

27. Note, "Intracircuit Nonacquiescence," p. 592.

28. Ibid.

29. *Judicial Review of Agency Action: HHS Policy of Nonacquiescence: Hearing before the Subcommittee on Administrative Law and Governmental Relations of the House Committee on the Judiciary*, 99th Cong., 1st Sess. (1985), p. 128 (statement of Professor Lea Brilmayer, Yale University Law School) (hereafter *Judicial Review of Agency Action*).

30. Mashaw, et al., *Social Security Hearings and Appeals*, p. 110.

31. Note, "Judicial Supervision of Agency Action," p. 162.

32. *Judicial Review of Agency Action*, p. 132 (statement of Lea Brilmayer).

33. Unlike the National Labor Relations Board, the Social Security Administration does not ordinarily seek certiorari after losing in circuit court. SSA has filed only two petitions for certiorari from 1979 to 1984 for cases involving interpretation of the Social Security Act as it relates to the disability program; see Gerald Heaney, "Why the High Rate of Reversals in Social Security Disability Cases?" *Hamline Law Review* 7(1984):10. See also *New York Times*, May 13, 1984, p. 27 for statement by Minnesota Federal District Court Judge Miles Lord on nonacquiescence.

34. 42 U.S.C. §221(a)(2) (1984).

35. *Disability Amendments of 1982: Hearings before the Subcommittee on Social Security of the House Committee on Ways and Means*, 97th Cong., 2d Sess. (1982), pp. 15–16 (statement of Louis Hays, associate commissioner for Office of Hearings and Appeals, Social Security Administration) (hereafter *Disability Amendments of 1982*).

36. The Social Security Administration issued eight formal nonacquiescence rulings from 1967 to 1983. From 1968 to 1979 only two were issued, from 1980 to 1982 there were six; see *The Role of the ALJ*, p. 25; Christine Fallon, "Social Security and Legal Precedent," *Case and Comment* (March-April 1984):6.

37. Aside from the medical improvement standard, SSA has also refused to acquiesce in court decisions setting standards for evaluation of pain, treating physicians' reports, alcoholism, multiple impairments, and failure to apply the grid in accordance with the regulations. *Judicial Review of Agency Action*, p. 85 (statement of Eileen Sweeney, National Senior Citizen's Law Center).

38. SSA's Office of Hearings and Appeals Handbook §§1–161 (cited in *The Role of the Administrative Law Judge in the Title II Social Security Disability Insurance Program*. Subcommittee on Oversight of Government Management of the Senate Committee on Governmental Affairs. 98th Cong., 1st Sess. (Comm. Print 1983), p. 24 (hereafter *The Role of the ALJ*); superceded by SSA's new ruling on nonacquiescence released on June 3, 1985 in Interim Circular 185; see *Judicial Review of Agency Action*, pp. 34–41.

39. *Stieberger v. Heckler*, 615 F.Supp. 1315, 1366 (S.D.N.Y. 1985).

40. Interview with District Court Judge Milton Shadur, October 17, 1986.

41. Interview with District Court Judge James Moran, July 8, 1986.

42. *Oversight of Social Security Disability Benefits Terminations: Hearing before the Subcommittee on Oversight of Government Management of the Senate Committee on Governmental Affairs*, 97th Cong., 2d Sess. (1982), p. 400 (hereafter *Oversight of Disability Terminations*).

43. Mashaw, et al., *Social Security Hearings and Appeals*, p. 112.

44. Eichel, " 'Respectful Disagreement,' " p. 485; *Stieberger*, 615 F.Supp. at 1364.

45. *Lopez v. Heckler*, 572 F.Supp. 26, 30 (N.D.Cal. 1983).

46. *Stieberger*, 615 F.Supp. at 1362.

47. *New York Times*, March 10, 1985, p. 33.

48. *Social Security Disability Program Reform: Hearings before the Senate Committee on the Budget*, 98th Cong., 2d Sess. (1984), p. 124 (statement of Administrative Law Judge Robert Laws) (hereafter *Disability Program Reform*).

49. *The Role of the ALJ*, p. 30.

50. Rule 11 of the Federal Rules of Civil Procedure, amended in 1983 to attempt to curtail abuses in pleading reads in relevant part:

The signature of an attorney or party constitutes a certificate by him that he has read the pleading, motion, or other paper; that to the best of his knowledge, information, and belief formed after reasonable inquiry it is well grounded in fact and is warranted by existing law or a good faith argument for the extension, modification, or reversal of existing law, and that it is not interposed for any improper purpose, such as to harass or to cause unnecessary delay or needless increases in the cost of litigation. . . . If a pleading, motion, or other paper, is signed in violation of this rule, the court, upon motion or upon its own initiative, shall impose upon the person who signed it, a represented party, or both, an appropriate sanction, which may include an order to pay to the other party or parties the amount of the reasonable expenses incurred because of the filing of the pleading, motion, or other paper, including a reasonable attorney's fee.

51. *Jones*, 583 F.Supp. at 1252.

52. *Jones*, 583 F.Supp. at 1256–57 n.7.

53. 663 F.2d 745 (7th Cir. 1981).

54. *Switzer v. Heckler*, 742 F.Supp. 382, 384 n.1 (N.D.Ill. 1984).

55. *New York Times*, September 23, 1984, p. 54. See Donald Horowitz, *The Jurocracy* (Lexington, Mass.: Lexington Books, 1977) for a discussion of litigating by government attorneys.

56. *Social Security Disability Insurance Program: Hearing before the Senate Committee on Finance*, 98th Cong., 2d Sess. (1984), p. 118 (statement of Carolyn Kuhl, deputy assistant attorney general, Department of Justice) (hereafter *Disability Program Hearing*).

57. 579 F.Supp. 985, 1002 (D.N.C. 1984), *vacated and remanded to Secretary of Health and Human Services*, 757 F.2d 1455 (4th Cir. 1985). The district court's order to the Secretary to follow the Fourth Circuit ruling of *Dotson v. Schweiker* was vacated in light of Congress' refusal to impose an absolute ban on nonacquiescence.

58. *Hyatt*, 579 F. Supp. at 1001.

59. *Stieberger*, 615 F. Supp. at 1359.

60. *Stieberger*, 615 F.Supp. at 1361.

61. 713 F.2d 1432 (9th Cir. 1983).

62. *Lopez*, 713 F.2d at 1441 (Pregerson, J., concurring).

63. Such cases include *Polaski v. Heckler*, 585 F.Supp. 1004 (D.Minn. 1984) *remanded on other grounds*, 751 F.2d 943 (8th Cir. 1984); *Holden v. Heckler*, 584 F.Supp. 463 (N.D. Ohio 1984); *Layton v. Heckler*, 726 F.2d 440 (8th Cir. 1984); *Chee v. Heckler*, 563 F.Supp. 1362 (D.Ariz. 1983); *Capitano v. Secretary of Health and Human Services*, 732 F.2d 1066 (2d Cir. 1984); *Doe v. Heckler*, 576 F.Supp. 463 (D.Md. 1983).

64. 575 F.Supp. 1203, 1204–5 (D.Col. 1983).

65. *Valdez*, 575 F. Supp. at 1205 n.3.

66. 715 F.2d 428, 430 (8th Cir. 1983).

67. *Hillhouse*, 715 F.2d at 430 (McMillian, J., concurring).

68. *Disability Program Reform*, pp. 124–25 (statement of Sen. Sasser).

69. *Judicial Review of Agency Action*, p. 4 (statement of Rep. Frank).

70. Ibid., p. 66 (statement of Dr. Arthur Flemming, former Secretary of Health, Education, and Welfare).

71. Ibid., p. 105.

72. Ibid., p. 116 (statement of Herbert Hoffman, American Bar Association).

73. January 7, 1982 memo entitled "Adjudicatory Policy," addressed to SSA administrative law judges from Louis Hays, quoting a statement by Frank Dell 'Acqua, deputy assistant general counsel, Social Security Administration, cited in *The Role of the ALJ*, p. 24.

74. Social Security Ruling 82–49c (1982); see also Social Security Ruling 82–10c (1982). Although the Ninth Circuit utilized a medical improvement standard in *Finnegan v. Mathews*, 641 F.2d 1340 (9th Cir. 1981), the facts of this case were limited to "grandfatherees" who transfered from the state public assistance plan to the federal SSI program. *Patti v. Schweiker*, 669 F.2d 582 (9th Cir. 1982), following a year later, affirmed that the medical improvement standard was not simply limited to "grandfatherees."

75. *Lopez*, 572 F.Supp. at 29. The requirements for obtaining an injunction include proof of either a likelihood of success on the merits and the possibility of irreparable injury or a showing that serious legal matters are involved and the balance of hardships are sharply in plaintiffs' favor.

76. *Lopez*, 572 F.Supp. at 32.

77. *Lopez v. Heckler*, 713 F.2d 1432, 1437 (9th Cir. 1983).

78. The criteria for an emergency stay by a Supreme Court Justice sitting as a Circuit Justice are based on the probability of four justices granting certiorari, the likelihood of success on the merits, and the balance of equities.

79. *Heckler v. Lopez*, 463 U.S. 1328, 1331 (1983) (Rehnquist, J., Circuit Justice).

80. *Lopez*, 463 U.S. at 1335, quoting *Weinberger v. Salfi*, 422 U.S. 749, 766 (1975).

81. *Lopez*, 463 U.S. at 1336.

82. *Heckler v. Lopez*, 464 U.S. 879, 886 (Brennan, J., dissenting).
83. *Lopez*, 464 U.S. at 887 (Brennan, J., dissenting).
84. *Lopez v. Heckler*, 725 F.2d 1489, 1503 (9th Cir. 1984).
85. *Heckler v. Lopez*, 469 U.S. 1082 (1984).

8

Passage of the 1984 Disability Reform Act

By 1984 there was a stalemate between the courts and the executive branch. The disability program was in gridlock and it was apparent that remedial action was required "to clear up the chaotic situation in the State disability agencies and the Federal courts."[1] Because judicial authority was, by itself, unable to bring about compliance in the face of a recalcitrant bureaucracy, terminated disability beneficiaries were forced to seek relief in other policymaking arenas as well. Following the example set by other public interest litigants, demands for a new disability standard expanded beyond the courtroom and moved onto the political agenda.

The problems within the disability program were evident at all levels of adjudication. At the local level, state agencies began a revolt against the Social Security Administration and, throughout 1983, a growing number of states—under orders from governors and state welfare executives—joined the ranks and refused to process disability terminations. In January 1984, 26 states were refusing to carry out SSA procedures as ordered.[2] By February, the number had risen to 38.[3]

Lobbying groups and legal aid services represented claimants' interests in and out of the courtroom. Media attention was focused on the plight of terminated beneficiaries. Congress was inundated with letters requesting investigation of the review process and pleading for congressional intercession to restore benefits. The growing sense of crisis among disability recipients was mirrored in their pleas to Congress to bring order to the disability program by setting legislative standards for SSA's continuing eligibility policy.

The Social Security disability litigation demonstrates that a realistic appraisal of the impact of the federal courts on the policymaking process requires a broader perspective of the notion of judicial impact and necessitates an examination of the extent to which litigation serves as an influence on, or catalyst for, other actors in the policymaking process. In this case, the impact of plaintiffs' courtroom victories was attenuated by the Secretary's nonacquiescence policy challenging traditional notions of judicial review of administrative adjudication. Thus, although plaintiffs were often successful in appealing their individual termination decisions, the litigation was less successful in changing the continuing review process. Federal court rulings on the medical improvement standard nevertheless served two vital functions: first, they legitimated the beneficiaries' demands for disability reform; second, they provided legal support for the legislative imposition of a medical improvement standard in continuing eligibility cases.

There was unanimous agreement among people intimately involved in the disability program during the years of struggle over periodic review that the courts played an essential role in the formulation of new disability policy. Susan Collins, majority staff director of the Senate Subcommittee on Government Management, assessed the courts' role as "critical" in leading to the reform legislation, adding that they gave "credibility" to the reform movement.[4] Similarly, Patricia Dilley, of the Social Security Subcommittee staff, pointed out that the "courts were used as evidence that there was a real problem by Congress."[5] When asked his opinion of the role of the litigation in prompting disability reform, Robert Lehrer, deputy director of the Legal Assistance Foundation of Chicago, answered that the cases lent "invaluable support to the political efforts because they allowed legislators to feel righteously indignant" about current disability policy.[6] Eileen Sweeney, staff attorney of the National Senior Citizens Law Center, simply said "Thank God for the courts," when asked about the importance of the courts in disability reform.[7]

EARLY LEGISLATIVE ACTION

Throughout 1982 there was evidence of increasing congressional concern over administration of the disability program. At the beginning of the year, however, legislative attention was not focused on periodic review. In March 1982, Representatives Jake Pickle and Bill Archer, chair and ranking minority member of the Social Security Subcommittee respectively, introduced H.R. 5700, a bill entitled the Disability Amendments of 1982.[8] Intended as a comprehensive reform of the disability program, the bill did not address problems of the continuing eligibility review process. Hearings on H.R. 5700 were held during March.

Although insisting that its positive changes were not extensive enough, disability advocates appeared generally supportive of the proposed legislation.[9] The bill was marked up in Subcommittee and reported out to the Ways and Means Committee on April 1, 1982.[10] Favorably reported out of Ways and Means and sent to the Rules Committee, H.R. 5700 was later withdrawn from committee because of a conflict over the rule under which it would be considered. The Disability Amendments of 1982 never reached the House of Representatives for debate.

Other legislative proposals, designed to extricate the disability program from the morass into which it had sunk, were offered in the summer of 1982. Most of these bills were now specifically linked to the problems created by CDR, although the medical improvement standard did not figure prominently in these proposals. Some bills, such as S. 2725,[11] introduced by Republican Senator William Cohen of Maine and Democratic Senator Carl Levin of Michigan, and S. 2730,[12] introduced by Republican Senator John Heinz of Pennsylvania, were intended only as interim measures to offer short-term relief for terminated beneficiaries. The Levin and Cohen bill, S. 2725, would have continued disability and medicare benefits through appeal to the ALJ level and would have directed the Secretary to slow down the rate of disability reviews prescribed under the 1980 Amendments. The Heinz measure, S. 2730, would have simply proscribed disability reviews, except for diaried cases, until January 1983.[13]

Another bill introduced by Senator Levin alone, S. 2674,[14] was intended as a more comprehensive reform of the adjudication process and focused on the medical improvement standard as a solution to the growing disability crisis. The bill also proposed to revitalize the initial stages of eligibility determinations by establishing face-to-face interviews with state DDS officials before decisions were finalized and to continue disability and medicare benefits through appeal to the administrative law judge.[15]

Finally, in September, the Senate Finance Committee marked up a bill, S. 2942,[16] introduced by Senator Cohen and nineteen cosponsors. This bill, like its predecessor, S. 2725, proposed a slowdown of the review process and payment of benefits through the appeals process. By voice vote the Committee weakened the measure by sunsetting the payment through ALJ provision and only permitting curtailment of periodic review selectively on a state-by-state basis.[17]

H.R. 7093

After receiving Finance Committee approval, at the request of its chair, Senator Robert Dole, the provisions of S. 2942 were added to an unrelated House bill, H.R. 7093.[18] House Bill 7093 was amended on the Senate floor and approved on December 3 by a vote of 70 to 4. It returned again to the House for consideration on December 14, and the final Conference bill was approved by both chambers on December 21. The vote in the House on the final bill was 259 to 0; the Senate approved it by voice vote and President Reagan signed it into law on January 12, 1983.[19]

When this "relatively noncontroversial"[20] bill was enacted, the battle between the judiciary and the bureaucracy over eligibility for continuing disability had not yet reached crisis proportions. The Senate floor debate over the proposed reform bill indicates that the federal courts had not yet begun to play a major role in disability policymaking. The major impetus to congressional action in passing H.R. 7093 was the failure of the administrative review process. Citing the high number of reversals by ALJs—two-thirds of those appealing—as evidence of the frequency of erroneous DDS decisions, Congress voted to continue the benefits of terminated individuals through the ALJ hearing stage. (Benefits would be subject to recovery as overpayment if the ALJ affirmed the state's finding.) The Act authorized the Secretary to slow down the flow of cases to the state agencies and to offer the states additional money for implementation of the review process. It also required the Secretary to provide an opportunity for a face-to-face eviden-tiary hearing at the state reconsideration level by January 1, 1984.

H.R. 7093 was designed to provide temporary relief to victims of the ces-sation process. During the floor debate, Senator Cohen noted that its purpose was "to provide immediate relief to the thousands of disabled people whose benefits are being erroneously terminated and subsequently restored after a lengthy appeals process has run its course." The Senator characterized the situation as "both absurd and cruel [because] it makes no sense to inflict pain, uncertainty, and financial hardship on disabled workers and then tell them, 'sorry, we made a mistake.' "[21]

Enacted by the lameduck 97th Congress, H.R. 7093 was characterized as an "emergency" measure and not envisioned as a comprehensive response to the "key structural problems in the disability insurance program."[22] The statute was only designed as a temporary solution for the more egregious administrative problems created by the 1980 Act.[23] Passage of the bill was achieved in short order because it was largely perceived as an interim mea-sure to deal "with extremely complicated provisions of law in a very short period of time."[24] Seeking to erase any misunderstanding about his reason for voting in favor of the bill, Senator Dole expressed his continued support for periodic review and emphasized that this Act did "not in any way rep-resent a reversal of the 1980 mandate that the Social Security Administra-tion work diligently to remove ineligibles from the benefit rolls."[25]

Congress paid little attention to the issue of the medical improvement standard during debate over the Act. A Senate-proposed amendment to H.R. 7093 providing that the Secretary is not precluded "from finding an individual to be ineligible . . . even if such individual's medical condition has not improved or otherwise changed since any prior determination of his eligibility," was stricken from the final bill without comment.[26]

The Congressional Record shows that a few Senators made passing ref-erence to the need to resolve the ambiguities in the Social Security Act and some, such as Senator Cohen, spoke of a need for "long-term reforms, in-cluding a medical improvement standard."[27] Senator Dole, however, warned his colleagues that insistence on a medical improvement component in the bill would have aroused controversy and prevented it from being brought to the floor under the unanimous consent provision.[28] Ohio Senator Howard Metzenbaum stated that "the bill is not intended to change any current case law on the subject of when a showing of medical improvement is required."[29] It was not clear from the Senator's remarks whether he was aware of the growing judicial movement toward imposition of the medical improvement standard.

STATES IN REVOLT AGAINST SSA

The events of 1983 showed that the partnership between SSA and the states was becoming increasingly tenuous. The Agency's termination policy placed states in an unenviable position. They were contractually obligated to follow SSA's guidelines in the continuing disability reviews, and, as the proximate cause of the termination notices, they received the brunt of the complaints and negative publicity.[30] In testimony before the House Select Committee on Aging in June 1983, Governor Bill Clinton of Arkansas described his frustration as "a Governor with nominal responsibility for a program which includes the power to hire and fire the person who is running it, but with virtually no real power to affect the substantive decisions which were made or the decisionmaking process."[31] He told the Committee that his predecessor, the former Governor of Arkansas ordered the state letterhead changed to delete his name from the termination notices sent out by the state. Governor Clinton called this tactic "a highly intelligent move" and noted that if he had been in office he "would probably have done the same thing." He added that he wished "there was some way to take the 'State of Arkansas' off the stationery."[32]

Impact on State Finances

Governors, such as Clinton, were not merely concerned with maintaining a favorable public image; they were alarmed about the impact of the disability terminations on their states' treasuries. Removing persons from the disability rolls created enormous financial problems for the states as terminated beneficiaries quickly applied for state welfare assistance to replace federal disability payments. And, as the terminations in her state progressed, Barbara Blum, New York's commissioner of Social Services, predicted that "many people losing Federal benefits would end up on state-financed public assistance because they are poor and have little prospect of finding a job."[33]

When the federal government instituted these cost-shifting measures, it reduced disability recipients from the status of federal social insurance beneficiaries to the status of state public assistance applicants. It was estimated that every dollar saved by the Social Security Administration resulted in a cost of 84 cents to state and local governments who were faced with the prospect of adding many thousands of people to the state welfare rolls.[34] And because many state governments did not possess, or did not wish to commit, resources to meet these demands, the income level of former disability recipients who were forced to rely upon state welfare aid was reduced by 60 percent.[35]

Partially in self-defense, local governments fought back against SSA's termination policy. As part of their efforts to combat the federal government's cost reduction plan, some states, such as New York, allocated millions of dollars to subsidize legal services agencies to provide representation for ex-disability beneficiaries to avoid their reliance on the state relief program; it was estimated that this policy could save as much as $7 to $10 million dollars a year.[36] Illinois also encouraged suits against the Social Security Administration by providing attorneys fees for persons successfully restored to SSI rolls from state welfare assistance. And, in at least one instance, New York City and State became part of a class action suit against SSA for illegal removal of mentally impaired persons from the disability rolls.

The logic of the states' efforts against SSA was obvious; New York District Court Judge Jack Weinstein commented, "it makes financial sense for cities and states to undertake class actions and to provide individual legal assistance to their disabled citizens because, through welfare, public hospitals, and shelters for the homeless, the local governments must bear much of the cost of caring for those who do not receive federal benefits."[37]

States also objected to their role in the CDR process because SSA increased its demands on their productivity without giving them adequate staff or resources to conduct the reviews.[38] Herbert Brown, administrator of the Tennessee DDS, testified before the Senate Oversight Subcommittee in May 1982 that his agency had been understaffed for the last four years. He emphasized that staffing had not been increased to accommodate the new workload when periodic review was thrust upon them. Because of the priority accorded to CDRs, state agencies shifted their resources within the agency to process the reviews. A shift, according to Brown, that "so adversely affected our performance that for three consecutive quarters, our processing time exceeded the maximum acceptable according to regulation, which brought Social Security on our back because of poor performance."[39]

The states' rebellion against the Social Security Administration was aided by the House Select Committee on Aging. The impetus for this Committee's involvement in the disability crisis in early 1982 arose from its function of investigation and oversight of policies and programs for the elderly.[40] The Aging Committee perceived the federal-state relationship as "its handle" on the disability crisis, that is, as a focal point for Committee action. According to the staff director of the Subcommittee on Retirement Income and Employment, Allen Johnston, the committee served "as a national network" by keeping states apprised of the way in which other states were reacting to the disability crisis and informing them of the range of available responses. The Committee accomplished these goals in part by holding a series of hearings around the country to publicize the states' disaffection with the disability program.[41]

State Moratoria

The battle of the states against SSA was also facilitated by the growing number of federal court decrees imposing a medical improvement standard on SSA adjudications. State executives, such as West Virginia's Governor John D. Rockefeller, were able to point to judicial rulings on the medical improvement standard to support their recalcitrance in implementing Agency policy. He ordered the West Virginia Disability Determination Service to rely on "federal court decisions most favorable to beneficiaries" which would "generally require a showing of medical improvement."[42]

The growing impact of the federal courts on disability policy was manifested in the number of state disability agencies operating under court decree; at the end of August 1984, the *New York Times* was reporting that 45 states were under court orders blocking them from carrying out terminations without using a medical improvement standard.[43] Assessing the importance of courts in the battle of the states against the Social Security Administration, Staff Director Johnston indicated that the "courts were very helpful because they gave the governors a legalistic framework in which to take executive action."[44] Echoing this sentiment, Aging Committee staff member Lowell Arye noted that the states were in tune with the courts and were encouraged to withstand SSA pressure because they felt "the courts were behind them."[45]

Despite the legal constraints upon them, by the end of 1983, just over half the states were not "acquiescing" in SSA policy. During that year the chief executives of eight states: Alabama, Illinois, Massachusetts, New York, Arkansas, Maine, Michigan, and Ohio called a halt to CDRs within their states. Some of these states, such as Ohio, Michigan, and New York, were simultaneously under a state-declared moratorium as well as under a court-imposed medical improvement standard. Another group of states, mostly in the Ninth Circuit, including Washington, Montana, Maryland, Oregon, Hawaii, Colorado, Nevada, Idaho, Arizona, Alaska, California, and West Virginia, were conducting CDRs under a court-imposed medical improvement standard. Six states—New Jersey, South Carolina, Virginia, North Carolina, Pennsylvania, and Delaware—were awaiting litigation decisions on the medical improvement standard in the federal district courts in their states. The remaining 24 states continued to process CDRs as required by the Social Security Administration.

SSA Intervenes

On December 7, 1983 SSA called a temporary halt to terminations. The Agency cited uncertainty about the renewal of the payment through appeal provision enacted in the 1983 Act as well as the need to prepare for the face-to-face interviews mandated under the Act. State agencies were told to continue reviewing cases but to refrain from sending termination notices to beneficiaries.

In January 1984, the Secretary sent notices to all state agencies ordering them to resume processing disability reviews and to initiate the reconsideration interviews. Reflecting the lack of coherency in the disability review process, four different types of letters were sent. SSA accorded no legitimacy to the states with self-imposed moratoria on terminations and governors in these states were instructed to begin processing CDRs and send cessation notices beginning in early February.[46]

Secretary Heckler's letter to George Wallace of Alabama, one of the governors who imposed a moratorium on disability terminations, assured him that "we [SSA and the states] can resume our full-processing of this program in a way assuring fair and humane treatment for our citizens."[47] Her letter to Governor DuPont of Delaware, one of the litigation-pending states, recognized the court's role in the review process by acknowledging that "there is pending medical improvement litigation that may have a bearing on the standard to be used in deciding whether disability continues." She told him that although other states would be ordered to begin processing, his state should "continue to hold all medical cessations pending further consideration of the litigation issues."[48] The Secretary's letter to Governor Sheffield of Alaska, cognizant of the Ninth Circuit's ruling on the medical improvement standard, ordered his state DDS to resume the processing and notification procedure "beginning in February in accordance with court imposed standards. . . . "[49] Governors in the last category of states were simply told that the SSA-initiated moratorium on CDRs was ended and they were to continue processing reviews.

The flurry of letters between SSA and the state executives evidenced a fractionalized disability policy. Despite SSA's stated desire to avoid variation within its termination policy, the combination of federal court rulings and state revolts was subjecting disability beneficiaries to the vissicitudes of geographic fortune. Ironically, the Agency's nonacquiescence policy had been justified by SSA's need to maintain national standards of adjudication. By sending four versions of the letter, SSA was admitting that it was unable to maintain uniformity within the program.

EXTRAJUDICIAL LITIGATION TACTICS

SSA's refusal to acquiesce in adoption of a medical improvement standard forced disability reform advocates to expand their litigation strategy into the legislative arena. While continuing their legal efforts by appealing the Agency's termination decisions, they also demanded that Congress enforce judicial rulings by legislative adoption of a medical improvement standard.

Beginning in early 1982, members of Congress became inundated with requests to intercede with the Social Security Administration to prevent termination of benefits. One congressional staffer reported that 90 percent of congressional casework during the CDR period concerned disability cases.[50] In a statement submitted to the Senate Oversight Subcommittee in May 1982, Senator Donald Riegle of Michigan reported that the number of people seeking his help with a disability problem had increased by about 95 percent in the last year.[51] The success of the disability reform advocates in attracting congressional attention was reflected in the 27 hearings on the disability program from March 1982 until May 1984.[52]

Litigants also sought to create a public debate over their battles against the bureaucracy. Their efforts were enhanced by representatives of interest groups, attorneys for terminated beneficiaries, and state and local political figures who contributed to the clamor for disability reform. Not surprisingly, disability recipients had little difficulty in gathering public support for their side; they were the disabled Davids struggling against the governmental Goliath. Increasing media interest and public expressions of sympathy for terminated disability beneficiaries demonstrated the success of their strategy.

Media Involvement

The media attention accorded to the disability crisis played a key role in the litigation strategy by bringing the issue into public view and creating a favorable environment for legislative change.

Newspapers around the country from the *New York* and *Los Angeles Times* to the *Roanoke Times & World-News* and the *Quincy Patriot Ledger* all helped publicize the plight of terminated beneficiaries. Investigative reports on television newscasts, such as the one entitled "Disabled Workers" on WBEZ-TV in Massachusetts, succeeded as well in bringing this issue to public attention.[53] A documentary called "Disabled" that aired on national public television in June 1983 also drew a sympathetic picture of disability beneficiaries caught in the review process. Reviewing the documentary, a *New York Times* critic wrote, " 'Disabled' suggests that fiscal policy, not medical and humanitarian reasons, determined the outcome of some reviews."[54]

The case of Roy Benavidez, retired Master Sergeant in the Army Special Forces, was an especially poignant one that captured public interest. Wounded twice in Vietnam, Sergeant Benavidez had been awarded the Medal of Honor by President Reagan in a White House ceremony in February 1981. Retired from the military in 1976 with an 80 percent disability classification, Sergeant Benavidez told a *New York Times* reporter in a telephone interview in May 1983 that "a punctured lung and two pieces of shrapnel in [my] heart were two of many Vietnam War injuries that qualify [me] for civilian and military disability benefits."[55]

Sergeant Benavidez, whose story was publicized in the *Readers Digest* and the *New York Times*, was invited to testify before the House Select Committee on Aging in June 1983. He reported that he had been on the disability rolls for seven years when he received a termination notice from the Texas Human Resources Department in 1982. In his prepared statement to the committee, the sergeant pleaded for "this nation's veterans who have ensured this Freedom over the years [and who] now need your intervention and assistance on this very critical issue of disability entitlements. Please do not forget them," he said, "our future as a nation devoted to Duty Honor and Country are at stake."[56]

Stories about people committing suicide following receipt of termination notices also evoked public sympathy, especially when the stories were about mentally impaired individuals who had their benefits terminated.[57] A *New York Times* story in May 1982 reported that two people with histories of mental disabilities took their lives after being sent termination notices.[58] A year later a *Times* editorial criticized the disability program's cessation decisions and cited two more termination tragedies to support its anti-SSA stance. The first account was of a woman suffering from "arthritis, spinal disease, and severe depression" who committed suicide following the termination of her benefits; she left a note addressed to the Department of Health and Human Services saying that she was getting a "message" from them to "either work or die." The other suicide story was about a "49-year-old Illinois man [who] wrote to his wife that 'Social Security keeps turning me down,' and then shot himself."[59]

Aside from the suicides, there were other dramas reported in the newspapers about people with terminal illnesses whose benefits were terminated, about people with mental impairments who were barely able to function—much less able to work, and about doctors describing patients they certified as totally unable to work who were declared fit by SSA. The effectiveness of the publicity in attracting congressional attention was evident in the steady stream of newspaper articles placed in the Congressional Record by sympathetic members of Congress. In their private discussions on the disability program as well, members of Congress often recounted a favorite "horror" story to illustrate the problems of the program and to demonstrate the need for disability reform.[60]

Attorney Advocates

While it was to be expected that the legal profession would play a crucial role in the conflict over CDR as claimants' legal representatives, they also were critical to the publicity efforts outside the courtroom. Disability attorneys were frequently sought after to testify at congressional hearings or quoted as experts in newspaper reports on the disability program. Their dual role as advocates inside and outside the judicial arena represented an important part of the overall litigation strategy to force bureaucratic compliance with judicial authority.

Not-for-profit public interest law organizations such as legal services offices and law school clinics bore the brunt of representing disability clients.[61] Additional legal support came from organizations such as the Eastern District Pro Bono Panel in New York in which twenty law firms and over three hundred lawyers volunteered their services to help beneficiaries struck from the disability rolls.[62] As terminations increased, private attorneys, accepting cases on a contingency fee basis, played an increasingly important role in the disability litigation.

Although a private disability bar had existed in the late 1970s, it took on new life with the onset of periodic review and the tremendous influx of termination clients. The increased interest in disability law was evident in newsletters, procedure manuals, and continuing legal education classes on representing disability clients in the administrative process and in federal court. The efforts of such groups as the Social Security Law Committee of the Chicago Bar Association, formed in 1981, served an educational function to "provide a forum to keep people abreast of what's happening and to share problems."[63]

The automatic withholding and payment of past-due benefits to attorneys by the Social Security Administration was "an attractive feature for lawyers" that was at least partially responsible for the private bar interest in disability cases.[64] Private disability attorneys appeared to be motivated by nonfinancial factors as well; many members of the private disability bar were former legal services attorneys who saw the termination struggle as a continuation of their legal services commitment.[65]

Attorneys also became an integral part of the publicity and lobbying efforts when the litigation activity was extended beyond the courtroom.[66] Aside from their courtroom litigation efforts, representatives of the private disability bar and legal services, especially the latter, were familiar figures on Capitol Hill. From 1982 to 1984 it was rare for a congressional hearing to be held without testimony or a written statement for the record from attorneys involved in disability litigation. Committee hearings in field locations around the country included testimony from the local Legal Services office such as the Tennessee Legal Services, the Memphis Area Legal Services, and Greater Boston Legal Services, the Atlanta Legal Aid Society, and the Legal Assistance Foundation of Chicago.

In addition to appearing before congressional committees, attorneys also played a role in bringing the disability crisis to public attention through interviews and press releases. Staff attorneys for the National Senior Citizens Law Center, the Manhattan Legal Aid Society, the Mental Health Law Center, and the Community Legal Services of Philadelphia were frequently quoted in the *New York Times* as experts on disability law. Many took advantage of this public forum to appeal for disability reform.

Advocacy Groups

The record number of disability terminations and the bureaucracy's refusal to obey judicial rulings on medical improvement also spawned a flurry of interest group activity that lobbied Congress for a disability reform measure. The large number of regional and national groups that arose in response to the disability crisis moved on several fronts to attract attention to the needs of the beneficiaries. According to staffmembers of the Social Security Subcommittee and the House Aging Committee, advocacy groups spent much time lobbying individual members of Congress during the critical years of 1982 and 1983.[67] Like the attorney advocates, representatives of these groups were also frequently quoted in the media on their positions against the continuing disability review process.

A number of organizations, the Alliance of Social Security Disability Recipients, the Ad Hoc Committee on Social Security Disability, the Consortium for Citizens with Developmental Disabilities, the Disability Rights Center, and the National Organization of Social Security Claimants' Representatives, sent representatives to testify at committee hearings on the disability program. Additionally, spokespersons for the Mental Health Law Project, the United Vietnam Veterans Association, the Save Our Security Coalition, and People United for Self Help frequently volunteered testimony at committee hearings. Finally, representatives of the American Psychiatric Association, the American Bar Association, and the National Association of Disability Examiners all testified before congressional committees and urged reform of the disability program.

REACTION FROM SSA

Responding to criticism from all directions—state agencies, disability attorneys, members of Congress, and health professionals—the Social Security Administration signaled a change in policy in the summer of 1983. Citing the need for reevaluation of standards, on June 7, 1983, Secretary Margaret Heckler ordered a moratorium on periodic reviews for about 135,000 mentally impaired beneficiaries with functional psychotic disorders.[68] The policy also increased the permanently disabled category to more than one million and exempted an additional 200,000 individuals from review.[69]

In discussing these changes, Secretary Heckler stated that she "had no idea that the sudden, three-year review of millions of cases we then mandated might result in hardships and heartbreaks for innocent and worthy disability recipients. . . . "[70] However, she was also quoted in the *New York Times* as saying that the Agency had "no reason to believe that there have been any unjust findings," adding that while the "process has been very insensitive," "the results have been fair."[71]

SSA Moratorium

It was almost another year before the Social Security Administration announced a further change in the disability review policy. On April 13, 1984, Secretary Heckler ordered a moratorium on the continuing disability review process affecting about 250,000 individuals with reviews scheduled through the end of September. She also announced that the Agency would restore or continue benefits to about 40,000 persons with terminations on administrative appeal. Acknowledging that the disability policy was "splintered and divided," Secretary Heckler attributed the problem in part to "nationwide 'confusion' because Federal courts have issued conflicting orders and many governors have refused to comply with rules issued by the Social Security Administration." The Secretary added that she awaited "new disability legislation" that "can be effectively implemented."[72] The Secretary's action did not affect individuals who had already filed federal court appeals; at the time of the moratorium, there were over 30,000 cases in the federal courts involving over 100,000 people.[73]

LEGISLATIVE DISABILITY REFORM

Although events were set in motion during the year, no legislative disability reform was enacted in 1983; it was a period described by Senator Jim Sasser of Tennessee as "a year of inaction."[74]

On February 15, 1983, Senators Cohen and Levin introduced a bill, S. 476,[75] proposing the adoption of a medical improvement standard for termination reviews. Later that year, Senator Levin indicated an intention to amend S. 476 to clarify the original bill and to require the Social Security Administration to consider the combined effect of an individual's impairments. In November Senators Cohen and Levin offered a bill with essentially the same provisions as S. 476 as an amendment to H.R. 3959,[76] a supplemental appropriations bill. The amendment was opposed by Senators Long and Dole because they wanted to place the bill before the Finance Committee first; it was tabled on a 49 to 46 Senate vote. The other major Senate impetus for change during that year came from Senator Heinz of the Special Committee on Aging who proposed a bill, S. 1144,[77] to reform the procedure for evaluation and termination of persons with mental impairments.

On the House side, Representatives James Shannon and Fortney Stark of California introduced H.R. 2987,[78] a bill that proposed a number of significant changes in the disability program, most importantly, a medical improvement standard for terminations. The Shannon and Stark bill became the basis for another proposed bill developed by the Social Security Subcommittee staff; the new bill was marked up by the Subcommittee during the summer of 1983. Upon completion of the markup, the bill was introduced by Representative Pickle as H.R. 3755[79] on August 3 and sent to the full Committee. In September, H.R. 3755 was marked up by the Committee on Ways and Means and reported favorably to the House.

The House Ways and Means Committee decided to include H.R. 3755 as part of a tax reform measure which was then favorably reported out of Committee. Because of controversy over the tax provisions of the bill, the House voted 214 to 204 not to consider it.

No further action was taken by Congress during 1983.

It was clear by the start of 1984 that the disability program was in crisis—a crisis that was largely attributable to the deteriorating relationship between the courts and the executive branch—and that Congress no longer had the luxury of slow deliberation of reform proposals. The Congressional Record shows that members of Congress were aware of their role as mediator between the executive and judicial branches. Stressing the need for urgency in finding a legislative solution, Representative Pickle reminded his colleagues that the federal courts were "being beseached [sic] and besieged." He pointed out that there were "over 40,000 disability review cases [in the federal courts] affecting nearly 200,000 former beneficiaries. These appeals," he warned, "represent the largest part of the Federal court caseload and are costing us millions of dollars in legal fees and court costs."[80]

H.R. 3755

Responding to pressure emanating from a variety of sources, the House passed a disability reform package early in 1984. The way was paved when the House Ways and Means Committee reported out a tax proposal on March 5. Two days later, the House Rules Committee agreed to consider this bill under a modified closed rule that allowed the disability provisions to be deleted from the more controversial tax bill. On March 14 the House Ways and Means Committee reported out an amended version of H.R. 3755 and on March 27, H.R. 3755 was overwhelmingly passed by the House in a 410 to 1 vote, with Representative Philip Crane of Illinois casting the only negative vote.

The future of disability reform was less certain in the Senate and a reform measure was not enacted there until the end of May. The year started with the Senate Finance Committee holding hearings on the tax reform bill that contained the disability reform provisions. One of the witnesses was Martha McSteen, acting commissioner of Social Security, testifying against the bill. Focusing on the medical improvement standard, she informed the committee that "the Administration strongly opposed section 901 of HR 4170 [the medical improvement standard] which would establish a separate standard of disability for those already on the rolls."[81] There was strong support for the bill from disability reform advocates, including Governor Bill Cinton of the National Governors Association.

While this bill was under consideration, Senators Cohen and Levin, always in the forefront of the battle over the disability termination issue, renewed their efforts to bring S. 476 to the Senate floor. They initially intended to offer it as an amendment to a boat safety bill but agreed not to do so when Senator Dole promised to bring it to the Finance Committee for markup and have it on the Senate floor by early May. On May 16, the Finance Committee finally approved an amended version of the Cohen and Levin bill and, on May 22, S. 476 was passed by the Senate (under the title of H.R. 3755) on 96 to 0 vote.

After lengthy negotiations throughout the summer, the Conference Committee reached informal agreement on September 14 and reported out their version of the bill on September 18. On September 19 the House voted 402 to 0, and the Senate 99 to 0, to approve the Conference report. The bill was signed into law by President Reagan on October 9, 1984.

The Judiciary as Catalyst

Congressional debate over passage of the 1984 Act demonstrated near unanimity on the need for legislation to restore order to "the chaos in the program which has produced the constitutional conflict between the executive branch and the States and Federal courts."[82] Moreover, the debate also showed that reform of the disability program claimed widespread bipartisan approval with support and opposition distributed throughout both parties. Two of the Senate reform leaders, Senators Cohen and Heinz, were Republicans while Democratic Senator Long ardently opposed loosening the disability criteria. Although some Republicans, such as Senator Dole and Representative Bill Archer of Texas hastened to remind their colleagues that periodic review was instigated by the Carter administration and a Democratic Congress, members on both sides of the aisle in the House and Senate blamed the Reagan administration for using the 1980 legislation to cut social welfare spending without regard for the human consequences.[83]

Members of both houses acknowledged that the social security disability litigation played a major role in spurring congressional reform of the continuing eligibility reviews. Massachusetts Representative Silvio Conte, for example, commented that the legislation "addresses the problems created by Federal court concerns over lack of a medical improvement standard. . . . "[84] Almost every member of Congress speaking on the proposed bill noted the impact of the judicial decrees on adjudication of disability standards in their own states and nationwide. They particularly pointed to the need to reassert congressional control over disability policy by ending the stalemate between the courts and the bureaucracy.

A few congressional leaders, namely, Senators Dole and Long, and Representative Barber Conable of New York, criticized the courts for acting like "regional legislatures" and for exceeding congressional intent in broadly construing social security legislation.[85] Representative Conable urged Congress to "simplify or expedite an adjudicative process which has in these past 4 years—with the assistance of the Federal courts—become chaotic and unmanageable."[86] Russell Long, an old foe of disability reform, attacked the courts for substituting their own judgment for the Secretary's criteria of disability.[87] Senator Dole accused the courts of complicity in causing the current crisis by "making all of this policy that far exceeds the intent of Congress"; a role, he added that "is not unusual for courts."[88]

During House debate over H.R. 3755, the prevailing view among members of Congress was support for the judiciary's insistence on a medical improvement standard in the termination decision. Representative Bruce Vento of Minnesota lauded the federal judges who acted "to convince the administration to come to its senses and to obey the law."[89] Representative James Jeffords of Vermont, member of the House Aging Committee, pointed out that the proposed legislation endorsed the judiciary's policy toward termination of benefits; "the medical improvement standard in H.R. 3755 will codify the standard that has been developed by the courts and advanced by the States."[90] Representative Roybal also noted that "nationwide, the courts have ordered SSA to use a medical improvement standard and . . . [that] to date the administration has yet to win a single decision which affirms their policy of failing to use a medical improvement standard."[91]

The debate shows quite clearly that litigation strategy successfully moved the issue from the courtroom to the floor of Congress and allowed Congress to justify legislative imposition of the medical improvement standard as compliance with judicial doctrine. By refusing to accept the agency's interpretation of standards for the continuing eligibility review process, the courts were serving the litigants' purpose of catalyzing legislative action. Several statements by members of Congress demonstrated their awareness of the relationship between the courts and the legislative process.

Speaking to the House on behalf of the Conference Committee Report, Representative Pickle stressed the need for congressional action by pointing to the disorder in disability policy caused by the litigation. "Already in over half the states the disability program is being run by Federal court order or by orders of the governor in opposition to the federal guidelines set forth by the Secretary of Health and Human Services; as a result," he said, "we have no uniform national disability program today."[92]

In the Senate, New York's Daniel Moynihan pointed out that "SSA's policies have provoked a rash of court cases involving individuals suing the Government to overturn their termination decisions. This situation, in the words of SSA, is a 'major crisis in litigation,' and has led to a huge volume of adverse court decisions." He added that "circuit courts throughout the nation have ruled against SSA and have ordered the evaluation of thousands of disabled individuals under a medical improvement standard."[93] Senator Robert Byrd of West Virginia underscored the importance of the courts' role by announcing that "over half of the states, either of their own accord . . . or upon orders from the courts, ceased enforcing the Federal review and termination requirements."[94] Speaking on behalf of S. 476, Senator Heinz of Pennsylvania informed his colleagues that the "courts in virtually every circuit have ruled that SSA must adhere to a medical improvement standard."[95] Senators Dave Durenberger of Minnesota and Bill Bradley of New Jersey similarly acknowledged the impact that the courts were having on their states by reversing thousands of social security disability decisions.[96]

Finally, in his House speech in support of the Conference agreement, Illinois Representative Dan Rostenkowski, chair of the House Ways and Means Committee, summed up the urgent need for reform by reminding the House that "hundreds of thousands of beneficiaries have lost their benefits, thousands of appeals are clogging our Federal court dockets, twenty-nine states have refused to follow the Administration's instructions for termination of benefits, and two hundred federal courts all over the country have threatened the Secretary of Health and Human Services with contempt of court citations for refusing to pay benefits when ordered."[97]

Committee Reports

When originally approved by each chamber, the House and Senate bills differed in a number of ways. Reflecting the views of Finance Committee members Long and Dole, the Senate measure demonstrated a greater concern with containment of costs and proposed a less radical reform of the program. "A major purpose of this legislation," according to the Finance Committee report accompanying the bill, "is to resolve the current controversy over the medical improvement issue, without unnecessarily increasing the cost of the disability program by broadly applying the new standard to thousands of individuals who had effectively accepted the finding of ineligibility and abandoned their claims by not following prescribed procedures for seeking review of the denial of benefits."[98]

In contrast, the House Ways and Means Committee report explained that "the overall purpose of the bill is, first, to clarify statutory guidelines for the determination process to insure that no beneficiary loses eligibility for benefits as a result of careless or arbitrary decision-making by the Federal Government [and]... to provide a more humane and understandable application and appeal process for... beneficiaries appealing termination of their benefits."[99]

The Burden of Proof

Although there was basic agreement between the Senate and the House over the adoption of a new continuing eligibility standard that included a medical improvement component, consensus rapidly eroded on the interpretation of the new standard. The Senate bill made it clear that the burden of proof remained with the beneficiary to demonstrate lack of improvement, that is, the claimant would have to show that the condition had worsened or stayed the same. The House bill placed the burden on the Secretary to show improvement and essentially adopted the prevailing judicial interpretation of a presumption of continuing eligibility for the current beneficiary. The Senate proposal also would have limited retroactive application of the new standard, and, additionally, would have sunsetted the medical improvement standard by December 31, 1987.

The Conference Committee essentially adopted the House version and specified that benefits could be terminated with substantial evidence of medical improvement in the impairment (or if one of the exceptions to medical improvement applied) and the individual was able to engage in substantial gainful activity.[100] The Committee opted for a middle ground between the House and Senate bills on the burden of proof issue; it removed the burden from the claimant but disallowed the presumption of continuing disability which court decisions had given to the beneficiary. The Conference report specified that decisions about continuing eligibility were to be made on the "basis of the weight of the evidence" and "without any preconception or presumption as to whether the individual is or is not disabled."[101] The three-year sunset provision was also deleted.

Retroactivity

One of the thorniest differences of opinion between the House and Senate concerned the application of the new standard to beneficiaries with claims currently under review—administrative or judicial—as well as to beneficiaries who had been terminated and had not complied with the appeal requirements. Decisions on limiting retroactivity were vitally important because of the thousands of appeals pending against the Agency and the thousands of beneficiaries who had been terminated under the old standard who would seek redetermination under the new standard. Moreover, at the time of Finance Committee deliberation, there were over 30 class action or putative class action suits pending in the federal courts.[102] Without some measure of retroactivity, a huge number of disability beneficiaries would be eclipsed from the benefits of the reform legislation.

The House-endorsed measure would have simply provided for adjudication of continuing eligibility under the medical improvement standard for all disability determinations pending in administrative or judicial review on the date of enactment of the law. The Senate version of the bill sought to limit the judicial role in disability adjudications by requiring the courts to remand pending cases to the Secretary for adjudication. It specified that the new standard would be applicable to upcoming continuing eligibility determinations and to individuals with claims on administrative appeal, but not for cases on appeal to the federal courts. The bill evidenced particular concern about the large numbers of individuals nationwide with current claims for judicial review as part of class action suits.[103]

The Finance Committee report warned against extending the deadline for filing claims because "a future certification of one or more class actions— or even a nationwide class action might give the Committee decision much broader retrospective effect (and for higher cost) than the Committee intends."[104]

The Conference agreement reconciled these two views by ordering the application of the medical improvement standard to all future continuing eligibility determinations and to all cases pending in administrative review on or after enactment. The Conference Committee basically settled on the Senate treatment of litigants under judicial review but extended the permissible date for filing claims in federal court from May 16 to September 19, the date of congressional approval of the Conference report.

Individual litigants and *named* members (those identified in the pleadings as class representatives) of class action suits pending as of September 19 would be remanded by the courts to the Secretary for review under the new standard. Individuals with requests for judicial review made during the period beginning March 15, 1984 and ending 60 days after enactment were also remanded to the Secretary for adjudication under the medical improvement standard. *Unnamed* plaintiffs in class action suits certified before September 19 would be remanded to the Secretary for notification of their right to request administrative review within four months. The report stipulated that no class action suits alleging an improper termination of benefits could be certified by the courts after the September 19 deadline.[105]

Unsettled Issues

The new law also touched upon some other sources of conflict between the courts and SSA but failed to provide firm guidelines for resolution of a number of them, most notably, the battle over nonacquiescence. It permanently established the payment-through-appeal for SSI beneficiaries and continued this provision for SSDI claimants for termination decisions through December 1987 with benefit payments allowed through June 1988.

The bill also set forth a temporary standard for evaluating pain and a commission was ordered to complete a study on the role of pain in disability determinations by December 31, 1985. A new version of the sequential evaluation was created whereby the Agency would consider the combined effects of impairments even if no single one would by itself be considered severe. The Secretary was ordered to publish a revised Listing of Mental Impairments within four months and a moratorium on mental impairment reviews was ordered until new criteria for evaluating mental impairments were established. Addressing itself to the conflict between the states and SSA, the law also required the Secretary to take over disability determinations within six months after a finding that states were not in compliance with federal law.

SSA NONACQUIESCENCE IS UNRESOLVED

Another difference of opinion between the Senate and the House concerned their attitudes toward the issue that precipitated the constitutional crisis and the standoff between the courts and the Agency—specifically, the legitimacy of SSA nonacquiescence. The Committee reports accompanying the bill reflected the differing perspectives of each chamber on the role of judicial supremacy over Agency action.

The House Committee report announced that one of the "overall" purposes of the legislation was "to standardize the Social Security Administration's policy-making procedures through the notice and comment procedures of the Administrative Procedures Act, and to make those procedures conform with the standard practices of Federal law, through acquiescence in Federal Court of Appeals rulings."[106] The Senate Committee report stressed that the adoption of the medical improvement standard was necessitated because "in recent months, due both to independent actions by States that are in violation of Federal law and guidelines *and to Court actions*, the social security disability insurance program is no longer being administered in a nationally uniform manner, consistent with the goals of the Federal program" (emphasis added).[107]

The differing approaches to nonacquiescence were mirrored in the two versions of the Reform bill. Section 302 of the House bill would have ordered the Secretary either to appeal to the Supreme Court if it disagreed with an appellate court's interpretation of the law or to acquiesce in the decision. If the Supreme Court denied review, acquiescence would be required until the Court ruled on the issue in another case. Although stressing that it should not be interpreted as sanctioning the practice of nonacquiescence, Section 6 of the Senate bill would have merely required the Social Security Administration to publish a statement in the Federal Register indicating its intention to acquiesce or not to acquiesce in a particular circuit court ruling.

The Conference Committee report deleted both versions. It expressed concern about its possible unconstitutionality and "urge[d] that a policy of nonacquiescence be followed only in situations where the Administration has initiated or has the reasonable expectation and intention of initiating the steps necessary to receive a review of the issue by the Supreme Court." Citing the need "to achieve consistent uniform administration of the program" and the negative consequences of having "major differences in statutory interpretation between the Secretary and the courts remain unresolved for a protracted period of time," the Conference Committee strongly urged the Secretary to seek Supreme Court review or a legislative remedy from Congress. Stressing the need to defer to congressional judgment in this area, the committee felt that the legislation would play a major role in resolving possible ambiguities in statutory language and congressional intent.[108]

A New Nonacquiescence Policy

Notwithstanding the Conference Committee's optimism, the legislation did not provide guidelines for avoiding future disputes between the executive and judicial branches of government. Responding in part to the concern voiced by the committee, however, on June 3, 1985, the Secretary of Health and Human Services announced a change in SSA's nonacquiescence policy. She reported that the Social Security Administration would begin to follow precedent in circuit court rulings within the same circuit. "Our new approach," Secretary Heckler stated, "will reconcile to the maximum extent possible, the Congressional requirement for uniform standards and the need to abide by judicial precedents with which we disagree."[109]

In testimony before the House Judiciary Committee, Martha McSteen further explicated the new policy. She promised that ALJs and the Appeals Council "will apply circuit court decisions, following special Social Security Rulings, in adjudicating claims in the circuit." She explained that where conflict arose between the courts and SSA policy where the latter would lead to a denial of benefits, "the ALJ will issue a recommended decision favorable to the claimant." The Appeals Council will review the ALJ's decision and, according to McSteen, "in most cases will adopt the ALJ recommended decision and the claim will be allowed." If, in the opinion of the Appeals Council, an issue should be relitigated within the circuit, the Council "will draft an unfavorable decision." Only after review by the Department of Justice and a special Policy Review Committee will HHS refuse to follow circuit precedent; in those circumstances, promised McSteen, the Agency is prepared to litigate the issue "all the way to the Supreme Court, if necessary."[110]

The new policy did not, however, include orders to the state agencies to apply circuit court decisions in their determinations of eligibility. *Plus ça change, plus c'est la même chose.* The failure to acknowledge the judicial rule of law at the state agency level obviously disturbed Representative Barney Frank when it was explained to him at a Judiciary Subcommittee hearing. Reacting to testimony from deputy assistant attorney general Carolyn Kuhl, Representative Frank pointed out to her that "they [SSA] are still going to nonacquiesce within the circuit at the determination and redetermination level. You're [the Department of Justice] off the hook, but the disabled person is not. No assistant U.S. attorney will get beat up by a judge for defending a nonacquiescence policy, but a disabled person would still be denied."[111]

Disability attorneys, city and state officials, and other members of Congress also expressed concern about the Agency's new acquiescence posture. In language reminiscent of the height of the termination crisis, attorneys and other disability advocates pointed out that very little had changed. Attorney Eileen Sweeney identified the problem with a reminder that only "persistent people who appeal may get the benefit of Circuit Court precedents" while those "who do not appeal will not."[112] "In my opinion, the situation remains disastrous," Robert Abrams, attorney general of New York State, said. "Under the new policy on nonacquiescence, only the few claimants who possess the resources, physical stamina and time to pursue an appeal may benefit from the relief afforded by judicial order."[113] Representative James Jones, Democrat from Oklahoma, new chair of the Social Security Subcommittee, characterized the new policy as "180 degrees opposite of what Congress intended."[114] Thus, while the debate over nonacquiescence was temporarily shelved, the issue of the supremacy of the rule of law over SSA's procedural autonomy has not been resolved; it seems quite likely that before too long, the controversy will resurface and Congress will be forced to confront it again.

POST-ACT REGULATIONS

The 1984 Act also instructed the Secretary to prescribe regulations establishing standards for continuing review of eligibility for social security disability benefits within six months, specifying that until such regulations were promulgated, an individual may not be subjected to periodic review more than once. On April 30, 1985, SSA issued a set of proposed rules for implementation of Section 2 of the Disability Reform Act.[115]

Noting the concern of the Conference Committee that SSA find an appropriate way to deal with the presumption of continuing eligibility, the proposed regulations announced that decisions on continuing eligibility "will be made on a neutral basis without any initial inference as to the presence or absence of disability" merely because of an earlier finding of disability.[116]

The major thrust of the regulations was to create a new sequential evaluation to judge whether the individual remained legally disabled. Under the new evaluation, SSA adjudicators would essentially follow the steps utilized in the previous one through the Listings inquiry. The question of medical improvement, defined as an increase in functional ability to perform basic work activity, would not arise until the end of the review process. Consistent with the Agency's view that the definition of disability must be legal rather than medical, the new standard for continuing eligibility would be measured by an increased ability to do work rather than by an improvement in a medical condition.[117]

These proposed regulations were published amidst controversy over whether they were consistent with the intent of Congress. There was consternation at the way in which SSA intended to apply the medical improvement standard because it appeared contrary to the legislative intent exhibited in the congressional debate over the Reform Act.

Analysis of the legislative history of the Reform Act shows that Senator Levin had indicated in the floor debate over the bill that his intent had been to apply the medical improvement test immediately after ascertaining that the beneficiary was not currently working and before the evaluation proceeded to the second step. He was on record as saying that "if the Secretary finds after looking at all the available acquired evidence that the beneficiary has in fact improved . . . then the Secretary must determine if the individual is able to perform substantial gainful activity using the sequential evaluation process."[118] Similarly, the Senate Finance Committee report had stated that "if any of these factors [improvement or an exception] are met, the Secretary would then determine whether the individual can perform substantial gainful activity."[119]

Final rules were published in the Federal Register on December 6, 1985. SSA noted that it had received comments from the public, including members of Congress, expressing concern about the sequential evaluation. The comments warned that unless medical improvement was the first step, "a negative mind set" would develop and the adjudicator will be "compelled" to reach a finding that medical improvement had occurred. Partially succumbing to these arguments, SSA agreed to advance the medical improvement query to the third step in the sequential evaluation. The Agency justified its refusal to accede to suggestions that the process begin with an appraisal of medical improvement by arguing that it was beneficial to settle the current work and Listings questions early in the adjudication process. It denied that any "mind set" would be created by placing these two steps before the improvement step in the evaluation.

Comments on the proposed regulations also indicated a fear that the definition of disability, focusing on the increase in functional capacity, would allow benefits to be terminated following an "arbitrary finding of medical improvement based on ascribed 'functional' change in the face of unchanged medical findings." In response to this concern, the Social Security Administration announced that the new test for improvement would be based on a "decrease in severity [of the impairment] as shown by symptoms, signs and laboratory findings." Unless changes occurred, the regulations stated, there would be no finding of medical improvement. And if the condition were changed, "there must be a finding that the change is related to the ability to work."[120]

Following the announcement of the new regulations, disability attorneys, such as Eileen Sweeney and Jonathan Stein, long involved in the termination crisis, expressed concern over the resumption of continuing eligibility reviews and predicted that the problems were far from resolved.[121] At this time it is still too early to know whether, and to what extent, these fears are warranted.

NOTES

1. 130 Cong. Rec. S11452 (Sept. 19, 1984) (statement of Sen. Dole).

2. *Social Security Disability Reviews: A Costly Constitutional Crisis: Hearing before the House Select Committee on Aging*, 98th Cong., 2d Sess. (1984), Appendix (hereafter *A Costly Constitutional Crisis*).

3. *Social Security Disability Program Reform: Hearings before the Senate Committee on the Budget*, 98th Cong., 2d Sess. (1984), p. 20 (hereafter *Disability Program Reform*).

4. Interview with Susan Collins, majority staff director, Subcommittee on Oversight of Government Management of the Senate Committee on Governmental Affairs, August 28, 1986.

5. Interview with Patricia Dilley, professional assistant, Subcommittee on Social Security of the House Committee on Ways and Means, May 8, 1986.

6. Interview with Robert Lehrer, deputy director, Legal Assistance Foundation of Chicago, September 10, 1986.

7. Interview with Eileen Sweeney, staff attorney, National Senior Citizens Law Center, May 8, 1986.

8. H.R. 5700, 97th Cong., 2d Sess. (1982). This bill would have provided benefits through the reconsideration level, established a Social Security court, closed the record after reconsideration to prohibit further introduction of evidence, clarified the Agency's policy toward evaluation of pain, and established uniform standards by applying Social Security Rulings and the POMS at all levels of adjudication.

9. Katherine Collins and Anne Erfle, "Social Security Disability Benefits Reform Act of 1984: Legislative History and Summary of Provisions," *Social Security Bulletin* 48 (April 1985), p. 15.

10. During markup by the full committee, Representative Pickle introduced another disability bill, also entitled the Disability Amendments of

1982, containing essentially the same provisions as H.R. 5700. The new bill was H.R. 6181, 97th Cong., 2d Sess. (1982). Pickle requested the committee to delay consideration of the new bill until further agreement among members could be reached.

11. S. 2725, 97th Cong., 2d Sess. (1982).

12. S. 2730, 97th Cong., 2d Sess. (1982).

13. *Staff Data and Materials Related to the Social Security Disability Insurance Program.* Senate Committee on Finance, 97th Cong., 2d Sess. (Comm. Print 1982), p. 119 (hereafter *Materials Related to the Disability Program*).

14. S. 2674, 97th Cong., 2d Sess. (1982).

15. Three other bills introduced in the Ninety-Seventh Congress (S. 2731, S. 2739, and S. 2776) were also designed to ease the disability crisis and contained essentially the same provisions as the Levin bill, S. 2674.

16. S. 2942, 97th Cong., 2d Sess. (1982).

17. The original sunset date of July 1, 1983 was extended in committee to September 30, 1983. At the beginning of October 1983, when it became apparent that comprehensive legislation was not forthcoming, Congress extended the payment provision. In an amendment to H.R. 4101, a supplemental unemployment compensation bill, Congress authorized a 67-day extension of the September 30 deadline until December 7, 1983. H.R. 4101 (Public Law 98–11) was passed by the Senate and House on October 6, 1983 and signed into law by President Reagan on October 11, 1983.

18. H.R. 7093, 97th Cong. 2d Sess. (1982). On September 20, 1982, the House had passed H.R. 7093, a bill to allow a reduction on taxes on certain investment income earned from sources within the Virgin Islands.

19. The Virgin Islands Source Income—Social Security Disability Benefit Apeals Act, Pub. L. No. 97–455, 96 Stat. 2497 (1983).

20. 128 Cong. Rec. H10673 (Dec. 21, 1982) (statement of Rep. Archer).

21. 128 Cong. Rec. S13856 (Dec. 3, 1982) (statement of Sen. Cohen).

22. 128 Cong. Rec. S13851 (Dec. 3, 1982) (statement of Sen. Dole).

23. See S. Rep. No. 648, 97th Cong., 2d Sess. (1982).

24. 128 Cong. Rec. H10674 (Dec. 21, 1982) (statement of Rep. Archer).

25. 128 Cong. Rec. S13851–52 (Dec. 3, 1982) (statement of Sen. Dole).

26. Unprinted Amendment 1413 provided in relevant part:

Nothing in the preceding sentence shall be considered to preclude the Secretary from finding an individual to be ineligible on the basis that such individual is not disabled within the meaning of the term disability for purposes of initial determinations under this title even if such individual's medical condition has not improved or otherwise changed since any prior determination of his eligibility. 128 Cong. Rec. S13854 (Dec. 3, 1982).

27. 128 Cong. Rec. S13857 (Dec. 3, 1982) (statement of Sen. Cohen).

28. 128 Cong. Rec. S13859 (Dec. 3, 1982) (statement of Sen. Dole).

29. 128 Cong. Rec. S13854 (Dec. 3, 1982) (statement of Sen. Metzenbaum).

30. See *New York Times*, September 12, 1983, pp. 1, B13.

31. *Social Security Disability Reviews: A Federally Created State Problem: Hearing before the House Select Committee on Aging*, 98th Cong., 1st Sess., (1983), p. 61 (statement by Gov. Clinton) (herafter *A Federally Created Problem*).

32. Ibid., p. 63.

33. *New York Times*, February 8, 1982, p. B2.

34. Bob Wyrick and Patrick Owens, "The Disability Nightmare," Special Reprint, *Newsday*, 21 March 1983, p. R6. See also William Johnson, "Disability, Income Support, and Social Insurance," in Edward Berkowitz, ed., *Disability Policies and Government Programs* (New York: Praeger, 1979), p. 120.

35. In Suffolk County, New York, for example, there was a three-fold increase in expenditures budgeted for home relief from 1980 to 1983. $8.6 million was budgeted for home relief in fiscal 1980 and $21.5 million for fiscal year 1983. See Wyrick and Owens, "The Disability Nightmare," p. R5.

36. *New York Times*, August 7, 1983, p. 29.

37. Jack Weinstein, "Equality and the Law: Social Security Disability Cases in the Federal Courts," *Syracuse Law Review* 35 (1985), p. 936.

38. Interview with Lowell Arye, research assistant, Subcommittee on Retirement Income and Employment of the House Select Committee on Aging, August 28, 1986; see also *Oversight of Social Security Disability Benefits Terminations: Hearing before the Subcommittee on Oversight of Government Management of the Senate Committee on Governmental Affairs*, 97th Cong., 2d Sess. (1982), pp. 120–22 (statement by Herbert Brown, administrator of the Tennessee DDS) (hereafter *Oversight of Disability Terminations*).

39. *Oversight of Disability Terminations*, p. 121 (statement by Herbert Brown).

40. Interview with Lowell Arye, August 28, 1986.

41. Interview with Allen Johnston, staff director, Subcommittee on Retirement Income and Employment of the House Select Committee on Aging, May 8, 1986.

42. *New York Times*, September 12, 1983, p. B13.

43. *New York Times*, August 26, 1984, p. 12.

44. Interview with Allen Johnston, May 8, 1986.

45. Interview with Lowell Arye, August 28, 1986.

46. Several state chief executives wrote back to the Secretary reminding her of the problems caused by the review process and pointed to the divergence between judicial rulings and SSA regulations on terminations. The governors of Illinois and Massachusetts, calling attention to the court action in their states, requested consideration as states under court order so that they could legally avoid processing CDRs.

47. *A Costly Constitutional Crisis*, p. 84.

48. Ibid.

49. Ibid., p. 85.

50. Interview with Patricia Dilley, May 8, 1986.

51. *Oversight of Disability Terminations*, p. 231 (statement of Sen. Riegle).

52. Fourteen committee hearings were held in Washington, D.C. and thirteen were conducted in field locations around the country.

53. See examples of media coverage in *Social Security Disability Reviews: A Federally Created State Problem: Hearing before the House Select Committee on Aging*, 98th Cong., 1st Sess. (1983) (hereafter *A Federally Created Problem*); and *Social Security Disability Insurance Program: Cessations and Denials: Hearing before the House Select Committee on Aging*, 97th Cong., 2d Sess. (1982) (hereafter *Cessations and Denials*).

54. *New York Times*, June 20, 1983, p. C14.

55. *New York Times*, May 29, 1983, p. 25.

56. *A Federally Created State Problem*, p. 19 (statement of Master Sergeant Roy Benavidez, United States Army).

57. The mentally impaired were the most vulnerable and seemingly the largest single target of the Agency's eligibility review policy. Because of SSA's policy of presuming individuals with mental disability capable of work if they did not meet the Listings, this group constituted 11 percent of the disability rolls and yet were 27 percent of the terminated population. *Social Security Disability Reviews: The Human Costs: Hearing before the Senate Special Committee on Aging*. 98th Cong., 2d Sess. (1984), p. 78 (hereafter *The Human Costs*); see also *Social Security Disability Benefits Terminations: New York: Hearing before the Subcommittee on Retirement Income and Employment of the House Select Committee on Aging*. 97th Cong., 2d Sess. (1982) (hereafter *Disability Terminations: New York*). The New York hearing focused on the problems of terminating benefits for the mentally disabled.

58. *New York Times*, May 19, 1982, p. B5.

59. *New York Times*, May 23, 1983, p. 18.

60. Interview with Patricia Dilley, May 8, 1986.

61. Interview with Robert Lehrer, September 10, 1986.

62. Weinstein, "Equality and the Law," pp. 935–36.

63. Interview with Barbara Samuels, disability attorney, September 19, 1986.

64. Interview with Deborah Spector, disability attorney, September 24, 1986. The statute and regulations allow the Secretary of HHS to compensate attorneys for services performed at the administrative level by fixing a "reasonable fee" and certifying the payment out of past-due benefits up to a maximum of 25 percent of such benefits. When a client is awarded back benefits by a court, a "reasonable fee" for services not to exceed 25 percent of past-due benefits may be allowed by the court and the Secretary may also certify the payment to the attorney out of these benefits. 42 U.S.C. §406(a,b) (1984).

The financial benefits offered by the automatic withholding provision were offset to some extent by the problems caused by cash flow limitations and subjecting payment of their fees "to fluctuations in government work flow" as well as problems caused by the requirement of government approval of the fee.

65. Interview with Henry Rose, director, Loyola University Community Law Center, September 12, 1986. Eileen Sweeney also felt that legal services

background was an important motivation for many members of the private bar.

66. In broadening the scope of their involvement, attorneys were fulfilling a role that had been urged upon them by Stuart Scheingold; see Stuart Scheingold, *The Politics of Rights* (New Haven: Yale University Press, 1974).

67. Interview with Patricia Dilley, May 8, 1986; Interview with Lowell Arye, August 28, 1986.

68. Collins and Erfle, "Disability Benefits Reform Act," p. 21.

69. This change meant that 37 percent of the total number of workers on the disability rolls were now considered permanently disabled and exempt from review. Secretary Heckler also announced that SSA was abandoning the "profile" method of selecting disability recipients for review and indicated that she was proposing legislation to remove SSA's obligation to review two-thirds of all state allowances that had been mandated in the 1980 Act.

70. Department of Health and Human Services News Release, reprinted in *A Federally Created Problem*, pp. 518–34.

71. *New York Times*, June 8, 1983, p. 17.

72. *New York Times*, April 14, 1984, pp. 11–12.

73. *New York Times*, April 14, 1984, p. 12.

74. *Disability Program Reform*, p. 5 (statement of Sen. Sasser).

75. S. 476, 98th Cong., 1st Sess. (1983).

76. H.R. 3959, 98th Cong., 1st Sess. (1983).

77. S. 1144, 98th Cong., 1st Sess. (1983). In June 1983 the Senate approved a House supplemental appropriations bill, H.R. 3069, which included a floor amendment with essentially the same provisions as S. 1144. On July 20, 1983, the Heinz provisions were dropped during conference at the request of Social Security Subcommittee chair Jake Pickle who argued against bypassing the authority of the Ways and Means Committee. See Collins and Erfle, "Disability Benefits Reform Act," for history of legislative proposals for disability reform from 1981 to 1984.

78. H.R. 2987, 98th Cong., 1st Sess. (1983).

79. H.R. 3755, 98th Cong., 1st Sess. (1983); this bill was enacted as the Social Security Disability Benefits Reform Act of 1984, Pub. L. No. 98–460, 98 Stat. 1794 (1984).

80. 130 Cong. Rec. H9836 (Sept. 19, 1984) (statement of Rep. Pickle).

81. *Social Security Disability Insurance Program: Hearing before the Senate Committee on Finance*, 98th Cong., 2d Sess. (1984), p. 100 (statement of Martha McSteen, acting commissioner, Social Security Administration) (hereafter *Social Security Disability Program Hearing*); the Tax Reform Act was H.R. 4170, 98th Cong., 1st Sess. (1983).

82. 130 Cong. Rec. H9837 (Sept. 19, 1984) (statement of Rep. Roybal).

83. 130 Cong. Rec. S6207 (May 22, 1984) (statement of Sen. Dole); 130 Cong. Rec. H1973 (Mar. 27, 1984) (statement of Rep. Archer). For the contrary position see, for example, 130 Cong. Rec. H1960 (Mar. 27, 1984) (statement of Rep. Perkins); 130 Cong. Rec. H1966 (Mar. 27, 1984) (statement of Rep. Jenkins); 130 Cong. Rec. H1968 (Mar. 27, 1984) (statement of Rep. Oaker); 130 Cong. Rec. H1971 (Mar. 27, 1984) (statement of Rep. Fowler); 130 Cong. Rec. H1975 (statement of Rep. Dyson) (Mar. 27, 1984).

See also 130 Cong. Rec. S6223 (May 22, 1984) (statement of Sen. Cranston); 130 Cong. Rec. S6225 (May 22, 1984) (statement of Sen. Pell).

84. 130 Cong. Rec. H1963 (Mar. 27, 1984) (statement of Rep. Conte).

85. 130 Cong. Rec. S6211 (May 22, 1984) (statement of Sen. Long).

86. 130 Cong. Rec. H9834 (Sept. 19, 1984) (statement of Rep. Conable).

87. 130 Cong. Rec. S11457–8 (Sept. 19, 1984) (statement of Sen. Long).

88. 130 Cong. Rec. S6209 (May 22, 1984) (statement of Sen. Dole).

89. 130 Cong. Rec. H1962 (Mar. 27, 1984) (statement of Rep. Vento).

90. 130 Cong. Rec. H1978 (Mar. 27, 1984) (statement of Rep. Jeffords).

91. 130 Cong. Rec. H1964 (Mar. 27, 1984) (statement of Rep. Roybal).

92. 130 Cong. Rec. H9836 (Sept. 19, 1984) (statement of Rep. Pickle).

93. 130 Cong. Rec. S11463 (Sept. 19, 1984) (statement of Sen. Moynihan).

94. 130 Cong. Rec. S11467 (Sept. 19, 1984) (statement of Sen. Byrd).

95. 130 Cong. Rec. S6215 (May 22, 1984) (statement of Sen. Heinz).

96. 130 Cong. Rec. S6226 (May 22, 1984) (statement of Sen. Durenberger); 130 Cong. Rec. S6223 (May 22, 1984) (statement of Sen. Bradley).

97. 130 Cong. Rec. H9834 (Sept. 19, 1984) (statement of Rep. Rostenkowski).

98. S. Rep. No. 466, 98th Cong., 2d Sess. 14 (1984).

99. H. Rep. No. 618, 98th Cong., 2d Sess. 2 (1984).

100. Section 2 of the Social Security Disability Benefits Reform Act of 1984 specified the following list of exceptions to medical improvement: a finding of no disability may be based upon that advances in medical or vocational technology have rendered the impairment less disabling and the individual is therefore able to engage in substantial gainful activity; new diagnostic techniques demonstrating that the condition is not as disabling as was originally thought to be, or a finding that the prior determination of disability was erroneous. 42 U.S.C. §423 (5)(A) (1984).

101. H. Rep. No. 1039, 98th Cong., 2d Sess. 26 (1984).

102. S. Rep. No. 466, 98th Cong., 2d Sess. 14 (1984).

103. The Senate bill proposed that the claims of individual litigants and *named* plaintiffs in class action suits with cases properly pending in the courts by May 16 (the date of Committee approval) would be taken out of the courts and remanded to the Secretary for review under the new standard. (Individuals who properly requested judicial review of their denials from March 15, 1984 to 60 days after enactment of the law would also be remanded to the Secretary for consideration under the new standard). *Unnamed* plaintiffs in class actions with suits certified before May 16 would be remanded to the Secretary for notification of their right to request a review of their claim within two months. By not properly requesting review, claimants waived their right to seek further administrative or judicial review of the Secretary's decision. The new standard would not apply to any cases where final administrative decisions had been made prior to May 16, 1984 and judicial review had not been properly requested.

104. S. Rep. No. 466, 98th Cong., 2d Sess. 13 (1984).

105. See *Kuehner v. Heckler*, 778 F.2d 152 (3d Cir. 1985); *Polaski v.*

Heckler, 751 F.2d 943 (8th Cir. 1984) for explanations of how the Act applies to class action suits.

106. H. Rep. No. 618, 98th Cong., 2d Sess. 2 (1984).

107. S. Rep. No. 466, 98th Cong., 2d Sess. 9 (1984).

108. H. Rep. No. 1039, 98th Cong., 2d Sess. 37 (1984).

109. *New York Times*, June 4, 1985, p. 1.

110. *Judicial Review of Agency Action: HHS Policy of Nonacquiescence: Hearing before the Subcommittee on Administrative Law and Governmental Relations of the House Committee on the Judiciary*, 99th Cong., 1st Sess. (1985), p. 8 (statement of Martha McSteen) (hereafter *Judicial Review of Agency Action*).

111. *Judicial Review of Agency Action*, p. 15 (statement of Rep. Frank).

112. *New York Times*, June 4, 1985, p. 20.

113. *New York Times*, June 9, 1985, p. 31.

114. Ibid.

115. 50 Fed. Reg. 18432 (1985).

116. 50 Fed. Reg. 18434 (1985).

117. See 50 Fed. Reg. 18436–37 (1985). The proposed sequential evaluation would have determined the following: first, if the individual were presently engaging in substantial gainful activity; second, if the individual currently has a severe impairment or combination of impairments; third, if the impairment meets or equals the severity of impairments in the Listings; fourth, if the impairment does not meet or equal the Listings, a comparison of the original residual functional capacity to the current residual functional capacity will be made. If the latter shows medical improvement, that is, an increase in the individual's functional ability to perform basic work activities, or one of the exceptions to medical improvement applies, there will be a finding of noneligibility. Thus, in the proposed regulations, medical improvement would be the last step in the continuing eligibility judgment.

118. 130 Cong. Rec. S6230 (May 22, 1984) (statement of Sen. Levin).

119. S. Rep. No. 466, 98th Cong., 2d Sess. 8 (1984).

120. 50 Fed. Reg. 50121–22 (1985).

121. *New York Times*, December 6, 1985, p. 1. Attorneys that I interviewed also expressed concern about a new round of reviews and were not convinced that the disability crisis had been put to rest.

9

Summing Up

The social security disability insurance program has always reflected the inherent contradictions in the goals of its planners. In shaping the contours of disability protection, the disability policymakers never quite resolved the tension among the social insurance, public aid, and market insurance elements in the program. Underlying the legal arguments over disability entitlement was a deep-seated conflict among policymakers over the role of the disability program in the American social welfare scheme.

Disability insurance was inaugurated during the 1950s and, despite the initial reluctance by some, the program enjoyed steady growth for the next two decades. As the program incorporated more beneficiaries and increased the value of a disability claim, it assumed a larger role in the coverage provided by the Social Security Act. Beginning around 1975, however, there appeared to be a reaction to the program's expansiveness manifested by a harsher climate of adjudication for disability claimants. The impetus for this change came in part from the executive branch and in part from Congress.

There were a number of indicators of the program's narrowing approach to disability protection and the shift in direction created hard times for hopeful disability claimants as the Social Security Administration became increasingly restrictive in awarding benefits. The Agency's attempt to restrain growth in the program was largely focused on potential beneficiaries until 1981 when it established a new policy of reviewing the eligibility of current beneficiaries every three years. The effect on beneficiaries was especially dramatic because the Agency had also instituted a more rigorous method of determining whether individuals were no longer disabled. The reviews, mandated by Congress in the 1980 Amendments, resulted in the termination of benefits to an unprecedented number of disability recipients.

The targets of the reviews, beneficiaries who had been led to believe they were virtually guaranteed benefits for life, felt betrayed as they became aware that they were being subjected to new rules, or at least new interpretations of the old rules. The beneficiaries demanded that the Social Security Administration prove they recovered from their disabilities before determining that they were no longer entitled to benefits.

In the furor that arose over the continuing eligibility reviews and termination of benefits, disability beneficiaries reached out and sought aid from the federal courts, the executive branch, and the legislature in an effort to force a return to the previous rules of the game for cessation of benefits.

Following the pattern established by their expansive interpretation of private disability insurance plans, the courts reacted favorably to requests by terminated beneficiaries to reinstate their benefits. Urged by disability beneficiaries to become active participants in the disability policymaking process, the courts reviewed administrative determinations of disability entitlement and, by doing so, had a major impact on social security disability policy.

The litigation precipitated by social security continuing eligibility reviews created the atmosphere for persuading other policymakers to join on the side of the disability beneficiaries. As beneficiaries sought judicial imposition of a medical improvement standard in eligibility reviews, the federal courts became the focal point for the process of seeking change in social security disability policy.

In advancing the interests of the disability claimants through judicial rulings against Agency determinations that beneficiaries were no longer disabled, the federal courts provided a counterforce to the budgetary restraints that appeared to be motivating the social security bureaucracy. The conflict over judicial policymaking in the disability program escalated as the courts were increasingly asked to rule in favor of disability beneficiaries. Against this backdrop of growing political turmoil, the courts were urged by others to leave disability policymaking to the legislature and bureaucracy.

The Courts as Catalyst

The Social Security Administration's policy of continuing eligibility review offered an opportunity to explore the catalytic effect of the federal courts on disability policymaking by examining the actions and reactions of the actors in this policymaking process. By acting as a catalyst to bring about legislative intervention, the courts were able to play a crucial role in instigating changes in bureaucratic policies.

Judicial impact studies typically are concerned with the end results of the judicial decree, that is, bureaucratic compliance or implementation. They do not deal with the process by which the judicial ruling leads to a shift in bureaucratic or legislative policy nor with interactions among policymakers. This analysis of the social security litigation examined the way in which the three branches formulated their own disability policy and showed *how* the federal courts prompted reactions by the decisionmakers at the legislative and executive levels.

The termination cases showed that structural factors identified in previous studies as favorable to judicial policymaking were present in this litigation as well. While the norms of statutory interpretation ordinarily demand deference to legislative intent, there is a greater propensity for judicial statutory policymaking when the legislature fails to provide guidance for the courts by signaling its intentions unambiguously. Deference to the statutory language and the intent of the legislature under these circumstances is difficult. In the case of the continuing disability review process, there were varying and equally plausible interpretations of the legislature's intentions. And, as the Social Security Administration's cessation policy assumed political overtones, discerning the meaning of the Act and legislative intent became even more problematic.

The disability litigants demonstrated the power of litigation to affect changes in public policy, yet, at the same time, they illustrated its fragility as a weapon against bureaucratic power. The social security disability litigants used lawsuits to generate publicity and bring the plight of disability beneficiaries to public awareness. In so doing, they eventually succeeded in catalyzing the legislature into action and overcoming bureaucratic resistance. The plaintiffs thus prevailed over the Agency by ultimately persuading Congress to change the standard for terminating benefits.

Litigation Strategy

The lawsuits helped to make the issue salient to Congress and the rest of the nation and to legitimize the demands of the terminated beneficiaries. Media attention was focused on the disability appeals in the federal courts as well as on the extrajudicial litigation strategy. Newspapers accounts and television documentaries highlighted the effects of the termination of benefits on persons plagued by physical and mental illness yet described by the Agency as no longer disabled. By attracting public attention, the litigants were able to achieve their goals of overturning their termination decisions and changing the standards for the periodic review process. Whether Congress would have been equally responsive to the urgings of groups and individuals in the absence of the litigation strategy remains open to speculation. But the conclusion appears inescapable that members of Congress were very much aware of the federal courts' role in reshaping the continuing eligibility review process.

The social security litigation strategy was also characterized by the skillful use of lobbying activities that presented the terminated beneficiary as the victim of a heartless bureaucratic machine. National lobbying organizations of the disabled were mobilized to present testimony at congressional hearings. Beneficiaries were able to claim the attention of individual legislators through letters from severely ill terminated recipients, or sometimes, even more dramatically, from their next of kin after their death.

Disability beneficiaries were aided in their campaign against the bureaucracy by state and city officials who were forced to assume financial responsibility for terminated beneficiaries; by administrative law judges who considered themselves pressured by the Social Security Administration to produce administrative denials of benefits; and by members of the bar who were often ideologically committed to serving this population and, in the case of private attorneys, were attracted by the fee withholding provisions of the statute and regulations.

Judicial Capacity

The Social Security Administration's litigation stance raised questions about the effectiveness of judicial oversight of the executive branch. And the Agency's policy of nonacquiescence transformed the social security disability lawsuits from a contest between litigants and the Agency into a struggle between two branches of government. The conflict arose because while the Social Security Administration complied with the court's holding in the case at bar, adjudication of individual cases did not bring about immediate changes in national social security disability policy until great numbers of litigants challenged Agency determinations and standards for cessation of benefits.

The Social Security Administration justified its nonacquiescence policy by claiming that, as a national bureaucracy, it required insulation from the reach of appellate court holdings. Stating that it was subject only to the rulings of the U.S. Supreme Court, the Agency refused to assign precedential weight to the rulings of the circuit courts.

The social security disability experience showed that the success of a litigation reform movement must be measured by more remote and indirect indices than victory in the courtroom. The nonacquiescence posture adopted by the Social Security Administration challenged the effectiveness of litigation as a tool for changing social policy. Because of nonacquiescence the individual lawsuit did not cause a revision of the Agency's administrative procedure; and winning the lawsuit did not secure bureaucratic compliance with the policy change. Though disability plaintiffs frequently won their suits, these individual victories were not translated into social reform for the entire group of disability plaintiffs. It required the aggregation of thousands of lawsuits around the country and the support of interest groups and a virtual media blitz before the litigation strategy was successful.

The disability litigation also illustrated the limits of judicial control of executive agencies. Thwarted by the Social Security Administration's policy of nonacquiescence, the judiciary was not, by itself, powerful enough to impose its authority upon the Agency and therefore, while the policy changes were pursued in court, litigants were forced to fight against bureaucratic power in other arenas. More than in other types of litigation campaigns, publicity and national consciousness-raising were necessary adjuncts of the litigation and, with court decisions serving as a catalyst, Congress was eventually persuaded to change the disability policy.

Despite their position as the final review over agency actions, courts were shown to have only a limited capacity to coerce administrative agencies into changing public policy. The impasse between the Social Security Administration and the courts, revolving around the Agency's nonacquiescence policy, demonstrated the differing perspectives of the bureaucracy and the judiciary on the issue of judicial review of administrative decisionmaking. This disagreement over the proper role of the judiciary required congressional intervention to resolve the conflict between the courts and the Social Security Administration.

Bibliography

BOOKS

Agresto, John. *The Supreme Court and Constitutional Democracy*. Ithaca, N.Y.: Cornell University Press, 1984.

Ball, Howard, ed. *Federal Administrative Agencies*. Englewood Cliffs, N.J.: Prentice-Hall, 1980.

Berger, Raoul. *Government by Judiciary*. Cambridge: Harvard University Press, 1977.

Berkowitz, Edward, ed. *Disability Policies and Government Programs*. New York: Praeger, 1979.

———. *Disabled Policy*. Cambridge: Cambridge University Press, 1987.

Berkowitz, Edward, and McQuaid, Kim. *Creating the Welfare State*. New York: Praeger, 1980.

Berry, Jeffrey. *The Interest Group Society*. Boston: Little, Brown, 1984.

Bickel, Alexander. *The Supreme Court and the Idea of Progress*. New Haven: Yale University Press, 1978.

Blasi, Vincent, ed. *The Burger Court*. New Haven: Yale University Press, 1983.

Bryner, Gary. *Bureaucratic Discretion: Law and Policy in Federal Regulatory Agencies*. New York: Pergamon Press, 1987.

Calabresi, Guido. *A Common Law for the Age of Statutes*. Cambridge: Harvard University Press, 1982.

Casper, Jonathan. *Lawyers before the Warren Court*. Urbana, Ill.: University of Illinois Press, 1972.

Choper, Jesse. *Judicial Review and the National Political Process*. Chicago: University of Chicago Press, 1980.

Cofer, Donna. *Judges, Bureaucrats, and the Question of Independence*. Westport, Conn.: Greenwood Press, 1985.

Derthick, Martha. *Policymaking for Social Security*. Washington, D.C.: Brookings, 1979.

Dickerson, Reed. *The Interpretation and Application of Statutes*. Boston: Little, Brown, 1975.

Dixon, Robert. *Social Security Disability and Mass Justice*. New York: Praeger, 1973.

Dolbeare, Kenneth, and Hammond, Phillip. *The School Prayer Decisions: From Court Policy to Local Practice*. Chicago: University of Chicago Press, 1971.

Dubois, Richard, ed. *The Analysis of Judicial Reform*. Lexington, Mass.: Lexington Books, 1982.

Dworkin, Ronald. *Taking Rights Seriously*. Cambridge: Harvard University Press, 1977.

Ely, John Hart. *Democracy and Distrust*. Cambridge: Harvard University Press, 1980.

Epstein, Lee. *Conservatives in Court*. Knoxville, Tenn.: University of Tennessee Press, 1985.

Everson, David, ed. *The Supreme Court as Policy-Maker: Three Studies on the Impact of Judicial Decisions*. Carbondale, Ill.: Southern Illinois University Public Affairs Research Bureau, 1968.

Gambitta, Richard; May, Marlynn; and Foster, James, eds. *Governing through Courts*, Beverly Hills: Sage, 1981.

Gardiner, John, ed. *Public Law and Public Policy*. New York: Praeger, 1977.

Graglia, Lino. *Disaster by Decree: The Supreme Court's Decisions on Race and Schools*. Ithaca, N.Y.: Cornell University Press, 1976.

Halpern, Stephen, and Lamb, Charles, eds. *Supreme Court Activism and Restraint*. Lexington, Mass.: Lexington Books, 1982.

Handler, Joel. *Social Movements and the Legal System*. New York: Academic Press, 1978.

———. *Protecting the Social Service Client*. New York: Academic Press, 1979.

Handler, Joel, and Zatz, Julie, eds. *Neither Angels Nor Thieves: Studies in Deinstitutionalization of Status Offenders*. Washington, D.C.: National Academy Press, 1982.

Horowitz, Donald. *The Courts and Social Policy*. Washington, D.C.: Brookings, 1977.

———. *The Jurocracy*. Lexington, Mass.: Lexington Books, 1977.

Johnson, Richard. *The Dynamics of Compliance: Supreme Court Decision-Making from a New Perspective*. Evanston, Ill.: Northwestern University Press, 1967.

Katzman, Robert. *Institutional Disability*. Washington, D.C.: Brookings, 1986.

Kluger, Richard. *Simple Justice*. New York: Alfred A. Knopf, 1976.

Lieberman, Jethro. *The Litigious Society*. New York: Basic Books, 1981.

Light, Paul. *Artful Work: The Politics of Social Security Reform*. New York: Random House, 1985.

Lilly, Graham. *An Introduction to the Law of Evidence*. St. Paul: West, 1978.

Lowi, Theodore. *The End of Liberalism*. New York: W. W. Norton, 1969.

Mashaw, Jerry, et al. *Social Security Hearings and Appeals*. Lexington, Mass.: Lexington Books, 1978.

———. *Bureaucratic Justice*. New Haven: Yale University Press, 1983.

McDowell, Gary. *Equity and the Constitution*. Chicago: University of Chicago Press, 1982.

Melnick, R. Shep. *Regulation and the Courts: The Case of the Clean Air Act*. Washington, D.C.: Brookings, 1983.

Miller, Arthur. *Toward Increased Judicial Activism*. Westport, Conn.: Greenwood Press, 1982.

Milner, Neal. *The Court and Local Law Enforcement: The Impact of Miranda*. Beverly Hills: Sage, 1971.

Mnookin, Robert, ed. *The Interest of Children*. New York: W. H. Freeman, 1985.

Neely, Richard. *How Courts Govern America*. New Haven: Yale University Press, 1981.

O'Connor, Karen. *Women's Organizations' Use of the Courts*. Lexington, Mass.: Lexington Books, 1980.

Olson, Susan. *Clients and Lawyers*. Westport, Conn.: Greenwood Press, 1984.

Perry, Michael. *The Constitution, the Courts, and Human Rights*. New Haven: Yale University Press, 1982.

Posner, Richard. *The Federal Courts*. Cambridge: Harvard University Press, 1985.

Rodgers, Harrell, and Bullock, Charles, III. *Coercion to Compliance*. Lexington, Mass.: Lexington Books, 1976.

Scheingold, Stuart. *The Politics of Rights*. New Haven: Yale University Press, 1974.

Shapiro, Martin. *The Supreme Court and Administrative Agencies*. New York: Free Press, 1968.

Soule, Charles. *Disability Income Insurance*. Homewood, Ill.: Dow Jones-Irwin, 1984.

Stone, Deborah. *The Disabled State*. Philadelphia: Temple University Press, 1984.

Vose, Clement. *Caucasians Only*. Berkeley: University of California Press, 1959.

Weaver, Carolyn. *The Crisis in Social Security*. Durham, N.C.: Duke University Press, 1982.

Weisbrod, Burton; Handler, Joel; and Komesar, Neil. *Public Interest Law*. Berkeley: University of California Press, 1978.

Wright, Charles. *Law of Federal Courts*. St. Paul: West, 1979.

Yarbrough, Tinsley. *Judge Frank Johnson and Human Rights in Alabama*. University, Ala.: University of Alabama Press, 1981.

ARTICLES

Arner, Frederick. "The Social Security Court Proposal: An Answer to a Critique." *Journal of Legislation* 10(1983):324–50.

"The Bellmon Report." Reprinted in *Social Security Bulletin* 5(May 1982).

Bork, Robert. "The Impossibility Of Finding Welfare Rights in the Constitution." *Washington University Law Quarterly* (1979):695–701.

Brubaker, Stanley. "Reconsidering Dworkin's Case for Judicial Activism." *Journal of Politics* 46(1984):503–19.

Cass, Ronald. "The Meaning of Liberty: Notes on Problems within the Frater-
     nity." *Journal of Law, Ethics & Public Policy* 1(Summer 1985):777–
     812.
Chambers, Donald. "Policy Weaknesses and Political Opportunities." *Social
     Service Review* 59(March 1985):1–17.
———. "The Reagan Administration's Welfare Retrenchment Policy: Ter-
     minating Social Security Benefits for the Disabled." *Policy Studies
     Review* 5(November 1985):230–40.
Chassman, Deborah, and Rolston, Howard. "Social Security Disability Hear-
     ings: A Case Study in Quality Assurance and Due Process." *Cornell
     Law Review* 65(1980):801–22.
Chayes, Abram. "The Role of the Judge in Public Law Litigation." *Harvard
     Law Review* 89(May 1976):1281–1316.
———. "Public Law Litigation and the Burger Court." *Harvard Law Review*
     96(November 1982):4–311.
Cofer, Donna. "The Question of Independence Continues: Administrative
     Law Judges within the Social Security Administration." *Judicature*
     69(December-January 1986):228–35.
Collins, Katherine, and Erfle, Anne. "Social Security Disability Benefits Re-
     form Act of 1984: Legislative History and Summary of Provisions."
     Social Security Bulletin 48(April 1985):5–32.
Cortner, Richard. "Strategies and Tactics of Litigants in Constitutional
     Cases." *Journal of Public Law* 17(1968):287–307.
Cowan, Ruth. "Women's Rights through Litigation: An Examination of the
     American Civil Liberties Union Women's Rights Project, 1971–1976."
     Columbia Human Rights Law Review 8(1976):373–412.
Denvir, John. "Toward a Political Theory of Public Interest Litigation." *North
     Carolina Law Review* 54(1976):1133–60.
Diver, Colin. "The Judge as Political Powerbroker: Superintending Struc-
     tural Changes in Public Institutions." *Virginia Law Review*
     65(1979):43–106.
Eichel, Steven. " 'Respectful Disagreement': Nonacquiescence by Federal
     Administrative Agencies in United States Courts of Appeals Prece-
     dents." *Columbia Journal of Law and Social Problems*
     18(1985):463–503.
Eisenberg, Theodore, and Yeazell, Stephen. "The Ordinary and the Extraor-
     dinary in Institutional Litigation." *Harvard Law Review 93(January
     1980):465–517.*
*Failinger, Marie, and May, Larry. "Litigating against Poverty." Ohio State
     Law Journal* 45(1984):2–56.
Fallon, Christine. "Social Security and Legal Precedent." *Case and Com-
     ment* (March-April 1984):3–10.
Fiss, Owen. "The Forms of Justice." *Harvard Law Review* 93(November
     1979):1–58.
Freeman, Gary, and Adams, Paul. "Ideology and Analysis in American Social
     Security Policymaking." *Journal of Social Policy* 12(January
     1983):75–95.
Glassman, Beth. "Terminating Social Security Disability Benefits: Another

Burden for the Disabled." *Fordham Urban Law Journal* 12(1983):195–217.

Glazer, Nathan. "Towards an Imperial Judiciary." *The Public Interest* 41(Fall 1975):104–23.

———. "Should Judges Administer Social Services?" *Public Interest* 50(Winter 1978):64–80.

Goldhammer, Alan, and Bloom, Susan. "Recent Changes in the Assessment of Pain." *Administrative Law Review* 35(Fall 1983):451–83.

Grey, Thomas. "Do We Have an Unwritten Constitution?" *Stanford Law Review* 27(February 1975):703–18.

Heaney, Gerald. "Why the High Rate of Reversals in Social Security Disability Cases?" *Hamline Law Review* 7(1984):1–17.

Horowitz, Donald. "The Courts As Guardians of the Public Interest." *Public Administration Review* 37(March-April 1977):148–54.

Howard, J. Woodford. "Adjudication Reconsidered as a Process of Conflict Resolution: A Variation on Separation of Powers." *Journal of Public Law* 18(1969):339–70.

———. "Book Review: The Courts and Social Policy." *Washington University Law Quarterly* 4(1978):833–39.

Johnson, Frank. "In Defense of Judicial Activism." *Emory Law Journal* 28(1979):901–12.

Lamb, Charles. "Book Review: The Courts and Social Policy." *University of California at Los Angeles Law Review* 26(1978):234–52.

Lando, Mordechai; Farley, Alice; and Brown, Mary. "Recent Trends in the Social Security Disability Insurance Program." *Social Security Bulletin* 45(August 1982):3–14.

Levant, Michael. "A Unified Corps of Administrative Law Judges—The Transition from a Concept to an Eventual Reality." *Western New England Law Review* 6(1984):705–21.

Liebman, Lance. "The Definition of Disability in Social Security and Supplemental Security Income: Drawing the Bounds of Social Welfare Estates." *Harvard Law Review* 89(1976):833–45.

Liebman, Lance, and Stewart, Richard. "Book Review: Bureaucratic Justice." *Harvard Law Review* 96(1983):1952–68.

MacIntyre, Angus. "A Court Quietly Rewrote the Federal Pesticide Statute: How Prevalent is Judicial Statutory Revision?" *Law and Policy* 7(April 1985):245–79.

Maranville, Deborah. "Book Review: Bureaucratic Justice." *Minnesota Law Review* 69(1984):325–47.

Mashaw, Jerry. "The Management Side of Due Process: Some Theoretical and Litigation Notes on the Assurance of Accuracy, Fairness, and Timeliness in the Adjudication of Welfare Claims." *Cornell Law Review* 59(1974):773–824.

Milner, Neal. "The Right to Refuse Treatment: Four Case Studies of Legal Mobilization." *Law and Society Review* 21(1987):447–85.

Moss, Kathryn. "The Catalytic Effect of a Federal Court Decision on a State Legislature." *Law and Society Review* 19(1985):147–57.

Note. "Administrative Agency Intracircuit Nonacquiescence." *Columbia Law Review* 85(1985):582–610.

Note. "Judicial Supervision of Agency Action: Administrative Nonacquiescence in Judicial Decisions." *George Washington Law Review* 53(November 1984-January 1985):147–67.

Note. "Intent, Clear Statements, and the Common Law: Statutory Interpretation in the Supreme Court." *Harvard Law Review* 95(1982):892–915.

Note. "Collateral Estoppel and Nonacquiescence: Precluding Government Relitigation in the Pursuit of Litigant Equality." *Harvard Law Review* 99(1986):847–61.

O'Connor, Karen, and Epstein, Lee. "The Rise of Conservative Interest Group Litigation." *Journal of Politics* 45(1983):479–89.

O'Neill, Timothy. "The Imperial Judiciary Meets the Impotent Congress." *Law and Policy* 9(1987):97–117.

Ogilvy, J. P. "The Social Security Court Proposal: A Critique." *Journal of Legislation* 9(1982):229–51.

Rabin, Robert. "Preclusion of Judicial Review in the Processing of Claims for Veterans' Benefits: A Preliminary Analysis." *Stanford Law Review* 27(1975):905–23.

Rehnquist, William. "The Notion of a Living Constitution." *Texas Law Review* 54(May 1976):693–706.

Reich, Charles. "The New Property." *Yale Law Journal* 73(1964):734–87.

Rosenbloom, David. "The Judicial Response to the Rise of the American Administrative State." *American Review of Public Administration* 15(Spring 1981):29–51.

Rosenblum, Victor. "Contexts and Contents of 'For Good Cause' As Criterion for Removal of Administrative Law Judges: Legal and Policy Factors." *Western New England Law Review* 6(1984):593–642.

Rowland, Landon. "Judicial Review of Disability Determinations." *Georgetown Law Journal* 52(1963):42–87.

Russo, Anthony. "The Social Security Disability Programs: Representing Claimants under the Changing Law." *Stetson Law Review* 14(1984):131–63.

Van Alstyne, William. "The Demise of the Right-Privilege Distinction." *Harvard Law Review* 81(1968):1439–64.

Wald, Michael, et al. "Interrogations in New Haven: The Impact of Miranda." *Yale Law Journal* 76(July 1967):1519–1648.

Wasby, Stephen. "Book Review: The Courts and Social Policy." *Vanderbilt Law Review* 31(1978):727–61.

Weinstein, Jack. "Equality and the Law: Social Security Disability Cases in the Federal Courts." *Syracuse Law Review* 35(1985):897–938.

Wyrick, Bob, and Owens, Patrick. "The Disability Nightmare," Special Reprint, *Newsday*, March 21, 1983.

Zankel, Norman. "A Unified Corps of Administrative Law Judges Is Not Needed." *Western New England Law Review* 6(1984):723–44.

GOVERNMENT DOCUMENTS

Code of Federal Regulations.

Congressional Record.

Disability Amendments of 1980—H.R. 3236. Subcommittee on Social Security of the House Committee on Ways and Means, 96th Cong., 2d Sess. (Comm. Print 1980).

Disability Amendments of 1982: Hearings before the Subcommittee on Social Security of the House Committee on Ways and Means, 97th Cong., 2d Sess. (1982).

Disability Insurance Legislation: Hearings before the Subcommittee on Social Security of the House Committee on Ways and Means. 96th Cong., 1st Sess. (1979).

Federal Register.

H.R. Rep. No. 100, 96th Cong., 1st Sess. (1979).

H.R. Rep. No. 944, 96th Cong., 2d Sess. (1980).

H.R. Rep. No. 618, 98th Cong., 2d Sess. (1984).

H.R. Rep. No. 1039, 98th Cong., 2d Sess. (1984).

Issues Related to Social Security Act Disability Programs. Senate Committee on Finance, 96th Cong., 1st Sess. (Comm. Print 1979).

Judicial Review of Agency Action: HHS Policy of Nonacquiescence: Hearing before the Subcommittee on Administrative Law and Governmental Relations of the House Committee on the Judiciary, 99th Cong., 1st Sess. (1985).

"More Diligent Followup Needed to Weed Out Ineligible SSA Disability Beneficiaries," General Accounting Office, HRD–81–48, March 3, 1981.

Oversight of Social Security Disability Benefits Terminations: Hearing before the Subcommittee on Oversight of Government Management of the Senate Committee on Governmental Affairs, 97th Cong., 2d Sess. (1982).

Oversight of the Social Security Administration Disability Reviews. Subcommittee on Oversight of Government Management of the Senate Committee on Governmental Affairs, 97th Cong., 2d Sess. (Comm. Print 1982).

"Report on Controls over Medical Examinations Necessary for Better Determinations of Disability by the Social Security Administration," General Accounting Office, HRD–79–119, October 9, 1979.

The Role of the Administrative Law Judge in the Title II Social Security Disability Insurance Program. Subcommittee on Oversight of Government Management of the Senate Committee on Governmental Affairs. 98th Cong., 1st Sess. (Comm. Print 1983).

S. Rep. No. 408, 96th Cong., 1st Sess. (1979).

S. Rep. No. 648, 97th Cong., 2d Sess. (1982).

S. Rep. No. 466, 98th Cong., 2d Sess. (1984).

Social Security Act Disability Program Amendments: Hearings before the Senate Committee on Finance, 96th Cong., 1st Sess. (1979).

Social Security Disability Benefits Terminations: New York: Hearing before the Subcommittee on Retirement Income and Employment of the House Select Committee on Aging. 97th Cong., 2d Sess. (1982).

Social Security Disability Insurance: Hearing before the Subcommittee on Social Security of the House Committee on Ways and Means, 98th Cong., 1st Sess. (1983).

Social Security Disability Insurance Program: Cessations and Denials: Hearing before the House Select Committee on Aging, 97th Cong., 2d Sess. (1982).

Social Security Disability Insurance Program: Hearing before the Senate Committee on Finance, 98th Cong., 2d Sess. (1984).

Social Security Disability Program Reform: Hearings before the Senate Committee on the Budget, 98th Cong., 2d Sess. (1984).

Social Security Disability Reviews: A Costly Constitutional Crisis: Hearing before the House Select Committee on Aging, 98th Cong., 2d Sess. (1984).

Social Security Disability Reviews: A Federally Created State Problem: Hearing before the House Select Committee on Aging, 98th Cong., 1st Sess. (1983).

Social Security Disability Reviews: The Human Costs: Hearing before the Senate Special Committee On Aging. 98th Cong., 2d Sess. (1984).

Social Security Rulings.

Staff Data and Materials Related to the Social Security Disability Insurance Program. Senate Committee on Finance, 97th Cong., 2d Sess. (Comm. Print 1982).

Status of Continuing Disability Reviews: Hearings before the Subcommittee on Social Security of the House Committee on Ways and Means, 98th Cong., 2d sess. (1982).

Index

About the Author

SUSAN GLUCK MEZEY is Assistant Professor of Political Science at Loyola University of Chicago. She has published articles in *Journal of Politics*, *American Politics Quarterly*, *Policy Studies Journal*, and other journals.

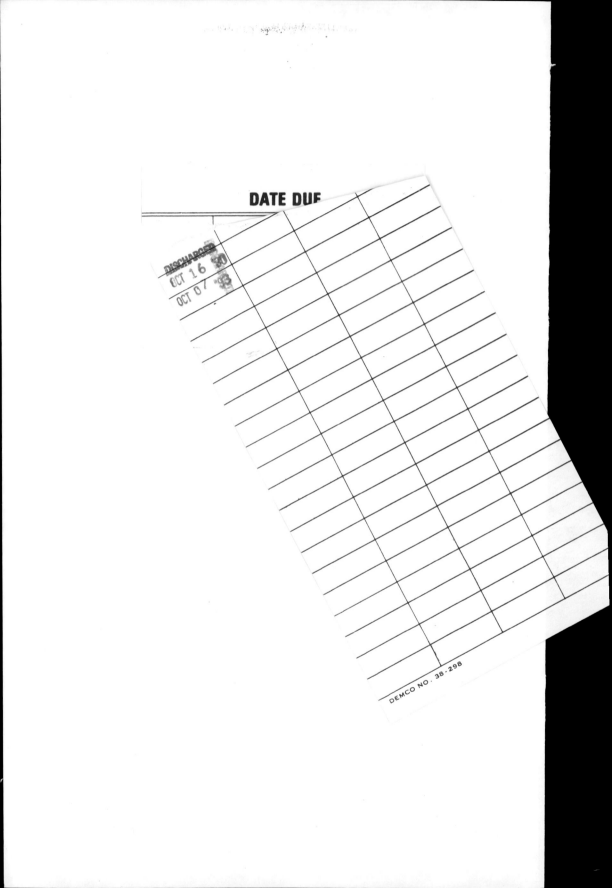

DATE DUE

DEMCO NO. 38-298